Dancing Past the Dark

Distressing Near-Death Experiences

Nancy Evans Bush

Foreword by
Bruce Greyson, M.D.

Dancing Past the Dark: Distressing Near-Death Experiences
Copyright © 2012 by Nancy Evans Bush

All rights reserved. No part of this book may be used or reproduced in any manner whatsoever without written permission from the author, except for brief quotations in critical articles and reviews, and fair use quotations in academic papers and other publications.

ISBN 978-1-936912-53-7

Includes a bibliography and index.

Publisher, Parson's Porch Books

Thanks to the International Association for Near-Death Studies for permission to use material from the *Journal of Near-Death Studies*. http://www.iands.org

Mark Nepo's poem "Upon Seeking Tu Fu as a Guide" is used by permission of CavanKerry Press, Ltd., Fort Lee, New Jersey.

Cover photograph of the Dumbbell Nebula, M27, from NASA and the Hubble Heritage Team (STScI/AURA), and C.R. O'Dell (Vanderbilt University)

Cover design by WebsiteGeographer, http://www.websitegeographer.com

Index by Wordmaps: http://wordmapsindexing.com

Interior Design by the eBook Artisans: http://ebookartisandesign.com

The website http://dancingpastthedark.com provides access to the Dancing Past the Dark blog, additional information and resources about near-death experiences, related articles, and contact information for the author.

Contents

Foreword	vii
Introduction	xi
Preface: Eden	xv
PART I NEAR-DEATH EXPERIENCE	
1 The Beginning	3
2 The End of Eden	17
3 The Experiences	25
4 Experiencer Responses	45
5 Common Questions	55
PART II INTERPRETATION: GOING BEHIND THE STORY	
6 First Views	65
7 Looking the Monster in the Eye: Hell	81
8 Personal Filters	113
9 Widening the Horizon	125
10 The Janus Self	141
11 The Cultural Milieu	161
PART III: DANCING PAST THE DARK	
12 Narrowing the Focus	181
13 Symbolic Language	199
14 Coping	209
15 More Questions	219
16 Bringing the NDE Home: Integration	225
17 Conclusions	241
Appendix 1: Interventions for Caregivers	249
Appendix 2: Experiencer Accounts	261
Appendix 3: IANDS, the International Association for Near-Death Studies	271
Acknowledgments	273
References	275
Index	xxi

Dedicated to my parents,

the Rev. Dr. Arthur Walwyn Evans and Mildred Pile Evans;

and, through them, to

Bishop William and Catherine Morgan,
the Rev. Dr. Morris Owen and Catherine Daniels Evans,
John and Mary Powell Milton, and
W. Clyde and Connie Duggins Pile

A cloud of witnesses

Foreword

Some 50 years ago, Nancy Evans Bush had a terrifying experience that jettisoned the world as she knew it. While giving birth to her second child, in what had seemed to be a normal pregnancy, she left her body and experienced a confrontation with soulless entities who conveyed the message that her whole life had been imagined, that nothing she knew and loved existed outside her imagination. There was at that time no public awareness of, or even a name for, such an experience, and so the despair that followed that experience remained locked inside her for decades, a grief she dared not share with anyone else. The truth was too horrible to reveal to others, and besides, those others didn't really exist, anyway. So that gut-wrenching experience remained her terrible secret.

Some twenty years later, desperate for a job, she answered a classified ad in the Sunday *Hartford Courant* for a temporary position as office manager for a start-up nonprofit housed at the University of Connecticut. That temporary position turned into a career working for the International Association for Near-Death Studies, eventually serving as its President and on its Board of Directors. In those first days as office manager for the organization, in a small, windowless room in the University's Psychology Department, Bush daily fielded telephone calls that began, "I hope you won't think I'm crazy, but…."

It was frightening enough for people who had blissful near-death experiences to speak about them in public; but it was unimaginably more difficult for the minority whose experiences were not blissful, but dreadful. Eventually, as awareness of near-death experiences spread throughout our culture, audiences yearned to hear about blissful reunions with deceased loved ones in heavenly realms. But no one wanted to hear (or talk) about the Other Kind. The problem with that denial is that we will never understand distressing experience by running from them, but only by getting to know them.

A major obstacle for people who have had distressing near-death experiences has been the almost complete absence of any helpful information about such events, from simple facts about how common they are and who has them, to what they might mean and how to cope with them. *Dancing Past the Dark* is the first comprehensive look at these experiences and at how we regard them, both collectively and individually. More importantly, this book is the first effective guide to understanding, living with, and learning from these experiences.

The topic of near-death experiences tends to evoke knee-jerk responses from many people desperately wedded to a particular way of seeing the world. Materialists tend to dismiss these profound events as meaningless hallucinations, whereas New Age spiritualists tend to sugar-coat them as encounters with a divine higher self. Somewhere in between, the work of the world goes on, and that is where you will find Nancy Evans Bush, trying to make sense of these experiences that defy facile explanation but cannot be ignored.

Bush starts from the reality that there can be no light without dark, no dark without light. From that truism, she shows that blissful and distressing experiences are different facets of the same underlying reality. As she puts it, both the heights of spiritual experience and the depths lie within the same mystery. Reality is both less than what we think it is and more. Bush reminds us that every enduring faith tradition describes spiritual quests involving confrontations with darkness as well as light, adversity and suffering as pathways to transformation. These quests may be frightening and painful and agonizing, but they are trials rather than punishments, and they may lead to invaluable spiritual gifts. They may not be gifts we expected, but we are never diminished by them.

Dancing Past the Dark progresses from the basic facts of distressing NDEs — what they are like, who has them, how they affect us; through our common attitudes toward them — our cultural ideas, beliefs, and fears; to what they mean — the challenges of understanding them and various ways of approaching and learning from them. Bush provides a clear rationale for treating distressing experiences as opportunities for growth, and concrete, practical suggestions for how to do that.

Nancy Evans Bush has spent a half century coming to terms with her own distressing experience. This book brings together the insights she came to through her own personal struggle, her master's degree in pastoral ministry, and her wide reading of the world's literature: not authoritarian answers but practical advice that you can try out for yourself. She writes with simple clarity, and with the humility, authority, and compassion of someone who has been there, a veteran who has "walked the walk" for fifty years and knows the route well.

Although this book was written by a person who has had a distressing near-death experience, it is not by any means a book *just* for them. This is a book for anyone who aspires to face the totality of the world in which we live. All of us have experiences for which we are unprepared, all of us at one point or another face frightening or distressing experiences, and all of us sooner or later need to master the art of dancing past the dark.

Bruce Greyson, M.D.
Chester F. Carlson Professor of Psychiatry & Neurobehavioral Sciences
Director, Division of Perceptual Studies
University of Virginia School of Medicine, Charlottesville, VA

Introduction

Over the years since 1975, when the modern world discovered near-death experiences, countless audiences have gathered to hear about these blissful experiences and their rapturous conclusions. Time and again, there has been the hush of a roomful of people bound together in hope and longing that these accounts might be true—that something like heaven may be waiting when we die. And there is a moment when a single person asks a cautious question: "I wonder…Is there…you know…is there the *other* kind of experience?" And the audience holds its breath.

The answer, we know now, is yes, that although the great majority of near-death experiences are beautiful beyond description, some are not. For almost one in five people coming away from a near-death experience, the memory may be not of joy but of profound distress. This book is the first concentrated look at those events and our cultural assumptions about them, which tend to be bleak at best. Perhaps surprisingly, the results of this more careful look are reassuring.

The Premise

We begin with good news. My premise in everything that follows is this: in everything we see, we are able to identify the darkness only in terms of its surrounding light. In other words, even the most frightening near-death experience is not conclusive.

Hubble photographs show that we are part of a universe that is an unceasing flow of radiance and darkness, violence and entropy, wholeness and fragmentation, the glory of dying novas and the implacable pull of black holes that may give birth to baby universes. Our experiences, all of them, are part of this same universe. Just as darkness is not the only reality in the universe, it is not conclusive in these experiences, either. The surest foundation for understanding and being able to live with the idea (or the memory) of a deeply disturbing near-death experience is to know about the radiant stories.

Those experiences are foundational, filled with light, and loving kindness, and a sense of wondrous, joyful discovery about the universe. There is more out there than what we have experienced, we who have had the distressing NDEs. There is more about the nature of the universe and our own experiences than what we know, just as there is more to nature itself than if we know only the desert of Baha Peninsula of California, the prairie of Protection, Kansas, or the granite of Mount Desert in Maine. They are all nature, yet astonishingly different—the scenes, the life forms, the scents, the required life skills, all quite different.

In this same universe, we do well to keep in mind that the seeming totality of a glorious or horrifying spiritual experience is not, in fact, *total*; it may still be enriched by understandings to be gained from a different landscape. One group represents the heights of spiritual experience; the other—the one this book is about—represents the depths. Both lie within the Mystery. This is the one about which the least is known.

That is why this book has been written.

The Book

Information always trumps ignorance, scrubbing away ungrounded fears and rumors. As a first step, then, the opening third of the book, chapters 1-5, deals with the basics of distressing near-death experiences—what they look like, the demographics, who has them, their effects, how people respond afterwards, common questions about them. The middle section of the book, chapters 6-11, looks at the most common expectations about the experiences—the ideas, beliefs, and fears our culture brings to them and which influence our understanding. The final section, chapters 12-18, clarifies the challenges of understanding such experiences and suggests avenues for approaching them from different directions, deepening the sense of their meaning and purpose. In terms of objectivity, the descriptive first section is the most factual, while the second and third are based in facts and scholarship laced with my own commentary and observations. The Preface tells the story of the earliest years of near-death studies and why they made a difference.

PREFACE
Eden

It is nearly the end of a movie, and the hero is dying. The scene has been set: a gauze curtain blows gently at the window; outside, rain spatters a mossy cemetery populated by stone figures—veiled women, mourning cherubs, weeping angels. The camera turns slowly back into the dim room, where a shadowy figure suggests the Grim Reaper. Moviegoers see the hero's hand rise weakly to touch the face of his beloved, and then…a slump, and the hand falls. Camera fade to Reaper. The audience knows the hero has died.

That scene, or one much like it, was the common theatrical deathbed scenario until toward the last decade of the 20th century. Then, abruptly, the imagery shifted. Characters began to die altogether differently. Now when a hero dies, a curtain may still drift gently at the window, but the gloomy cemetery is gone, along with the moss and the Reaper. Now the camera looks not *at* the failing hero but *with his eyes*. In a soft radiance, we rise with the camera and the vision of the leading man, then see his still body below. Coming mysteriously into the room, perhaps as if through mist, is the figure of a much-loved person who has died—the lost love, or a child or cherished army buddy. Behind that presence may be a splendid and welcoming light, or a great, brilliant Being; if the director has religious aspirations, the figure may be wearing a long robe and sandals. Scenes from earlier in the film flash across the screen, clips recognizable as the hero's life, and seeing them resolves unanswered questions. The hero, or what might be his spirit, rises to meet the lover, the child or friend, and together they move away, into the glorious light. The audience understands: the hero has died.

In the space of little more than ten years, the Grim Reaper virtually disappeared as the representative of death, replaced by a Being of Light. What happened to make such a dramatic shift? What happened was that through the work of two physicians the public came to know something startling and unprecedented about dying—that it didn't sound frightening or gloomy at all.

In the early 1970s Elisabeth Kubler-Ross (1969) was already well known for her work with dying patients and her description of emotional stages many go through as they struggle to accept the reality of their approaching death. She had become, unintentionally, a controversial figure in the medical community for her audacity in insisting that death is not a physician's failure but a natural part of the life cycle.

Thousands of people crowded her public lectures and workshops and heard stories of unexpected events reported around the time of death: dying patients had told Kubler-Ross they could see presences waiting for them; family members spoke of rooms filling with light. Science had no explanation for the accounts, other than to call them hallucinations.

In those same years, a young man with a PhD in philosophy, Raymond A. Moody, Jr., entered medical school. En route, he discovered and began quietly collecting curious accounts of people who had been close to death—some of them declared clinically dead by their physicians—who later told amazing stories of having had powerful, transcendent experiences during that time. Finding no existing term for the events they described, Moody called them *near-death experiences*.

Moody published a small book based on fifty of the accounts he had gathered (1975). The book, *Life After Life*, ran to fewer than 200 pages and was published by tiny Mockingbird Books of Georgia. No one, certainly not Moody himself or John Egle, his surprised publisher, was prepared for the response. The book took the world by a storm which has sometimes abated but never entirely calmed in the decades since. *Life After Life* became a best-seller, one of the most influential books of the twentieth century.

In an era notorious for its near-pathological avoidance of death, Moody began his book by asking openly, "What is it like to die?" (Moody, 9) His answer to the question, told through the near-death experiences, offered a view quite different from a dismal vision of the Grim Reaper.

The accounts in his collection echoed what Kubler-Ross was telling her audiences, but still it sounded fantastic. The stories came from different parts of North America, from people who had no contact with each other, but the commonalities were striking. Person after person described hovering outside of their physical body; rocketing through vast distances; finding strangely beautiful landscapes where they joyously encountered the presences of friends or loved ones who had previously died, and sometimes meeting a loving presence which appeared somehow to be surrounded by a radiant light, perhaps even made of light. Some people said it was God; Christians tended to describe the figure as Jesus or a favorite saint; deeply religious Jews said it was perhaps one of the Judges, or Elijah; the uncertain called it simply "a being of light." Many told of seeing a review of their life in which they felt the effects of their actions; of encountering some kind of barrier or boundary between life and 'beyond'; of being told that it was not time for them to be there, that they must return to the ordinary world.

For example, a ruptured appendix produced this experience:

> "I became very weak and I fell down. I began to feel a sort of drifting, a movement of my real being in and out of my body,

and to hear beautiful music. I floated on down the hall and out the door onto the screened-in porch. There, it almost seemed that clouds, a pink mist really, began to gather around me, and then I floated right straight on through the screen, just as though it weren't there, and up into this pure crystal clear light, an illuminating white light. It was beautiful and so bright, so radiant, but it didn't hurt my eyes. It's not any kind of light you can describe on earth. I didn't actually see a person in this light, and yet it has a special identity, it definitely does. It is a light of perfect understanding and perfect love. The thought came to my mind, 'Lovest thou me?' This was not exactly in the form of a question, but I guess the connotation of what the light said was, 'If you do love me, go back and complete what you began in your life.' And all during this time, I felt as though I were surrounded by an overwhelming love and compassion" (p. 59).

From a woman who had lost a lot of blood during childbirth:

"The doctor gave me up and told my relatives that I was dying. However, I was quite alert through the whole thing, and even as I heard him saying this I felt myself coming to. As I did, I realized that all these people were there, almost in multitudes it seems, hovering around the ceiling of the room. They...had passed on before. I recognized my grandmother and a girl I had known when I was in school...It was a very happy occasion, and I felt that they had come to protect or to guide me. It was almost as if I were coming home, and they were there to greet or to welcome me" (p. 53).

The pattern in the experiences emerging from Moody's and Kubler-Ross's work sounded very much—could it be?—like heaven. *Life After Life* also noted some aftereffects to the experience: People reported losing their fear of death, said they felt differently about themselves, expressed new belief in a continuation of life beyond death; a few noticed a deepening of their intuition.

> "The reason why I'm not afraid to die, though, is that I know where I'm going when I leave here, because I've been there before" (p. 91).

> "It was a blessing in a way, because before that heart attack I was too busy planning for my children's future, and worrying about yesterday, that I was losing the joys of the present. I have a much different attitude now" (p. 86).

Moody's book was published at a time when death and care of the dying had moved out of the household and the cycles of family life into the hospital. Dying had been professionalized as a medical condition, sanitized, distanced, and made foreign to the vast majority of people; now death was even more an "undiscovered country from whose bourne no traveler returns." But suddenly travelers were not only returning; they were in books and on talk shows everywhere, the subject of Hollywood movies and featured in favorite television shows. It was almost impossible to avoid them.

The impact was stunning. Audiences turned out by the hundreds of thousands to hear the stories, listening in absolute silence—their attention so focused they forgot to cough, to shift position, almost to breathe—then going out to tell their families and friends about what they had heard. From the miniscule audiences of small Rotary luncheons to the millions hearing Oprah, it seemed that everyone was hearing about near-death experiences. In less than the space of a single generation, it became hard to remember the earlier foreboding sense of death and dying, or the way the entire topic had been taboo in social conversation. The Grim Reaper seemed to be out of a job.

PART I
Near-Death Experience

1
The Beginning

Awakening

It was a clear, hot night in late July. In an old Hudson River town of New York State, I was in labor with my second child. At twenty-eight, I was healthy and the pregnancy had been easy; however, this was three weeks before the due date because an episode of premature labor the day before had moved the baby into the birth canal. When the obstetrician discovered that, he ordered an emergency induction. Now, ready to deliver, I was anesthetized according to common practice.

What I knew next was that I found myself awake and somehow flying over a building. A quick glimpse backward—oddly, with no sense of turning around—and I could see box-like structures on the roof of what I thought must be the hospital, because there, up the hill, was the window of the classroom where I taught. There was the town, receding swiftly below me, and then the dark outline of hills along the river, and the earth's curvature ("It's true, it really is round!"), and finally the planet becoming smaller, smaller while I continued into… where? Years later, I would describe it as hurtling into space "like an astronaut without a capsule," for the first astronaut had gone into space only a year earlier.

The speed was puzzling. It felt like drifting but covering enormous distances at what seemed to be an angle, headed northeast. (Is there a northeast in space?) The nighttime darkness turned into immensity and a different sort of dark: it was "thinner" somehow, shading inexplicably toward what might have been a paler horizon—except that there was no horizon. My impression was that God was over there. I was utterly alone. There was nothing but that strange twilight, and the awareness of being there, and emptiness.

There was a sense of form to me, I recall, or at least of presence, but no body. It was as if I were made of veiling—just insubstantial; but I was thinking. Did I *have* a mind, or was I *being* a mind? An unanswerable question.

A group of circles appeared ahead and slightly to my left, perhaps a half-dozen of them, moving toward me. Half black and half white, they clicked as they flew, snapping white-to-black, black-to-white, sending an authoritative message without words. Somehow its meaning was clear: "This is all there is. This is all there ever was. This is It. Anything else you remember is a joke. You are not real. You never were real. You never existed. Your life never existed. The world never existed. It was a game you were allowed to invent. There was never anything, or anyone. That's the joke—that it was all a joke."

The circles felt heckling but not evil, mocking, mechanistic, clicking without feeling. They seemed like messengers, certain of what they were saying, not ultimate authority themselves but with an authoritative message.

I argued passionately to prove them wrong, throwing out details of my mother's girlhood, stories of my husband's youth, facts from history—things I could not have experienced myself. Other people *must* exist; for how would I know these things if someone had not told me? And my first baby, the toddler Katy waiting at home—I knew that baby, the feel of the sturdy little body, the smell of her rosy babiness. I couldn't have made her up! And childbirth! Why would any woman (even an imaginary woman) invent childbirth? And what about this unborn baby?

"Whatever you remember is part of the joke. Your mother, your babies—they were never real," they mocked. "This is all there is, all there ever was. Just this."

But God? The thin darkness stretched off into nothingness, a thin not-quite-mist of dusk, and the circles kept clicking.

And then I was entirely alone. The circles had moved out of sight, and there was nothing left—the world unreal and gone, and with it my first baby, and this baby who would never be born, and all other babies. Everyone I knew and loved gone (but how had I known them, if they were never real?), and hills, and robins. There was no world, no home, no babies, not even a self to go home to. I thought that no one could bear so much grief, but there seemed no end to it and no way out. Everyone, everything, gone, even God, and I was alone forever in the swimming twilight dark.

And then I was groggily coming to in a hospital bed. My first waking thought: that I knew a terrible secret. "Calvin was right! Predestination, and I am one of the lost." That is what is out there, I thought, what it will be like when I die. There is something so wrong with my very being, even God has willed me not to be.

But why? Raised as a Congregational pastor's daughter in a denomination that emphasized the love of God and service to others rather than hell-fire, I was a questioner but deeply reverent, had belonged to youth groups, sung in choirs, taught Sunday School, was on staff at summer church conferences, had hoped for seminary. What had I ever done, that God would consign me to such emptiness? Despair moved like a tide.

The baby had been born cyanotic, the color of an over-ripe plum, and I was not allowed to see her. Was she real? Is that why I could not see her? I withdrew into silence and futile tears. No reassurances helped. My husband was there, and my mother and sisters; nurses clucked in sympathy, assuring everyone that the baby would survive. Were they real, the family, or the nurses, any of the world seemingly present, the baby I could not see—was any of it real? I was drowning in grief and despair, but could tell no one of the experience.

The hospital released me early because I was so upset—the baby's uncertain condition, they thought—and days went by, and the baby was allowed to come home. We finally met, she and I. Now it seemed there were two little ones. At night, hearing first one cry, then the other, I wondered, How can so much tiredness exist in a person who does not exist? Should I get up? If they are not real babies, do they really need to be fed?

Weeks became months, and slowly the experience receded. Its tide mark was always present and unmistakable; but what might or might not be life moved on, seeming easier when I repressed thinking about the message; and actual or not, little girls were fed and changed and tended to. Beneath the thinnest of emotional shells, though, despair ran roughshod. God had no place for me; the circles waited; nothing was real. I tried once to tell my husband about the experience, but stopped. Who can love a person and want to describe something so full of grief? I would not speak of it again, to anyone, for two decades.

Six years went by, and one afternoon I visited a neighbor, faculty member at a seminary nearby. Going into the kitchen to make tea, the friend gestured to a book on the table. "Jung's *Man and His Symbols*. It just arrived. Take a look."

The book was large, profusely illustrated, something about images, and I leafed through it with interest until, turning a page, I froze. From the left-hand page, one of the circles stared back. They were true! Someone else knew about the circles! My breath jammed in my throat, and in a storm of terror I hurled the book across the room and fled from the house, too frightened even to say goodbye. (Twenty-five years later, the friend would laugh and say, "Yes, I did think it odd that you simply disappeared.")

The image from which I fled, the circle whose message I had been repressing for years, was foreign, terrifying, and meaningless except as recalled from my own experience. I did not recognize it. It would be several years more before I discovered that it was the Yin/Yang, the ancient Chinese symbol of the seemingly opposed but always interdependent principles within all of human experience—the balance of yes/no, male/female, active/passive, light/dark, life/death, moving in a constant flow of interactions. It is the interconnection of opposites, the acceptance of ambiguity and paradox, the understanding that reality is both less than what we believe it to be and more. The circle comprises two nested tear-shaped halves, one black and one white, each containing a dot of the other. It was those halves that had been clicking back and forth, back and forth. Not only had I been I troubled by the experience itself, but now—how does an unrecognized ancient Chinese symbol became a message-bearer in the experience of a mainstream Protestant in New England?

Synchronicity

That experience and its aftermath were the genesis of this book. The year that baby turned twenty, I answered a small classified ad for temporary office work with a startup nonprofit organization housed at the University of Connecticut. It was just twenty minutes from my home. Convenient. The office was in the Psychology Building. Easy parking. I had never heard of the International Association for Near-Death Studies or near-death experiences, but it sounded possibly interesting. And so it has been.

Within a few weeks of being hired, I realized that my memory had a name, "near-death experience." I have remained in one capacity or another with that Association, called IANDS (*eye*-ands), for thirty years. I have been Executive Director, editor, something like house mother, and later President and a member of the Board of Directors. And always, the question of what we can know and what to say about the distressing experiences has been with me. I have written and lectured and taught and done research.

It has taken that long to bring this book into being. This is the story of distressing near-death experiences.

Is the universe friendly?

Albert Einstein is said to have remarked that the most important question facing humankind is this: "Is the universe a friendly place or not?" (Fox, 1998, p. 1) The question captures tens of thousands of years of human wonder and exploration—religion, philosophy, science, the substance of civilization. What's out there? Is it trying to get us? How does it work? Are we safe here?

Over the course of human history (geologically brief but ancient to our minds), the answers have varied. By the late twentieth century there were, at least in the Western mind, two conflicting views. The traditional, religious view was that we are part of a meaning-laden and cherished creation of the Lord of the Universe. On the other hand, after a few hundred years of revolutionary technological discovery, the philosophers of science had largely argued that data showed a mechanistic cosmology, seemingly meaningless history, and wishful thinking as a substitute for deep-rooted faith in a sacred reality. And the home place itself, said science, was merely a flying ember, the accidental cinder of a great explosion that happened so long ago as to be unimaginable.

Can such a universe be considered friendly? It is an irony that Einstein, the most famous scientist of the 20th century, is credited with asking the question, for it is one that science is not designed to answer. The subject will be discussed in more depth later on; for now it is important to note that it is the business of science to deal with *quantity*, not *quality*. By its own choice, science does not 'do' values other than those that are numerical. As Huston Smith puts it in *Forgotten Truth*: "A number is a number, and number is the language of science. Objects can be larger or smaller, forces can be stronger or weaker, durations can be longer or shorter, these all being numerically reckonable. But to speak of anything in science as having a different ontological status—as being better, say, or more real—is to speak nonsense" (Smith, 1977, 5).

In short, science cannot provide a friendly universe; it can provide only a description of what it observes physically: the planet Earth as a spinning bit of rubble toward the edge of a nondescript galaxy within a seemingly impersonal immensity. When Einstein asked, "Is the universe friendly?" the answer, according to materialism, was a resounding, No!

However, the residents of that bit of rubble are curiously designed to hunger after meaning and purpose, qualities that venture well beyond the realm of science. No wonder near-death experiences were greeted like food after famine! For the first time in centuries, here was abundant evidence of something meaningful beyond the sterile materialist model. At last, here were people who had directly experienced that "something," and it led them to proclaim that, yes, the universe is not only friendly but loving and welcoming, and it is safe to die.

Explorations

After that initial hush of hope came the question: Are these things scientific? Within three years of Moody's book, a handful of questioners had banded together to create the germ of "an association that would further the scientific study of NDEs and that would also serve as a support group of sorts for experiencers, as well as a clearinghouse of information for the public at large." The quote is from the earliest organizing document of the International Association for Near-Death Studies (IANDS), which quickly established a newsletter and peer-reviewed scholarly journal and began building a membership base.

The pace of publications began to pick up. Moody brought out *Reflections on Life After Life* (1977) to help answer the questions most frequently asked about the first book. A year later physician George Ritchie related his dramatic wartime near-death experience in *Return from Tomorrow* (1978). Meanwhile, at the University of Connecticut, social psychologist Kenneth Ring was doing research for his book *Life at Death* (1980), the first statistically-based report about near-death experiences and experiencers.

Moody and Kubler-Ross provided the initial stories, but Ring offered quantitative measures with the "Weighted Core Experience Index" (1980, 32), a scale by which to measure the experiences. Individuals who reported greater detail and/or depth of experience scored higher and were considered "core experiencers." From his first sample of forty-nine core experiencers, Ring developed a list of the ten most common descriptions of an NDE: peaceful, painless, no fear, relaxed, pleasant, calm; happy, joyful, quiet, warm (43). Statistics! And percentages! Here was the language of quantification, giving the reports a measure of scientific credibility.

Alongside Ring's statistics, the theme of wonder continued in the words of his study participants: ". . . I remember the feeling. I just remember this absolute beautiful feeling. Of peace…and happy! Oh! So happy!…The peace…the release…It was just absolutely beautiful" (43). Ring was able to conclude that "there is a consistent and dramatically positive emotional response to apparent near-death by experiencers" (45).

He examined the aftereffects of near-death experience in greater detail than Moody and discovered among his 49 respondents "a heightened inner religious feeling." Comparing their responses to those of 38 non-experiencers, he found 80% of the NDErs to have a lessened or lost fear of death, whereas 71% of the non-experiencers reported an increase or no change in their fear level (1980, Chapter 9).

The strongest response came in answer to questions about belief in life after death. Although the experiencers reported themselves as having been less inclined to believe in life after death before their NDE, they were significantly more inclined than the non-experiencers to believe in it afterward ($p<.01$).

About the aftereffects altogether, Ring concluded:

> "The typical near-death survivor emerges from his experience with a heightened sense of appreciation for life, determined to live life to the fullest. He has a sense of being reborn and a renewed sense of individual purpose in living, even though he cannot articulate just what this purpose is…The things that he values are love and service to others; material comforts are no longer so important. He becomes more compassionate toward others, more able to accept them unconditionally. He has achieved a sense of what is important in life and strives to live in accordance with his understanding of what matters" (157).

Life at Death would catapult Ring into the media ring. Within a year of the book's publication, Ring found office space for the Association (IANDS) at the University of Connecticut and was inaugurating its journal, soon under the editorship of psychiatrist Bruce Greyson at the University of Michigan.

Soon after, support for the observations of Moody and Ring came from a carefully crafted study by Atlanta cardiologist Michael Sabom and social worker Sarah Kreutziger (1982). Their *Recollections of Death: A Medical Investigation* was as readable as it was thoughtful and received widespread favorable attention, especially for its discussion of verifiable ("veridical") out-of-body experiences. Its publication coincided with another data treasury, *Adventures in Immortality*, by George Gallup, Jr. (1982), which included the stunning news that in the adult United States population alone, "about eight million have experienced some sort of mystical encounter along with the death event" (6).

The preliminary statistics of the Ring, Sabom, and Gallup studies offered a more systematic approach to NDEs than was possible with the earlier anecdotal books. By now it was relatively well accepted, at least within the field, that of people who have come close to death or been in a situation of extreme physical or emotional stress, 35-47% may later report a near-death experience; later hospital-based studies limited to NDEs reported after clinically monitored cardiac arrest would show rates as low as 8-10% (Zingrone & Alvarado, 2009). However, no pointers indicated who was or was not likely to have a near-death experience. The demographic variables (age, nationality, race, religious background, education, sexual preference, marital status) suggested not a clue about which people might be expected to report one. True, it seemed at first that women were more likely than men to have an experience; but closer investigation determined that they were simply more apt to talk about it.

The circumstances of coming close to death were likewise inconclusive. Experiences were reported after all manner of vehicle accident, near-drowning, surgery and post-surgery, childbirth, allergic reaction, falling out of an airplane, electrocution, heart attack, high fever, combat, rape and other criminal attack. Disconcertingly to a fair number of people, religious beliefs or the total lack of any religious belief seemed to have no impact on the likelihood of having an experience, and suicide attempts had produced some exceptionally radiant NDEs.

What had begun as great news with Moody was getting even better, so far as the media were concerned. A crush of requests for public appearances had already forced Moody to drop out of his residency in psychiatry; it would be ten years before he could complete it. Then came Ring's *Life at Death*; and shortly after its appearance, his phone began to ring. When Michael Sabom's *Recollections of Death* came out not long afterward, he, too, became a focus of media attention, and then George Gallup, Jr., with *Adventures in Immortality* and P.M.H. Atwater with *Coming Back* (1988), and Melvin Morse and *Closer to the Light* (1990)—and eventually *Transformed by the Light* (Morse, 1992 and Sutherland, 1992), *Embraced by the Light* (Eadie, 1992), *Beyond the Light* (Atwater, 1994), *Saved by the Light* (Brinkley, 1994), *After the Light* (Sharp, 1995)—everywhere, the Light!

The '80s were a time of public appearances. 'Experts' (the authors and researchers, now numbering at most a dozen) and a few telegenic near-death experiencers were in demand. At one end of the appearance scale were the local Rotary, Lions, and Kiwanis clubs, with an occasional PTA or church group. Speakers on near-death experiences populated professional conferences and retreat centers like California's Esalen, New York's Open Center and Omega Institute, and Boston's Interface. Prospecting authors wanted interviews with experiencers so they could write a book. And then there were the electronic media…

From the perspective of the IANDS office, media attention became a series of tsunamis, mountainous waves of requests bearing down and sweeping away everyone in their path. Because the important thing was to let people know the good news that they could be less fearful of death, no one wanted to refuse any request;

and if books were simultaneously promoted, that was a pleasant benefit. And so began a seemingly endless stream of radio talk shows across the United States and Canada, the task easy enough because calls could be patched to a home or office, with no need to travel.

Television, on the other hand, required presence in a studio, which meant travel and a multiplication of the hours involved in an appearance. Contrary to public belief, guests do not make money from appearances on informational shows. The larger programs take care of expenses but do not pay guests for their time and expertise; local shows often do not even reimburse expenses. What is more, there is no guarantee, especially with network shows, that an interview will actually air, no matter how much of a guest's time has been taken up. The amount of public service time and out-of-pocket money contributed by a handful of NDE researchers and experiencers has been astronomical.

The first national level shows to feature NDEs were out of network news departments—Good Morning, America; Today; CBS Morning News; then CNN, ABC's 20/20 and CBS's PM Magazine, and Unsolved Mysteries, The Other Side, Dateline, In Search Of, and others. Near-death experiences were a natural for television talk shows: Phil Donahue, Oprah Winfrey, Larry King, Sally Jessy Raphael, Geraldo Rivera, Rolanda. The calls went out from associate producers to authors directly and to the IANDS office—usually urgent calls pleading that a show needed immediate assistance with the recruitment of what came to be thought of as "a boxed set"—one or more experts, at least one articulate and photogenic experiencer, and a skeptic (preferably an MD). Almost never was there a request for clergy.

Take a map of North America and mark every city large enough to have a television station—say, a population of 50,000 or more. Now, assume that every one of the local news anchors and talk show hosts at those stations wants to locate and schedule a guest or two to talk about near-death experiences. It adds up. From the US and Canada, Britain, France, Belgium, Germany, Japan, Australia, Brazil, the requests kept coming. Researchers and experiencers flew from coast to coast. Television crews invaded homes and offices—good-looking, brisk, often charming young people who arrived with a great deal of expensive (and very large) technical equipment and sometimes less praiseworthy questions. An entire eight-person Japanese television crew, only one of whom spoke English, once spent two days filming in my living room—gracious, courteous, friendly young people who were delighted to discover American food. It was not the only such visit, though it was one of the most fun.

Where near-death books went, media attention followed, until the mid-1990s, when a positive frenzy over Betty Eadie's autobiographical *Embraced by the Light* and Dannion Brinkley's *Saved by the Light* appeared to wear everyone out, at least for a time.

A few of the programs were excellent; some were dreadful; all were over-simplified. The longer shows generally fared better, provided the host's ambition did not lean to sensationalizing. (The producers of one hour-long New England show about NDEs assured prospective guests that their objective was a balanced, thoughtful presentation—but aired the show at Halloween, with sepulchral music, clouds of spookily swirling fog, and horror film super-star Vincent Price as host.)

Whatever their quality, the shows accomplished what the tiny handful of researchers wanted, which was to implant awareness of near-death experiences squarely into public consciousness. In the early 1980s, a speaker could ask an audience, "How many of you know something about near-death experiences?" and a hand or two would go up. By the end of the decade, the question could be reversed: "Does anyone here *not* know something about near-death experiences?" In audience after audience, not a hand was raised. The Grim Reaper seemed to be out of a job.

If news of near-death experiences was a banquet, it was the authors who prepared it, the media who served it, and audiences who couldn't get enough. More than one speaker during the first decade or so found their audiences so hungering for information, for reassurance, for *anything* to suggest that life may hold meaning and promise, that the sheer sense of need was nearly overwhelming. The unanticipated danger was that a great many people, experiencer and non-experiencer alike, overfull of a materialist, secular worldview and naive to the point of ignorance about the range of religion or spirituality, had no vocabulary for such encounters, no adequate way of processing or understanding what they took in.

Unrecognized at first, the stage was set for what author and experiencer P.M.H. Atwater would later call "the myth of the near-death experience." (1994, 258) That myth is the expectation—even the insistence—that all NDEs are happy and peaceful, and that those who have them are effortlessly transformed, if not to saints then at least to paragons of enlightenment. Eventually, of course, the other shoe had to fall.

2
The End of Eden

Almost always, in the question period after a talk about NDEs, one brave person would venture the question, "All these experiences are so beautiful. Are there ever…you know…does anyone ever mention…well, the other kind?" And the auditorium would become utterly still. It was always difficult to know how to answer without bursting the bubble of hopefulness.

Raymond Moody (1997, 169) had been quite explicit: "[It] remains true that in the mass of material I have collected no one has ever described to me a state like the archetypal hell."

Kenneth Ring (1980, 45), like Moody, was firm: "Significantly, *no* person in our sample—including, of course, all our suicide attempt cases—recounted an experience that could be regarded as a 'journey to hell.' …Although some death experiences did include frightening aspects or moments of confusion and uncertainty, none was characterized by predominantly unpleasant feelings or imagery."

In Sabom's study (1982, 20), "In each case in which unpleasant emotions…were encountered…they were perceived to be but a momentary impression in an otherwise pleasant NDE. It is conceivable that this overall assessment might have been different (i.e., unenjoyable) if the experience had abruptly ended at the point at which the unpleasant emotion was perceived."

Indeed, of the 354 near-death experiences in eight major studies between the years 1975 and 2005, including the largest in-hospital investigations, there were no unpleasant reports (Bush, 2009, 65).

The dark cloud

In the heady rush of euphoria over blissful near-death experiences—the yearning of countless audiences to hear the good news, the intellectual excitement of new discovery, the seductiveness of television cameras, the wash of spiritual hope—no one wanted to hear that some experiences might point in a very different direction. But then…

"In 1978," Kenneth Ring would write years later, "a dark cloud of chilling testimony began to penetrate into the previously luminous sky of reports of near-death experiences" (1994, 5).

The "dark cloud" was a startling book published by Chattanooga cardiologist Maurice Rawlings (1978). In *Beyond Death's Door*, Rawlings described in grim detail another kind of near-death experience told by some of his patients being resuscitated from cardiac arrest. "Doc! Doc! Don't let me go under again—I'm in hell!" A chill went through just about everyone who read the book. An ancient and most unfriendly aspect of the universe had surfaced anew.

Beyond Death's Door made a deep impression in evangelical Christian circles, but overall nothing like the reception given *Life After Life*. Perhaps most obviously, the subject was unwelcome to readers who were happy to read about heaven-like experiences but not those interpreted as cosmic terror and a vengeful God. Many, especially those who felt harmed by organized religion, considered the Rawlings conclusions distasteful, even assaultive, while mainstream Christians tended to think of them as gauche.

From the research perspective, there were other problems. Most of the experiences in *Beyond Death's Door* were presented, not in the experiencers' own words, but as Rawlings's recollections of what patients had told him sometimes years before. Further, too many reported "facts" were shaky, if not downright in error: names were wrong, researchers' institutional affiliations were misstated, other research findings were inaccurately quoted. If such easily verifiable facts were wrong, what could be trusted in the rest of his work?

Most damaging of all, Rawlings was clearly less interested in objective reporting than in his conviction as a Christian fundamentalist that hell is waiting for anyone who does not live by conservative Christian theological doctrine. From that perspective, he was writing to save souls. While this position enhanced his reputation within the conservative Christian community, it was not well received elsewhere and strengthened the suspicion that terrifying near-death experiences were most probably associated entirely with hell-fire-and-brimstone religious beliefs.

In 1995, Dr. Rawlings was invited to speak at the IANDS North American conference. It was clear even to those who were horrified by his lurid presentation that his attitude of great caring stemmed from a desire to save people he believed to be destined for a dreadful fate; nonetheless, his sympathetic attitude did not deter several people from walking out of the lecture.

Overall, what Rawlings called hellish experiences were considered by the mainstream of near-death studies to be "negative experiences," a fringe matter. However, Rawlings was not alone. Despite the optimistic findings of the major studies that reported only pleasant experiences, there were hints, even in the early publications, that some NDEs were not entirely blissful.

Psychologist Charles A. Garfield reported as early as 1979 that of thirty-six people interviewed, eight described vivid demonic or nightmarish visions, while another four reported alternating blissful and terrifying features (1979, 5-7).

Three researchers from Washington State defined a negative NDE as "one that contains extreme fear, panic, or anger. It may also contain visions of demonic creatures that threaten or taunt the subject" (Lindley et al, 1981, 113). Their study reported finding eleven out of fifty-five NDEs "partially negative or hellish." They noted that "Most negative experiences begin with a rush of fear and panic or with a vision of wrathful or fearful creatures," but are "usually transformed, at some point, into a positive experience in which all negativity vanishes and the first stage of death [peacefulness] is achieved" (113).

Michael Sabom (1982, 20) had observed that "Momentary fright or bewilderment sometimes accompanied the initial passage into darkness," and quoted two of his patients as saying:

"There was total blackness around me...all you see is blackness around you. If you move very fast, you can feel the sides moving in on you....I felt lonely and a little frightened."

"'The next thing I remember, I was in complete total darkness....It was a very dark place and I didn't know where I was, what I was doing there or what was happening, and I started getting scared."

With George Gallup's *Adventures in Immortality* came an entire chapter entitled "Descent into the Abyss" (Chapter 6). In it, he reported, "[O]ur major national poll of those who had a close brush with death showed that only one percent said that they 'had a sense of hell or torment'" (76). Other investigators quickly adopted that one percent figure as the total percentage of distressing near-death experiences, neatly overlooking the conclusion of Gallup's paragraph: "But ... the picture is more complex than that ...[I]t does seem clear that many of these people...were reluctant to interpret their experience in positive terms."

Said a thirty-year-old, "I felt I was being tricked into death. In my mind, I was fighting with faces unknown to me, and I felt I had to have all my wits about me, to keep from dying" (Gallup, 78).

A middle-aged Illinois housewife: "I would [see] huge things coming toward me, like animals with baseball bats. Then, I'd be in this blue-green water, and out in front of me was this huge white, marblelike rock. At the top of the rock was this bright light, and as I got closer to the rock, I saw an image of a person standing on top of it in white clothing—like a robe. But I couldn't tell if it was male or female—I couldn't see the face at all" (Gallup, 79).

A pre-law student in his twenties told of his experience in an automobile accident: "My first thought was, 'I must be dead. This is what death must be.' But it certainly wasn't blissful. Just nothingness. I felt like a piece of protoplasm floating out on the sea. I thought, 'Maybe I'm lost, maybe I'm not going to heaven'" (Gallup, 80).

"[T]he negative near-death experiences in our study," Gallup summarized, "include some of the following features: featureless, sometimes forbidding faces; beings who are often merely present, but aren't at all comforting; a sense of discomfort—especially emotional or mental unrest; feelings of confusion about the experience; a sense of being tricked or duped into ultimate destruction; and fear about what the finality of death may involve" (Gallup, 83).

From Charles P. Flynn (1986, 82), a sociologist at Miami University in Oxford, Ohio, came the account of a woman who reported having seen "a realm of 'troubled spirits'":

"It's a dusky, dark, dreary area, and you realize that the area is filled with a lot of lost souls, or beings that could go the same way I'm going [to the Light] if they would just look up. The feeling I got was that they were all looking downward, and they were kind of shuffling, and there was a kind of moaning. There were hundreds of them, looking very dejected. The amount of confusion I felt coming off of it was tremendous. When I went through this, I felt there was a lot of pain, a lot of confusion, a lot of fear, all meshed into one. It was a very heavy feeling."

The Greyson/Bush study

So few of these reports of unpleasant NDEs made it into public awareness that when comparing medieval and modern near-death experiences in her blockbuster work *Otherworld Journeys*, religious scholar Carol Zaleski could make the often-quoted observation (1987, 7), "Gone are the bad deaths, harsh judgment scenes, purgatorial torments, and infernal terrors of medieval visions; by comparison, the modern otherworld is a congenial place, a democracy, a school for continuing education, and a garden of unearthly delights."

While heavenly near-death experiences were flooding publishing houses and other media, at the University of Connecticut offices of IANDS, a broader picture was unfolding. Not only did we have access to more published data than the public saw, but also contact with experiencers themselves. An occasional letter or phone call hinted at fear or unpleasantness during an experience—almost never an outright statement, but a hint. I knew from my own experience that the picture of NDEs as exclusively blissful was incomplete; so it was easy enough to begin inviting the hinters to say more. Further, psychiatrist Bruce Greyson had joined Kenneth Ring on the UConn faculty; head of the research division of IANDS and editor of the *Journal of Near-Death Studies*, he had professional reasons for wanting more information and had also begun a small collection of these disturbing NDEs. From our shared interest came the first study of frightening near-death experiences.

Methodology

The plan seemed simple enough. The unfunded study would be carried out as information became available. Its methodology was necessarily rudimentary. We would use only first-person accounts. As either of us sensed an unpleasant experience account, we would contact the person, sound out the situation, describe our interest in developing helpful information about these experiences, and invite the person to take part in a study. A coding system would guarantee anonymity. Participants would agree to write or tape-record the account of their NDE in as much detail as possible. They would sign a consent form permitting the anonymous use of the material and fill out a brief questionnaire requesting demographic information and a description of the circumstances under which the NDE had occurred. For additional information, we would contact the experiencer. The result would be the first descriptive study of these hidden experiences.

Easier said than done.

Medical social worker Kimberly Clark Sharp was the first to observe that this is a population that vanishes (Sharp, 1984). For many people with a painful NDE, simply admitting they have had such an experience is as much as they can do; describing it can seem impossible. Or they break through their fear just long enough to give an abbreviated account and promptly disappear. Sharp's observation, we found, was frustratingly true.

A person would hang far back after a program, sidle up to the speaker when the rest of the audience was out of earshot, and stammer, "I…I had an experience, but it was … I can't say. How come everybody else gets heaven and I got…that?" Was the person willing to say more about "that"? No.

A letter-writer wrote, "My experience was, I went to hell. Why don't you tell people the truth?" Would the person discuss it on the phone or write more in another letter? No.

Buried in an otherwise radiant NDE description one could sometimes find a terse comment: "One part of my experience was too frightening to talk about. I prayed to God, and it turned out all right." Would the person elaborate? No.

It took nine years to find fifty people who could give enough detail to create a coherent sense of such experiences. Despite our being able to draw on all the resources of IANDS, and despite contacts with several thousand experiencers overall, the "closeting" was so intense that even when our respondents could bring themselves to write their accounts, few were willing or able to complete the questionnaire, answer questions, or agree to an interview. (One participant, at the urging of her psychotherapist, eventually contacted one of the investigators [NEB] and agreed to be interviewed *nine years after the study.*)

To say the response was a slow trickle is to suggest substantially more speed than was the case. Follow-up produced consent forms but not much else. Demographic information about the participants is therefore extremely limited. Of those who completed the questionnaire, their age at the time of the experience ranged from nine years old upwards; their levels of education are from high school dropout to completion of graduate work. They include laborers, professionals, unemployed, and students, Christian, Jewish, without religious preference, and secular. Other studies have shown near-death experiencers to represent a broad cross-section of the population at large

(Ring, Sabom, Gallup, van Lommel), and there is no demonstrable reason to believe this sample to be otherwise. As a whole, experiencers appear no more likely than any random segment of the population to have emotional or psychological problems or outright mental illness (Greyson, 2000 and Holden, 2009). From what we know about these fifty individuals, they are a representative group of ordinary people who have had an extraordinary experience.

The basic finding of the study was quickly apparent: there is no universal "distressing experience." In fact, there was greater variety of phenomena within these accounts than among those of pleasurable experiences. Overall, they tend to follow the basic pattern of NDEs as described by Ring (1980, 32-36)) and Greyson (1983), provided the wording is broadened to accommodate more than specifically pleasant emotions.

As measures of pleasant NDEs, Ring's "Weighted Core Experience Index" includes: a subjective sense of being dead; intense feeling of peace, painlessness, etc. (the core affective cluster); sense of bodily separation; sense of entering a dark region; encountering a presence or hearing a voice; taking stock of one's life; seeing or being enveloped in light; seeing beautiful colors; entering into the light; and encountering visible 'spirits.' When worded neutrally, the Index applies as well to frightening experiences: for example, defining the core affective cluster as "intense emotions" rather than "feeling of peace, painlessness, etc." and "vivid sense impressions" in place of "seeing beautiful colors."

Patterns

Within the fifty accounts, three distinct types of experience emerged. The most common type featured the same elements as described in pleasurable NDEs, but experienced as terrifying. The second type was an experience of nothingness, of being without sensation and/or of existing in a limitless, featureless void. The third type, with by far the fewest accounts, corresponds more closely to the hell of the popular imagination. The study findings, first published in the journal *Psychiatry* (Greyson and Bush, 1993), form the basis of the next chapter.

3
The Experiences

It is easy to relate to the emotional tone of the beautiful experiences. The pleasurable accounts are told so passionately, with such care to set the scene, explain the circumstances, and describe the tiniest detail of the NDE, that it is easy to understand how a person would find glory in that kind of experience—emotions refined and vivid, description layered on top of description.

By contrast, a reader coming away from the account of a disturbing experience is apt to think, "Well, I don't know what all the fuss is about. It doesn't sound like much to me." Many of these accounts, especially those that are first tellings, sound almost grumpy, short to the point of abruptness, with few details and no commentary. Further, movie special effects are guaranteed to look far more fearsome than phenomena in the great majority of these NDEs. That being the case, what's so terrible about them?

In approaching other people's experiences, it is useful to remember that the thing with eight legs that is a bug collector's dream may send someone else into cardiac arrest. We do well not to pre-judge what another person will experience as ultimately terrifying. You, sitting there reading, have not just been pulled out of your body into a really weird neighborhood where incredible things are going on that you can't explain or deal with, and you don't know what is happening to you. Further, *threat* is a very real component of many experiences but is invisible (which is why great movie music gets an Oscar for creating moods when there's nothing to *see*). Put yourself in a late-night power outage in a strange house, standing at the door to a cavernous cellar from which you have been hearing noises. Carrying only a dim flashlight, you begin to open the door. Can you truly say, "Oh, it's nothing"?

To understand the fear involved—really to get it—you have to put yourself in the place of the person telling the experience. Vividly imagine yourself in the situation: *be* there, as if you were deep into a movie and it is now happening to *you*. This is the only way we know to get across the depth and power of these experiences in the lives of the people who so reluctantly tell about them.

Unless otherwise noted, experience accounts are from Bruce Greyson's and my files. Additional accounts of each type are in Appendix A.

Afraid of the light

In the first type, the elements of the experience (out-of-body event, movement, light, presences, and so on) may be identical to those found in a blissful account. What differs is the emotional response to them.

Here, for illustration, are two accounts of out-of-body experiences originating in severe allergic reactions. Nearly identical circumstances produce very different emotional responses. For the first young woman, this is definitely not a distressing experience:

Renée
"The swelling became substantially worse, and I had great difficulty breathing...Suddenly I found myself a few feet outside my body, watching with great curiosity as the firemen gave me mouth-to-mouth resuscitation and violently slapped my legs...Just as suddenly, I found myself

viewing this cosmically comic scene from slightly above the telephone wires… Delighted at my newly found freedom, I began to soar. I had become the phoenix, released at last from the limitations of the physical world. I was exhilarated. Everywhere around me there was music; the ether of my new universe was love, a love so pure and selfless that I only longed for more. . ." (Pasarow, 1981, 11)

Notice the words: "curiosity," "cosmically comic," "delighted," "freedom," "released from limitations," "exhilarated," "longed for more." Here is the classic feeling tone of the pleasurable NDE. Emphasis is on the experience itself rather than what was going on around her physical body or a fear of what could happen. The pronoun "I" is used seven times.

In contrast, with almost identical physical circumstances, a distressing account describes the massive anxiety of a thirty-eight-year-old woman:

Barbara

"Both my eyes were completely swollen shut, and I was having difficulty breathing…After a few minutes my body began to shake violently. I then experienced a sensation of floating above the room. I saw a clear picture of myself lying on the table. I saw the doctor and the nurse, whom I had never seen before, and my husband standing by my body. I became frightened, and I remember strongly feeling I didn't like what I saw and what was happening. I shouted, 'I don't like this!' but I was not heard by those in the room. After a while one eye opened a little [and] I saw that the room and the people were exactly as I had seen them during my floating sensation."

Whereas the first account described primarily *emotional* feelings, Barbara describes *physical* sensations: swollen eyes, trouble breathing, violent shaking, floating. Her attention is focused on what she can identify visually in the physical surroundings—the room, the attendants and husband, the table, her body, strange people "I had never seen before." Emotionally, she was "frightened, "I didn't like…," "I don't like." She tries to reconnect with the physical world, but "I was not heard." The pronoun "I" appears fourteen times.

Please note that we are not drawing conclusions at this point, only noticing details about the very different ways in which the women describe their experiences. We have no information to support an idea of why the two experiences were so diametrically opposite in affect.

Comments on the 'inverted' experience

This type of experience typically includes features like those of a pleasant experience but is felt in strongly unpleasant emotional tones. Kenneth Ring was the first to call them "inverted" experiences. As seen in the comparison above, what is frightening in this type of experience is not so much its objective content as the person's *subjective reaction to* the content. Situations move too fast; their incongruity makes them potentially dangerous; the experiencer feels helpless. For a materialist whose total faith is the certainty that only the physical world is real, there may be a terrifying realization that, as Ring has repeatedly said over the years, "They don't know what they encountered; they just know it wasn't supposed to be there." Reality is coming apart.

Here for the first time we see the conceptual difficulty of encountering a realm that is *other*. The world of science, remember, does not "do" the non-physical. Few of us are contemplative monks, saturated in the world of the transcendent and well versed in the history of spiritual practice; most of us have no language, no context for this kind of event. Three closely related concepts which bear on this are *control*, and *risk*, and *surrender*.

Control

Again and again in this type of experience one finds a description of events "out of control." For a person who is accustomed to being composed and in charge, this is a frightening loss of order. Things move too fast, others do not listen, there is nothing to grab onto to slow things down. A sense of careening down a slippery road pervades their telling of the experience. Safety lies in control. Especially for people whose preference in dealing with the world is cognitive, rational, analytical—the preferred mode in Western culture—the perception of chaos may be extremely alarming.

Risk

On the other hand, some people live for risk. Speedboat and race car drivers, for instance, and test pilots love the adrenaline rush, the feel of being "on the edge," the knowledge that something could go very wrong at any time. Part of being able to enjoy such risk is the belief in one's own skill to deal with whatever may occur.

For most of us, when a situation is beyond our knowledge or skill level, distress will follow. NDEs are risky. Like prayer and other spiritual practice, they function in the realm of non-physical encounter, where prediction stops working. Perhaps one reason that people respond so differently to an NDE lies in their ability to tolerate the radical riskiness of free-fall into *otherness*.

Surrender

Surrender is not a tolerable stance for people who value control and structure. Surrender makes a person vulnerable. In our highly competitive, entrepreneurial, individualistic society, being "vulnerable" is associated with weakness. And that's very scary.

Ram Dass (1989, 185) tells a wonderful story about a chicken and a pig walking down a street one morning, looking for breakfast. They come to a restaurant, and the chicken says, "Come on, let's get something to eat." The pig says, "Not me. I'm not going in any place advertises eggs and bacon." And the chicken says, "So? We'll order something else." "No," says the pig. "You don't get it. It's the principle: From you all they want is a contribution. From me they want total surrender."

In the same passage Ram Dass quotes Mahatma Gandhi as saying, "God demands nothing less than complete self-surrender as the price for the only freedom that is worth having. When a person loses himself/ herself, they immediately find themselves in the service of all that lives." Jesus said, "By gaining his life a man will lose it; by losing his life for my sake, he will gain it." We are all, in this sense, the Ram Dass pigs.

At the end of C.S. Lewis' *Narnia* series of books for children (1956), the many characters assemble to witness the end of the earthly kingdom of Narnia. The children and their multitudinous friends find themselves in the company of those they most love, with the great lion, Aslan, at a banquet of delicious foods spread under blue skies on a perfect day. They are deliriously happy. To one side, a group of dwarves huddle in a tight circle, convinced that they are captives in a dark and musty stable. Although the same blue sky is available to them, and the same warm air, and delicious food, the dwarves are unable to see them but register only hay, and old turnips, and a trough of dirty water. Perhaps something of the same phenomenon occurs with the first type of frightening NDE, and the task of the experiencer is to discern what is a delicacy and what is turnips. The difficulty of doing so will be discussed further, especially in Chapter 9.

The Void

What the second type of experiences have in common is some version of the Void, a palpable emptiness, a mental but otherwise nonsensory negation of self and world. Although the Void experience may at first seem like something altogether different than an NDE, a close look shows that despite showing fewer typical elements, the characteristics are present but subtler. These accounts include out-of-body episodes, a sense of movement and great speed, intense affect, darkness, strong messages, and a sense of ultimate Truth; there may be encounters with unfamiliar or hostile presences. Rarely is there a life review. The Light is not perceived; but that, of course, defines this type of experience, which may leave a pervasive residue of emptiness and fatalistic despair after the event. Several of the people whose experiences are included here were still in psychotherapy, some of them twenty years after their NDE.

Gary

A young artist lost control of his car on a snowy winter evening. As the car slid down an embankment and into a brook, he hit his head on the windshield and lost consciousness. He described leaving his body, watching as icy water filled the car, and:

> "I saw the ambulance coming, and I saw the people trying to help me, get me out of the car and to the hospital. At that time I was no longer in my body. I had left my body. I was probably a hundred or two hundred feet up and to the south of the accident, and I felt the warmth and the kindness of the people trying to help me. I felt their compassion and all the good feeling that was emanating from these people. And I also felt the source of all that kind of kindness or whatever, and it was very, very powerful, and I was afraid of it, and so I didn't accept it. I just said 'No.' I was very uncertain about it, and I didn't feel comfortable, and so I rejected it.

> "And it was at that moment that I left the planet. I could feel myself and see myself going way, way up into the air, then beyond the solar system, beyond the galaxy, and out beyond anything physical. At first I thought I'd just go with it, see where it went, and I stayed as calm as I could, just kind of went with the whole thing. And that part of it was all right for a while.

> "But then as the hours went on with absolutely no sensation, there was no pain, but there was no hot, no cold, no light, no taste, no smell, no sensation whatsoever. None, other than the fact that I felt a slight sensation of traveling at an extremely fast speed. And I knew I was leaving the earth and everything else, all of the physical world. And at that point it became unbearable, it became horrific, as time goes on when you have no feeling, no sensation, no sense of light. I started to

panic and struggle and pray and everything I could think of to struggle to get back, and I communicated with a sister of mine who passed away. And at that moment I went back into my body, and my body at that point had been moved to the hospital."

Helene
Like the experience in the Introduction, the next NDE occurred during childbirth.

> "Voices were laughing at me, telling me all of life was a 'dream,' that there was no Heaven, hell, or Earth, really, and that all I had experienced in life was actually an hallucination. I remember trying to tell the nuns, who were smiling in happy anticipation of the impending birth, 'How can you smile, when you've given your lives for religion, and there is no religion, no heaven or hell?' I passed through a stage of terrible thirst, and the voices kept laughing and telling me, 'You think this is bad? Wait 'til the next stage!'

> "I found myself hurtling towards the final torment: I was to be suspended in a total vacuum with nothing to see or do for eternity. I was naked, and I was sad about that because I thought, 'If only I had clothing I could pull the threads and knot them or reweave them for something to do. And, 'If only I were sitting in a chair I could splinter it and try to make something of the splinters.' And then the overwhelming realization that eternity was forever and ever, time without end! What to do in a vacuum forever?

> "...After all these years, the nightmare remains vivid in my mind. I assure you, the worst form of hell, in my mind at least, would be myself suspended, naked, in a vacuum!"

Comments on the Void

"The experience of the Void," says psychiatrist Stanislav Grof (1988, 147), "is the most enigmatic and paradoxical of all the transpersonal experiences. It is experiential identification with the primordial Emptiness, Nothingness, and Silence, which seem to be the ultimate cradle of all existence…This emptiness is thus, in a sense, pregnant with all of existence, since it contains everything in a potential form."

When encountered by a person who is by discipline and understanding ready for it, an experience of the Void represents a supreme achievement, the height of spiritual attainment. For a Buddhist this may be Nirvana, the objective of spiritual practice. For a Christian or Jew, it is the rhapsodic union described by the great mystics. By contrast, for the average Western person, a spiritual amateur, it is equivalent to being a novice skier on an Olympic ski jump. The problem with "everything in a potential form" is that what is potential is not yet visible; the event is experienced as an object-less emptiness, or annihilation.

Think about the education of those scientists we hold in the greatest esteem—astronauts, heart surgeons, Nobel Prize winners in chemistry and physics. They spend decades in training, learning obscure facts and difficult skills; they know things that most people have never heard of, which they discuss in such a specialized vocabulary that small-talk is almost impossible at parties; eventually they are truly comfortable only with each other. In other words, their professions demand that they become esoterics, keepers of knowledge hidden from the rest of us. We consider that perfectly normal: after all, they're astronauts and molecular chemists, and so on.

Another group of experts goes through much the same intensity of education. They spend decades training in obscure facts, difficult skills, a specialized vocabulary, knowledge hidden from the rest of us. Most don't even go to parties. They are technicians of the sacred, astronauts of the spirit—Benedictines and Trappists, Tibetan lamas and Sufi dervishes, heirs to the Baal Shem Tov. Their task is to venture into the deep space of consciousness and to describe what they encounter. Yet despite their scholarship and discipline, most of us will consider their learning fanciful and their skills impossible, because their expertise is in the non-physical life. Many of us could have that knowledge, just as we might become astronauts, if we were willing to undertake the discipline; but discipline sounds too much like oppression in today's world, and we suspect that only a neurotic person would put up with it. On the other hand, scientifically-minded people may admire the discipline but are almost guaranteed to discredit the skills.

Isn't it odd, as a friend once commented, that we practice guitar and saxophone and piano; we practice golf and gymnastics; we practice aerobics; but we rarely, if ever, practice anything in our inner life. We spend months planning a two-week vacation, but we do not plan to die—nor, for that matter, do we plan how to live. We tend to think it will just happen. And so, although we would not dream of asking an amateur to pilot a mission to outer space, we somehow expect ourselves to encounter inner space without training or assistance.

The result, when the Void comes, is too often the response described by Dorothee Soelle (1975, 85): "...the experience of being forsaken by God. In the depth of suffering people see themselves as abandoned and forsaken by everyone. That which gave life its meaning has become empty and void; it turned out to be an error, an illusion that is shattered, a guilt that cannot be rectified, a void. The paths that lead to this experience of nothingness are diverse, but the experience of annihilation that occurs... is the same."

One woman sums up the aftereffects mentioned by many people with this type of experience:

"On returning home, I found myself not wanting to talk to anyone. I felt that no one existed except me. I continued my duties as wife and mother, but I would wonder why. I would watch TV and think that I created all that was shown on it. Then I would wonder why I didn't know the outcome of a movie, and then I would rationalize that I was creating as I watched, so naturally I had not created an ending until the end. I wrote this poem a few weeks later:

> I have been to hell.
> It is not as you say:
> There is no fire nor brimstone,
> People screaming for another day.
> There is only darkness—everywhere."

Hell

Most people assume that all frightening near-death experiences will be hellish in the conventional sense; yet this was the least common type in the study, as it is in the IANDS archives and in the several online collections of NDE accounts. They are, however, the most frequent in book form (it's harder to be 'sexy' and published about, say, the Void). Although they are fewest in number, here is the widest range of images, a vividly felt catechism of horrors, not all of them visual.

The earliest information about these NDEs came in brief, sometimes abrupt letters, often from a family member of the experiencer, as in the quotes below.

> 1. "When [my mother-in-law] came to consciousness, she had the most terrified look I'd ever seen, and she said to me, 'I've just seen Dante's Inferno.' That was all, she wouldn't say any more."

> 2. "After he was able to speak, [my brother-in law] told of this experience. He felt himself slipping down some stairs and down and down in blackness and scared and a deep fear. He got to bottom and saw some very large rusty doors with a rusty lock and chain, people sitting outside on benches. He was so afraid of what he saw he was in a panic and knew he was at

the very doors of hell and with great effort climbed back up those stairs to the outside world again and realized they were working on him to get a heart beat."

3. "Hell is a pit and there is darkness, but there is also fire. I was in a place to which the Bible refers as 'outer darkness' and it is not pretty... After my experience, I could not talk about it. I did not want people to know that I had gone to hell...Some people may just want to laugh this 'hell business' off, but as real as this letter is, so is that place."

Fran

From a young woman who attempted suicide by drug overdose:

"The doctor leaned over close to me and told me I was dying. The muscles in my body began to jerk upward, out of control. I could no longer speak, but I knew what was happening. Although my body slowed down, things around me and things happening to me went rather fast. I then felt my body slipping down, not straight down but on an angle, as if on a slide. It was cold, dark, and watery. When I reached the bottom, it resembled the entrance to a cave, with what looked like webs hanging. The inside of the cave was gray and brown in color.

"I heard cries, wails, moans, and the gnashing of teeth. I saw these beings that resembled humans, with the shape of a head and body. But they were ugly and grotesque. I remember colors like red, green, and purple, but can't positively remember if this was the color of these beings. They were frightening and sounded like they were tormented, in agony. No one spoke to me.

"I never went inside the cave but stood at the entrance only. I remember saying to myself, 'I don't want to stay here.' I tried to lift myself up as though trying to pull myself (my spirit) up out of this pit. That's the last I remember."

Lou

A man in his late forties, despondent over persistent disappointments in his life, attempted to hang himself:

> "From the roof of the utility shed in my back yard I jumped to the ground. Luckily for me I had forgot the broken lawn chair that lay near the shed. My feet hit the chair and broke my fall, or my neck would have been broken. I hung in the rope and strangled. I was outside my physical body. I saw my body hanging in the rope: it looked awful. I was terrified, could see and hear but different—hard to explain. Demons were all around me. I could hear them but could not see them. They chattered like blackbirds. It was as if they knew they had me and had all eternity to drag me down into hell, to torment me. It would have been the worst kind of hell, trapped hopeless between two worlds, wandering lost and confused for all eternity.

> "I had to get back into my body. Oh my God, I needed help. I ran to the house, went in through the door without opening it, cried out to my wife but she could not hear me, so I went right into her body. I could see and hear with her eyes and ears. Then I made contact, heard her say, 'Oh, my God!'

> "She grabbed a knife from the kitchen chair and ran out to where I was hanging and got up on an old chair and cut me down. She could find no pulse; she was a nurse. When the emergency squad got to me my heart had stopped; my breath too was gone."

The hybrid experience

Some experiences include both pleasant and decidedly unpleasant scenarios. Perhaps because these are longer and more detailed accounts, they include the most graphic images. The next two accounts are examples of such a shift.

Rachel

"I have never related my experience [eight years ago] to anyone, because I was sure that they would think that I was a complete nut; and quite frankly, I am not all that convinced that I am not a complete nut. An article appeared in the Sunday supplement of the [newspaper] which prompted me to write this letter. If, in fact, you find me nuts, then merely disregard the following. I am not here to convince anyone of the following, as I, myself, am not totally convinced. I know that it all happened, and yet, logically, I cannot account for the happening—or possibly I just can't totally accept the reality of it—because I am Jewish and I do not believe in Jesus Christ. *I only believe in God.* [Emphasis in original.]

It was February, 1975. The roads were disastrous, covered with ice and snow. My husband and I were traveling to my mother-in-law's to drop off the two boys...[when] an oncoming vehicle slid over three lanes to hit us head on. The roof of our car collapsed, and my head was stuck between windshield, dash, and roof. Supposedly—I was unconscious to all onlookers, yet something weird was happening to me. Maybe I was dreaming—but it was so real; I really don't know. Maybe you will know and will be able to explain to me what actually occurred. I have asked God many times since then, why he just did not let me die as I so desired upon the touch of that hand.

"I was in a circle of light. I looked down upon the accident scene. I looked directly into the car that struck ours, and I saw a young woman with her head bent down resting on the steering wheel, and I knew that she was dead. I looked into my car and saw myself trapped and unconscious. I saw several cars stop and a lady taking my children to her car to sit and rest until the ambulance would arrive. I heard all the commotion and all the goings-on, and I saw it all. I heard [my husband] talk to me, and I saw me never moving and never answering. From the time that I left until the time that I returned was only a matter of minutes in reality; and yet my experience was so slow and quiet and peaceful from that time on when I was in the circle of light.

"[A] hand touched mine, and I turned to see where this peace and serenity and blissful feeling was coming from, and there was Jesus Christ—I mean the way he is made out to be in all the paintings, with white robe and beard and hood draped and so soft and sweet and so angelic—and I never wanted to leave this man and this place. I never looked or thought back upon the accident scene or earth again, until the final experience prodded me to do so.

"I was led around a well, because I wanted to stay with him and hold his hand. He led me from a side of bliss to a side of misery. I did not want to look, but he made me look, and I was disgusted and horrified and scared. It was so ugly. The people were blackened and sweaty and moaning in pain and chained to their spots. I had to walk through the area back to the well. One [person] was even chained to the evil side of the well. I hated it there. I couldn't wait to get to the well and go around it. He led me to it, but he made me go through it alone as he watched. Someone else followed me through and then stepped in front of me to help me walk over the debris on the ground (snakes or something). I never looked at this thing, but I know it was dark. The man was so skeletal and in such pain—the one chained by the side of the well—I wanted them to help him, but no one would—and I knew that I would be one of these creatures if I stayed, because of what I saw in the well. I knew that if I elected to stay because of the greatest, most serene feeling, that I would only have misery because he didn't want me to stay.

"I leaned over the well, and this young Jesus look-alike (maybe it was God himself, or maybe the Christians aren't as peculiar as I think they are) put his hand on my back as I looked in. There were three children calling, 'Mommie, Mommie, Mommie, we need you. Please come back to us.' There were two boys and a girl. The two boys were much older than my two little ones, and I didn't have a little girl. The little girl looked up at me (they were inside the well in water) and begged me to go back to life—and then all at once I was in the circle again (his hand still on my shoulder) and I saw the accident scene again, and I cried that I did not ever want to leave him—and then I heard my babies cry and saw the lady taking them to her car—and I knew I had to leave and get back. It was my responsibility. I moaned, awake in the car again, and I screamed for my children. I knew where they were, but I demanded that [my husband] tell me about the lady taking them to her car. I wanted to make sure that what I saw was real. And then the police and ambulance men tried to get me out of the wreck. Nobody wanted to tell me that the girl in the other car died—but I knew she had because I saw her, even if no one there knew that I did.

"Well, several years later I had a baby…I knew it would be the little girl in the well…

"It's strange, but at the time of the accident and following I knew that I no longer loved my husband, but I stayed with him. Right after the birth of my little girl, we got divorced... Many times these past years I thought about giving up my children to their father, because of the things he could do for them financially—but I always dismiss it because of my experience and how they cried and needed me. I am supposed to raise them, I know that. I also know that there is truly a higher being and something after this life. . . I know and yet I don't know."

Howard

In transcendent experiences, the pattern of death, resurrection, and rebirth is among the oldest and most widespread in human history. Throughout the world's tribal cultures, in shamanic initiation experiences it is common for initiates to sense being physically attacked or devoured by hostile entities and then reassembled into a "new being." However, if our study is representative, such attack may be uncommon in Western near-death experiences.

The first detailed account of this type to come to our attention was not part of the original Greyson/Bush study but came in an audiotape from Howard Storm, the first near-death experiencer who had the courage to "go public" with such an experience. The quotes here come from a newspaper article (Corneille, 1989); considerably later, Storm wrote his own memoir of the experience (2001).

Storm was a member of the art faculty at Northern Kentucky University and was accompanying a student field trip to Paris when he collapsed in agony with what was diagnosed as a perforated lower intestine. After many hours of delay at the hospital, he lapsed into unconsciousness. Regaining consciousness, he found himself standing next to the bed.

"I could feel my body perfectly. I didn't understand what was on the bed. I tried talking to my wife. She was sitting on the side of the bed staring at the ground. I got really angry and started shouting and swearing because she didn't respond. You have to remember, I had been unconscious and there I was suddenly standing next to the bed. It was then I heard male and female voices calling me."

Storm followed the voices into the hallway, where six or eight figures were waiting for him. He could not see their faces.

"I started becoming concerned the people around me weren't friendly. I could hear them whispering things like, 'Shhh...don't scare him off; he's going to be good.' I could sense their hostility. . . I didn't know how to get back to my room. It was at this time I started thinking, 'Maybe I'm dead,' but I didn't believe it because all my senses were working and I could feel my body."

Some of the figures attacked him—pushing, biting, scratching, gouging pieces out of his fingers—until Storm collapsed in pain and exhaustion. "In retrospect," he says, "I think they were beings who have no feelings of their own. The only way they can have senses is to fight with someone who has feelings."

Then—Storm struggles to explain this—it seemed that his own voice spoke from his chest, telling him to pray.

"I didn't know how. I started reciting parts of the national anthem, the 23rd Psalm, anything that had 'thees' and 'thous' in it. I didn't know where I was... if I was alive or dead. I smelled of something spoiled, like chicken. It gave me the impression I was decomposing, going putrid. I don't know how long I was there. I was in complete despair. I didn't become unconscious, I just stopped thinking. I just went blank."

Then, he says, the words of a Sunday School song came to him.

"'Jesus loves me, this I know...' I remember starting to think again. I thought, 'I'm going to try this.'" And as he began remembering the words of the children's hymn, "I was surrounded by bright light, brighter than an acetylene torch. I just knew it was a being. I just knew it knew me. It surrounded me with complete, unconditional love. It just loved me."

As this excerpt indicates, Storm's experience recapitulates the classic pattern of the shamanic initiation: suffering, death, and resurrection, or dismemberment, annihilation, and reconstitution. (See Chapter 6.) Following a long period of healing and adjustment, Storm later became the pastor of a liberal Protestant church in the Midwest, rebuilding its congregation and, with them, developing social action programs that reach out to meet community needs.

Comments on hellish experiences

A variety of sight and sound crowds these experiences, covering sensory extremes from clammy darkness to a rain of fire, from screeching blackbirds and moaning voices to insistent reed flutes. Demons are heard but not seen; other beings commonly appear with obscured faces. Landscapes, when mentioned, tend to be bleak or slimy.

With the hellish experience accounts more than the others, and excepting the Storm account, a close look at the contents often shows that the thing most feared is the fear itself, that it is the sense of dread rather than specific torments that creates the horror.

In a powerful article about responses immediately post-NDE, nurse educator Roberta Orne (1995) described the attitudes of a patient whose "interpretation of the NDE not only magnified her previous fear of death but precipitated such anguish that she signed out of the hospital against medical advice even though she had a life-threatening condition. 'I had to get out of there. I was afraid of what was gonna happen—again.' She had tried to put the NDE out of her mind, 'But I can't, it's there all the time.'"

About the "hybrid" experience, Michael Sabom observed as early as 1982 (41) that "Momentary fright or bewilderment sometimes accompanied the initial passage into darkness, as the person pondered: What is going on here? In time, however, these unpleasant emotions were replaced with calm, peace, or tranquility, as further elements of the NDE began to unfold."

Sabom's observation is echoed by psychologist Christopher Bache (1994, 42), whose substantial work with altered states of consciousness led him to declare that "a frightening near-death experience is an incomplete near-death experience."

In occasional instances, a pleasant NDE has become distressing rather than the other way around; but this is uncommon. The frightening-to-pleasant conversion pattern has become a helpful model in reassuring individuals and families who are severely traumatized by the thought of a hellish NDE.

In some accounts we find the suggestion that a shift toward the positive occurs when the individual stops fighting the unfamiliar experience and simply accepts it. Kenneth Ring has suggested that perhaps a few people get "stuck" in the frightening aspects of their NDE and are unable to move beyond it; if they could "go with it," he reasons, the fear might resolve into peace (Ring, 1980, 249).

In most hellish accounts, the people having the experience participate as observers, as in all but one of the accounts here. *Others*, they say, were moaning and in chains; *others* were tormented. Although in great fear or horror, they themselves were either personally escorted through the hellish scene or did not enter it at all but surveyed it from the periphery, sometimes from a considerable distance.

The quality of *detachment* in this group has been noticed in accounts of medieval European hellish experiences. Alice R. Turner, author of *The History of Hell* (1993, 102), comments that amidst the descriptions of demons, fiery coals, an infernal wheel, flocks of ravening birds, and boiling oceans, "Most visions...seem oddly distanced. The tortures don't really hurt and aren't nearly as nasty as in the old apocalypses; they're just part of the story." (102) The experiences to which she refers, like these contemporary accounts, seemed to be of the cautionary variety, suggesting a need for change in the person's life and/or a re-evaluation of what really matters—not power, not money but love, knowledge, and service.

4
Experiencer Responses

"Often," says Reed Anthony Carlson (2008), a young man who co-writes a particularly interesting blog, "a person experiences something unexplainable, a 'spiritual experience' if you will, and we find that he or she immediately begins making conclusions on what or who they encountered, why they had this experience, and what it is they needed to learn or act on because of it. These conclusions come primarily from worldview, not really from experience itself, and are inevitable, because they are necessary to the very human act of attempting to contextualize experience so that it can be understood."

And that summarizes the plight of almost every near-death experiencer—most especially those who have been devastated by the event. With only rare exceptions, the explanatory tools we bring *into* an NDE are only what we know beforehand. Sometimes that is not a help.

Writing for the *Journal of Near-Death Studies*, Christopher Bache (1994, 25) observed, "Survivors of frightening NDEs are doubly alienated in our culture. First they must manage the general failure of our society even today to accept the reality of their experience. Second, and more importantly, while the majority of NDErs report basking in divine light, they were taken to hell, or at least to its doorstep. How could they not take this as a devastating commentary on their life? How could they not conclude that they were deliberately singled out for harsher treatment by some higher intelligence? This reaction is reinforced by theological interpretations of frightening NDEs."

Against this background, individual people awaken from a redefining experience and either repress it, as Rawlings insists (1978), or go about the long-term task of making sense of it. *What was that?* The immediate need is for comprehensibility, for a definition of terms that leads to a sense of meaning.

Psychotherapist Miriam Greenspan (2004, 132), whose book *Healing Through the Dark Emotions* is highly recommended, notes, "Meaning-making is a defining characteristic of what it is to be human. Existing without purpose or meaning, for humans, is like existing without air. You can only go for so long before you choke."

Depth psychologist Leonard Corbett (1996, 73) offers, "It is useful to think of 'meaning' as the dispositional power of an event, or what it will cause us to think or do."

Following a terrifying near-death experience, then, what is its dispositional power—what do people tend to think, and how do they go about living their lives?

Over a good many years of observation, three distinct types of response have emerged in the making of meaning of NDEs. They apply to both pleasurable and terrifying experiences, and each links strongly with the ways in which the people involved will go about living their lives. Perhaps the most common is conversion, turning one's life around. Another is reductionism, replacing an alarming explanation by one that feels more manageable. The third response is a failure of resolution, which can range from bewilderment and a searching for one's life mission to a lingering disbelief and despair.

No claim will be made here that these three types of response are definitive or exclusive; however, they are clearly common. To these three types of response, repression might be added in the case of stark terror, as Maurice Rawlings has repeatedly claimed. There is at present neither reason to doubt him nor data to support the claim, as of course repressed experiences are invisible to investigation.

Although it is likely that these three response types apply to all types of NDE, discussion here deals solely with disturbing experiences.

Conversion

Conversion is not necessarily a change of religion but turning one's life around. This is the original meaning of the Greek word *metanoia*, meaning "to turn around," which in English is translated as *repent*. In colloquial terms, the response is probably what people mean when they say, "I needed that."

Among people with NDEs of types #1 and #3, genuinely terrifying and even hellish, it is likely that most fit this model. They understand the message of the NDE as simple: *This is a warning. Something in your life is wrong and must change, or there will be unwelcome outcomes.* Often with great anxiety, the experiencers search themselves for behaviors they think might have precipitated such an NDE, and they take steps to stop those behaviors. They look for avenues by which to modify their lives and temper their fear and residual anxieties. In some religious terms, they identify their sin and take steps to atone for it.

This literalized interpretation appears especially among people who described their experience as explicitly hell-like and have taken a concretistic attitude toward it.

"I was being shown that I had to shape up or ship out, one or the other. In other words, 'get your act together,' and I did just that" (Rommer, 46).

"The feeling I got was redemption. Hell was the place I was bound for, but not a place that I have to go now" (Rommer, 50).

"I too am not afraid to die now, because I made sure where I'm going when I die. I was a good person when I died, but being good will not get anyone to heaven…My priorities changed. There is definitely a place called hell. After my experience, I could not talk about it. I did not want people to know that I had gone to hell. I got out the Bible and really studied...Some people may just want to laugh this 'hell business' off, but as real as this letter is, so is that place." (Personal communication)

Here is the classic "saved" scenario of altar-rail conversion, though it is interesting that the behaviors experiencers typically identify as threatening to their salvation seem not so terrible: partying, petty shoplifting, drug use, not attending worship, or a legal misdemeanor. There may also be descriptions of a more internalized history of selfishness, quick temper, irresponsibility, problems forming relationships. None of the study participants mentioned major crime or sociopathology.

Movement toward a religious community, often a conservative one, is a common report in this group. Medical social worker Kimberly Clark Sharp (1986, 85), who, after Rawlings, was among the first to acknowledge hellish experiences, observed, "All the people I know who have had negative experiences have become Bible-based Christians...They might express it in various sects. But they all feel that they have come back from an awful situation and have a second chance." In Judaism, the equivalent is experiencers who have moved toward Orthodox observance, the pattern being the search for rules and order as protection against a recurrence of the NDE. Whether religious or secular, any fundamentalist belief system offers legitimization of deep-seated fear: the person is not hallucinating, not mad; there are, in fact, malevolent external forces at work in the world and in the human heart, and there are ways of dealing with them.

The role of fear in conservative religious groups has been well documented (Marty and Appleby, 1992; Spong, 1992, Bivens, 2007). That fear remains a powerful influence for these experiencers; but within those groups they find sanction for it, and a way out. Although a wrathful God is watching our choices; there are ways to counter the hazards. Within the group experiencers can find welcome and support: there will be affirmation of a truth in their experience and a language in which to talk about it, a theology to explain what happened, and a social community prescribing definite rules about how to live in the world so as to avoid another such encounter. What seem to outsiders like narrowly drawn boundaries, some frightened experiencers identify as safety nets promising, after all, the heaven that eluded them earlier.

> "I've stopped drugs, moved back to Florida, and now I'm in Bible college. I used to have a casual attitude toward death, but now I actually fear it more. So yes, it was a warning. I was permitted another chance to change my behavior on earth… I've taken my fear of death and given it to the scriptures" (Rommer, 43).

Reductionism

Reductionism is a well-known phenomenon among secular investigators who deny any spiritual claims about NDEs. For those accustomed to the clarity of hard evidence and replicable material data, it is more satisfying to be able to say, "It's only a lack of oxygen…only hallucination…only rapid eye movements"… (or any of the other "it's onlies") than it is to wonder about non-physical origins or to ask, "What does this mean to this person?"

Obviously, the work of those investigators may prove quite adequate to identifying the physiological correlates to an NDE. Nonetheless, reductionism is equivalent to knowing that having been kicked by a horse is what broke one's leg: while that may be useful knowledge, it does nothing to repair the shattered bone or live with the consequences. With near-death experience, a reductionist response provides the illusion of authority but is experientially useless.

Lionel Corbett (1996, 35), Professor of Depth Psychology at Pacifica Graduate Institute, describes this kind of disavowal as the "defense [that] allows one to repudiate the meaning of an event which does not fit into a safe category and to treat the event as if it did not matter."

From the University of Virginia, Justine Owens (1992, 72) said, "Even a good model of what was going on in the brain during a near-death experience would not explain it away, or explain the powerful aftereffects commonly reported, the sense of purpose and meaning in life."

Some experiencers, too, find the safely external and material explanations of reductionism a palatable answer to the question of "What was that?" The near-death experience of a young woman in New York City included first loving, then very frightening elements. Although reporting that her life had changed significantly and positively since the experience, she concluded,

> "There is a universe of people who have had experiences like mine. They have weekly Internet chats and meetings, and they write books with 'light' in the title: *Saved by the Light, Lessons from the Light.* They have their own shorthand, talking about NDEs (near-death experiences) and OBEs (out-of-body experiences). Their websites play plinky New Age music, and some talk about angels and aliens. My feelings about these people? Excuse me while I look around for Mulder and Della Reese [TV stars from shows about the paranormal]. There are actual rational explanations for what I experienced. British researcher Susan Blackmore says…[endorphins and cortical activity]. In the 1930s, a University of Chicago scientist, Heinrich Kluver, PhD, determined that…[anoxia]. University of Chicago neurobiologist Jack Cowan, PhD figured out that…[neural activity in the dying brain].] It's all very scientific" (Ingall, 2000).

The young woman seems quite aware of the positive effects of the experience on her life and untraumatized by its disquieting aspects. Her conclusion, based on scientific evidence, is that the experience has no particular meaning—except that actual dying won't be all that bad.

A different response entirely is that of a man in New England who for almost two decades had been on the near-death speaking circuit, telling groups about his light-filled NDE and exploring its significance. Then, in a second experience, he felt himself to be the prey of gigantic, brightly colored but sinister and threatening geometric forms that rushed at him with uncanny force and speed. Its effect was to "wipe out" the understandings he had ascribed to his earlier NDE, leaving him with a deep-seated pessimism and terror of dying.

The experience was so horrifying that he consulted an attorney about bringing a malpractice suit against his physician and the hospital. In Corbett's terms, the experience decidedly "does not fit into a safe category" and must be repudiated. Hearing that certain drug reactions commonly include perceptions of visual forms, he found a way out: The second experience was "only a drug reaction." He has no interest in exploring this event or why his reaction to it was so different from the first, and no amount of reassurance based on his earlier radiant NDE has eased his fear or his rage. He remains very fearful of dying. (Personal communication)

Kenneth Ring has put forward the argument (1994, 21) that, at least for women in childbirth, "such experiences—though highly real—are not true NDEs as such but are essentially emergence reactions to inadequate anesthesia…further intensified by initial resistance and fear." This argument is undercut by his exempting *blissful* experiences that occur under identical circumstances; they remain true NDEs while the distressing ones do not. Although inadequate anesthesia might in some instances explain causation, it begs the question so far as *experience* is concerned and seems a fair example of Corbett's (1996, 35) reductionism as a "defense [that] allows one to repudiate the meaning of an event which does not fit into a safe category."

The *experience* remains. To the individual, living with something that looks like a deeply distressing NDE, acts like an NDE, and talks like an NDE, "It's only a drug reaction" may provide a temporary buffer that, at least in the short term, masks questions and anxiety but does nothing to help resolve them.

Unresolved dismay and despair

It is not surprising that the New England experiencer—not yet able to defuse the dread he remembers from within the second experience or to recapture confidence in his first—remains fearful. The lack of resolution moves him from reductionism to this third group, in which the individuals have identified no comprehensible meaning in their near-death experiences. Especially following experiences of the Void but cutting across other types also, these are people who, years later, may still struggle with the existential implications of a frightening NDE.

The following quotes are from letters in my files:

> "I had an experience which has remained with me for 29 years… Over the years I read various books on life after death and everyone seemed to have good experiences…It has left a horror in my mind and I have never spoken about it until now…" (D.P.).

> "For twenty-six years I have been plagued by a fear of death [following an NDE] … As a result of this traumatic experience, I developed anxiety attacks, depression and feelings of depersonalization. These emotional problems grew into a generalized phobic response problem (agoraphobia). Although I have overcome these problems for the most part, I still harbor some fears about death" (C.B.).

> "For some reason, [thirty-one years later] all the memories are back and vivid, including the incident. It's like living it all over again, and I don't want to. I thought I had it all resolved and in its place, but I'm having a really bad time trying to put it away this time" (J.E.).

> "I have experienced some serious problems this year [including] depression. The weight of my unresolved NDE experience seemed, at least at times, to deplete the energy required to deal with current situations" (C.W.).

Conversations and correspondence indicate that these experiencers are typically articulate people haunted by the existential dimension of the event and searching for an explanation that is both intellectually and emotionally grounding. Intellectually unable to accept a literal reading of the event, they also find reductionist explanations inadequate, as the theories assign a cause but do not address the question of *meaning or integration*. Of the three groups, perhaps none has worked harder to find resolution. Their struggle is to find a way in which the encounter can make sense without destroying them (which is to say, their trust in the workings of the world) in the process.

More than the other experiencer groups, these experiencers mention having been in therapy, some of them for many years; without better data, it is not possible to say whether this indicates anything other than their openness to the idea of therapy and the financial means to pursue it. Their caregivers, for the most part, have been unable to reach the "real" issues: There are too many stories of medications prescribed to mask the questioning; of therapists who will not address the matter or who leave the client feeling blamed, or who so thoroughly romanticize spirituality they cannot deal with its dark side; of clergy who have no idea what to say or who reject the experience outright.

The religious element of these experiences is often an absence:

"I was filled with a sense of absolute terror and of being past the help of anyone, even God." (C.B.)

"Nobody was there, not even God." (BT)

"I expected the Lord to be there, but He wasn't. There was no God…I called on God and He wasn't there. That's what scared me." (Rommer, 53)

Overwhelmingly, their questions include some variant of, "What did I do to deserve this?" What is the truth about existence? What's wrong with me? What are the rules, if the rules I lived by don't work? What is there that I can't identify about myself, that this should happen? Not for a long time, if ever, do they lose their fear of death.

5
Common Questions

1. Are these things real?
What do you mean by "real"? There are at least two kinds of reality: a "real world" of material, physical objects and a "real world" of invisible, interior personal experiences that happen somewhere (and somehow) in our mind. Both are real, but differently.

The view of science for the past 300-plus years, and ferociously during the past century, has been that only physical reality is "real" reality; the rest has increasingly been dismissed as illusion. To say, "It's all in your mind" means that the "it" is not only unreal but unimportant.

This is obviously nonsense. Is loving someone less real than breaking your thumb with a rock? Is the political passion that starts a war less real than the rubble of a bombed city? Brain scans during deep prayer and meditation show activity in certain parts of the brain and demonstrate that something is happening; but scans are neither prayer nor meditation any more than a book of photos is a trip to Niagara Falls.

A near-death experience is a real experiential event in the life of the individual who has it. The instant it is told, it ceases to be that experience and becomes a story, a narrative that cannot be "known" to anyone else as it is to the experiencer. Does the memory point to a "real" reality of the material world? Could it be photographed? Any possible photos would be only of neural activity, not of the experience itself. There is no known geographical locality that matches what is described in NDEs. On the other hand, NDEs have real consequences, some of which may be physical, that are real enough to disrupt and reshape human lives. They belong to a category of events that have been known and respected around the world through time.

The sophisticated young blogger mentioned earlier (Carlson, 2008) makes some useful observations:

> The vast majority of human beings alive today, as well as those who have lived throughout history, never had a problem believing in supernatural activity that regularly affected their lives. …[C]onsensus never proves truth, but it should make us aware of our inevitable bias.

> Most cultures do not operate with strict codes denoting the "physical" and "metaphysical" realms. For the Pentecostal Christian communities in the bush in Africa, the spiritualist aboriginal cultures in the Pacific islands, and the Shamanistic nature religions in the remote mountains of South America, humans and spirits walk the same ground and live life side by side in a way a westerner cannot fully grasp. Seemingly miraculous healings/exorcisms/ demon sightings can and do occur—any cultural anthropologist will tell you this. But you will find alongside the "spiritual" explanation a "scientific" one that accounts for the same phenomena through Psychology, deceit, or nature. Acknowledging these other explanations should not force us to choose either side. It should simply make us wary when determining what can and cannot exist based solely off of what we can and cannot observe in the material realm. (http://theophiliacs.com/2008/09/14/demons/)

2. Where is the medical evidence that these NDEs happened?
The fact that this question keeps being asked is an indication that a great many people don't get the idea of "experience." *A near-death or similar experience is a private, personal happening in consciousness. It is not a public activity.* An NDE is not open to observers. A medical record tracks a person's physiological events and circumstances; it may register a blip in some function but it cannot "prove" that an NDE occurred or was absent during that blip. Only the patient can report an NDE.

3. Who are these people?
When their experiences happened, the fifty people in the Greyson/Bush study ranged from nine years old to their late 60s. At that time, they were Roman Catholic, Protestant (liberal, mainstream, and evangelical/ fundamentalist), Jewish (Conservative and Reform), agnostic, atheist, or had no religious identification at all; some were devout, others lackadaisical or nonobservant. We have no specific information about race, but based on what is known about the IANDS archive, the great majority would be Caucasian. They represent students, housewives, professionals, blue-collar and white-collar workers; several were retired at the time of their experience. They are heterosexual, bisexual, homosexual, single, married, divorced and widowed. In this particular study, most of the NDEs occurred somewhere in North America; a few took place in Europe.

Because these fifty people volunteered their information, they cannot, in strict research terms, be considered a random sample of experiencers. However, they are from a wide enough variety of background and circumstance that it is reasonable to believe they fairly represent "People who report frightening-NDEs" as well as "People who volunteer information about frightening NDEs."

4. What kind of lives did they live?
Isn't it tempting, the idea that everything that comes to a person is either a reward for good behavior or a punishment for wrong! This

way of thinking is a part of the conventional wisdom that goes back thousands of years—that good will be rewarded and wickedness punished—though experience shows us again and again that things don't necessarily work out this way, either in our own lives or in the world. (See Chapter 6.)

There are accounts of gloriously transcendent NDEs from people who, by the measure of conventional wisdom, did not deserve one. A man I know of is said to have been with the Mafia until a powerful near-death experience turned his life around. (The persisting rumor is that he was a hit man, though I strongly suspect that is a case of the public's ignorance of Family job descriptions.) By contrast, people doing their best to live a caring and responsible life, including saints in all of the world's enduring religious traditions, have reported terrifying spiritual experiences. "Deservingness" doesn't hold up.

This idea will be discussed in the next chapter.

5. Are these things common?

It was initially believed that troubling NDEs are extremely rare. However, a review of research reports made between 1975 and 2005 indicates that almost one out of five NDEs were identified as having some distressing elements (Bush, 2009).

6. What caused the NDE?

We can say what the *circumstances* were at the time of the NDE, and we can sometimes say what physiological *stimuli* were present. But no one can say what *caused* the experience itself.

Although stress seems to be a frequent issue with NDEs, there are no accurate predictors. Even as small a sample as these fifty experiences includes people who at the time of the NDE were in auto accidents, allergic reaction, cardiac arrest, childbirth, major or minor surgery, post-surgical complications, angina or heart attack, serious illness, infection, suicide by hanging or drug overdose, and other medical crisis; several were in psychological distress but no physical danger; one experience occurred spontaneously.

So far, no explanation accounts for all NDEs, although many theories have been put forward. It is common to think that oxygen deprivation is at fault; yet in accidents and clinically monitored surgery, individuals who were well oxygenated later reported an NDE. Despite the "dying brain theory," which requires some passage of time, many experiences occur in micro-seconds to people who are *not* close to dying. Even in the scientific journals, big headlines about "New Discovery Explains NDE" are questionable. Dozens of supposed "explanations" have in every case later been revealed to be based on only a single instance, or to apply only to one aspect of some NDEs, or to be disappointingly out in left field.

In the words of Bruce Greyson, MD, the most-published researcher in the field, "No one physiological or psychological model by itself explains all the common features of NDE" (Greyson, 2001). Reporting at a conference on thirty years of NDE research, Greyson (2009, 225) summarized, "Although physiological, psychological, and sociocultural factors may indeed interact in complicated ways in conjunction with NDEs, theories proposed thus far consist largely of unsupported speculations about what might be happening during an NDE. None of the proposed neurophysiological mechanisms have been shown to occur in NDEs."

For a thorough discussion of the many theories, see Chapter 10 of *The Handbook of Near-Death Experiences*, "Explanatory Models for Near-Death Experiences."

7. But what exactly is that?

A definition IANDS often uses is that "A near-death experience (NDE) is a profound psychological and spiritual event that typically occurs during a situation of physical or emotional trauma, health crisis, or when a person is near death."

From the *Handbook of Near-Death Studies* comes this: "NDEs are generally understood to be the unusual, often vivid and realistic, and sometimes profoundly life-changing experiences occurring to people who have been physiologically close to death, as in cardiac arrest or other life-threatening conditions, or psychologically close to death, as in accidents or illnesses in which they feared they would die" (Greyson, 2009, 213).

Most NDEs can be considered mystical experiences, which the great psychologist William James (1905, 319) defined as having four characteristics:

> Ineffability: It defies expression. No adequate report of its contents can be given in words. It follows from this that its quality must be directly experienced; it cannot be imparted or transferred to others
>
> Noetic quality: Although so similar to states of feeling, mystical states seem to those who experience them to be also states of insight into depths of truth beyond the ordinary intellect. They are illuminations, revelations, full of significance and importance, though they remain inarticulate; and as a rule they carry with them a curious sense of authority for aftertime. These first two qualities are enough to mark an experience as mystical.
>
> Transiency: Mystical states cannot be sustained for long. The experience itself may be extremely brief or may, except in rare instances, last half an hour, or at most an hour or two. They cannot be called up at will.
>
> Passivity: ...The mystic feels as if his own will were in abeyance, and indeed sometimes as if he were grasped and held by a superior power. Some memory of their content always remains, and a profound sense of their importance.

Bingo. Clearly, near-death experiences of all types belong in James's "mystical group."

8. Are these true NDEs?

At first look, frightening experiences like those in this study seem no more like the peaceful NDEs than a Russian wolfhound seems related to a Pomeranian. How can one decide which is True Dog? It seems paradoxical that the answer could be, both. So it is with these very different types of NDE.

Margot Grey (1985, 58) in her British study was the first to point out that they share an underlying pattern of elements, though with sharply diverging emotional content. Pleasurable or distressing, NDEs are likely to include an out-of-body episode, a sense of journeying, encounters with presences, and the familiar qualities of a transcendent experience described by William James: ineffability, noetic quality, transience, passivity. All types change lives. This observation was amplified by P.M.H. Atwater (1994, 43) in comparing "heaven-like cases" with "hell-like cases": friendly beings to lifeless or threatening apparitions; beautiful environments to barren expanses; dialogue to threats, screams, silence; acceptance and an overwhelming sensation of love to danger and the possibility of violence; warmth and a sense of heaven to temperature extremes and a sense of hell.

The overall pattern is consistent, although contents of the pattern elements differ greatly.

PART II
Interpretation: Going Behind the Story

6
First Views

The opening section of this book has been descriptive and as factual as possible. By contrast, Part II moves into speculation and interpretation, while Part III will tend to the practical. Chapter 6, dealing with initial impressions and assumptions, illustrates the unavoidable truth about NDEs: that from the narrative description of an experience, and after whatever clinical data has been reported, almost anything we can say will be conjectural. When the catalogue of observations becomes a personal story, hard science is left behind.

The conventional wisdom

The tinge of centuries colors the way we hear today's near-death experiences and what we make of them. Why should some individuals tell of blissful heights of spiritual experience while others believe themselves at the depths, lost in the stars or consigned to hell? (Behind the scenes, the unvoiced question of every listener: "And could that happen to me?")

The plain fact is that no one knows the answer. Theories abound, but nobody knows absolutely why one person's experience is gloriously life-affirming and another's so disturbing that it leads to years of turmoil. We are awash in assumptions but with a drought of data. Conventional wisdom teaches us that good people (however that may be defined) will be rewarded and the wicked will be punished or least left out of the good things. Embedded in our thought is the ancient assumption that people get—or should get—what they deserve. But is this a good thing, and does it work?

Theologian Marcus Borg (2002, 160) has observed, "Conventional wisdom leads to a performance and rewards view of life. The quality of our life depends upon doing things right. By making this connection, conventional wisdom also images life as orderly and, to that extent, under our control…But conventional wisdom has a cruel corollary. If your life fails to work out, it must be because you have done something wrong."

In religious language, this is expressed in terms of righteousness and sin. Moral virtue, moral failure. Live right, go to heaven; live wrong, there's hell. But this kind of categorizing is not limited to religious belief.

Truth to tell, a great many people who disdain organized religion and intensely dislike any concept of a literal heaven, hell, or 'divine judgment' immediately leap to an assumption about frightening near-death experiences that echoes the most conservative religious view. The difference is primarily that secular language replaces talk of sin with descriptions of psychological failure, spiritual weakness, or perhaps a characterological deficiency in the person who "attracted" the experience. Not many writers have theorized about people who have a disturbing NDE, but their adjectives are remarkably consistent: hostile, cold, repressed, suppressed, unloving, controlling, rigid, refusing surrender, hate-filled, guilt-ridden, non-God-loving, fearful, mean. Never mind the absence of data to support those conclusions, the belief remains firm.

One author (Atwater, 1992, 156) has sincerely claimed that the dark NDEs are "usually experienced by those who seem to have deeply suppressed or repressed guilts, fears, and angers, and/or those who expect some kind of punishment or accountability after death."

No data has been offered to support the claim of "usually." Physician Barbara Rommer (2001, 26) has been widely affirmed for reporting that a frightening NDE "may occur if the person has a...less than loving, or fearful mindset just immediately prior to the event...[or] if one grows up with negative programming expecting hellfire and brimstone, then that is what...one will be given to experience." No data supported the certainty of her claims.

As more than a century of psychological research has demonstrated, *everyone* has "deeply suppressed or repressed guilts, fears, and angers." They are part of the human condition, even for people who report dazzlingly transcendent experiences. Moreover, a good many people who *describe themselves* as having been guilt-ridden, fearful, and angry have reported beautiful mystical experiences. That bit of conventional wisdom is not enough.

Confident assertions in the absence of testable data seem largely a triumph of personal belief over objective evidence, whether the source is a researcher or a channeled entity. It does seem probable that something about an individual's emotional circumstances could influence an NDE; however, NDEs of all types demonstrate such great variability of situation and personal backgrounds that conclusiveness is a long way off. Certainly people are often challenged, after an NDE or any similar event, to make life changes; and their mindset may be hypothesized to have influence (though this begs the question of how suicide attempts and criminal attacks produce experiences of glory); however, unprovability is a significant problem when claiming flatly that experiences occur *in order to* effectuate a turnaround or *as a result of* the person's emotional status. It is not enough.

Curiously, to my knowledge, no researcher has ever raised similar speculations about how the people who have had a blissful NDE deserved it. There is no list of personal characteristics of those experiencers. Only the distressing experiences have drawn observers to such fascination.

Another common supposition is that religious belief determines the type of experience—that heavenly NDEs reward devout believers, while frightful ones go to agnostics, atheists, and the merely unobservant. This is another idea more logical than true, as no evidence supports it. Some individuals who believe in a wrathful god have reported terrifying NDEs; but others have reported bliss. Horrible experiences have been reported by people who believe with all their hearts that "God is love."

Here, for instance, is an excerpt from an account by Saint Teresa of Avila:

> "While I was in prayer one day, I suddenly found that, without knowing how, I had seemingly been put in hell...The entrance it seems to me was similar to a very long and narrow alleyway, like an oven, low and dark and confined; the floor seemed to me to consist of dirty, muddy water emitting foul stench and swarming with putrid vermin. At the end of the alleyway a hole that looked like a small cupboard was hollowed out in the wall; there I found I was placed in a cramped condition...I found it impossible either to sit down or to lie down, nor was there any room, even though they put me in this kind of hole made in the wall. Those walls, which were terrifying to see, closed in on themselves and suffocated everything. There was no light, but all was enveloped in the blackest darkness. I don't understand how this could be, that everything painful to see was visible." (Teresa)

If that could befall one of the greatest of all saints, what does that say about the conventional wisdom? Something more is involved than superficial judgments. These documented religious experiences of saints, like the range of *bardos* described by the Tibetan *Book of the Dead* and the images in psychedelic psychotherapy, indicate strongly that easy explanations point to over-simplification rather than real answers, and that deeper influences are at work.

There is, as of this writing, *absolutely no evidence* to support the conventional wisdom that deservingness has anything to do with having a glorious or dismal NDE. The psychological testing that has been done over decades provides no clue as to why people get the NDEs they do. Whatever germ of truth underlies these conventional conclusions, expanding it will require far subtler investigation and interpretation than these broad-brush declarations. It may even be that NDEs occur at random, like falling into a pothole on a road at night.

The unwelcome dark

"One does not become enlightened by imagining figures of light," said Jung (1945, 14) "but by making the darkness conscious." That is clearly a little-admired thought. Resistance to the subject of distressing experiences runs deep and has broad implications, both for experiencers and for the way in which society conceptualizes distress in general. Where does this enormous resistance to difficult NDEs come from?

What's out there?

A deep-seated dread of Something Terrible stalks humanity. It always has, throughout history. Perhaps the fear had a thoroughly practical origin in earthquakes, or lightning bolts, or saber-toothed tigers on the prowl. Or perhaps the origin lies in ourselves, in what seems to be the uniquely human recognition of our mortality—that each and every one of us and everything we know in the universe will die.

Philosophers have pondered this for as long as anything is known about philosophy. The dread stirs at the heart of the religious concept of salvation, and in the despair of much 20th century literature, and as Ernest Becker observed (1974), in the drivenness of robber barons yesterday and corporate hot-shots today to pile up incomprehensible amounts of power and wealth to ward off…what? This is *ontological fear*, a primal urge to hold onto our very *being*. Whatever the origin, this fear is basic. Some near-death experiencers remain invisible because something about their experience touched that dread; whatever the "something" was, it frightened them so badly they will not talk about it.

Medical social worker Kimberly Clark Sharp, herself an experiencer and long-time leader of IANDS Seattle, the oldest NDE support group in North America, reported (1984, 84):

> "People who have negative experiences are afraid of death. Not forever, but for a long time. Can you blame them? There's lots of problems with a negative experience...People will call and begin to talk about them, but then change their mind and say, 'Goodbye, I have to go.' And they often won't tell you who they are when they call. With someone who's had a positive experience, it takes about three or four attempts [for them to be able to talk about their experience]. With someone who's had a negative experience, it takes twice as long...[and] sometimes I won't hear from them ever again after they related it to me."

Retelling any powerful experience pulls it back to the surface of consciousness, where it can be remembered and, if necessary, dealt with; that is a function of reunions as well as psychotherapy. But if the emotions are *too* powerful, too threatening, and if the fear is too great, and if there is no one to help a person deal with any of it—it is natural to look the other way, get busy, keep the whole thing buried. Whatever was awe-full in the experience may seem too awful to approach and certainly too awful to share. As difficult as it is for a person who had a radiant NDE to tell others about an inbreaking non-physical encounter of peace, acceptance, and love, how much greater will be the resistance for the person who came away from the experience in ontological terror?

Who's saying

Experiencers have not been the only ones to turn away from discussion of fearsome NDEs. In the ordinary run of things, only daredevils (interesting word, that) *want* to experience cosmic terror or even to know about it, and very few people have any idea how to think about such a near-death experience. Bruce Greyson and I did not know, at the beginning of our study, *how* to think about them, or *what* to think. Further, researchers and academics were as captivated as everyone else by the accounts of radiant experiences; why would they want to go looking for a dark side? Ring's Weighted Core Experience Index and Greyson's influential NDE Scale, for example, asked nothing that might have led them to uncover frightening experiences. And so, because they did not know what questions to ask, and did not hear *completely* what they were told, and because they had not set out in the first place to look for terror, the early NDE researchers missed the signs that could have led them in this other direction.

When they *did* recognize the existence of distressing experiences, a good many people denied them or were simply repelled, leading one writer to describe difficult NDEs as the slums of a city, created by "the nature of the minds that are interacting to create this reality" (Ring, 1980). The author compared people with glorious NDEs to privileged passengers traveling as if through a subway tunnel protecting them from awareness of the slums just beyond. Intended simply as a descriptive analogy, this image unintentionally displays the same kind of linguistic shading found in stereotypes about poverty or racism: Distressing experiences are "the slums of a city," from which the privileged (the "core experience") traveler must be protected. It is the "nature of [their] minds" (inferior? distorted?) that strands those other experiencers in the "lower domain." By implication, therefore, the "nature of the minds" of the core experience traveler must be of a higher, more approved type. How this comes about, or how it differs, is not specified. The description is expressed as if sociologically, either with no awareness of the demeaning implications or rationalizing the suggestions away as having been unintended. The point of view is a variant of the one stating that "these people" must have been guilty of being unloving or hostile, mean or hate-filled.

There is no suggestion that there might be something worthwhile in those "slums," no suggestion that a privileged person might ever encounter such a thing, or how to respond if exposed to such a dreaded contact. There is certainly no hint that it could serve a useful purpose. Aversion to the dark experiences runs so deep that even ordinarily compassionate people turn their attention away.

Dealing

When my son was four, he came to me with a story to write down for him. He called it "The Best Nest in the West," about a baby bird who faced dangers with courage and good cheer. It contained two chapters. In the first, the bird was becoming aware that his world was full of dangers. In the second, he reached resolution. "Coyotes can't bother me," sang the little bird. "I'm allergic to them."

Unfortunately, as the four-year-old would discover, allergies don't work that protectively. Yet for the most part, adults take that attitude toward emotional states we do not want: if we can just be "allergic" enough, they won't get close. This leaves us wide open for disaster, because coyotes of the psyche can breach our illusion of defense in an instant, finding us completely unprepared.

"Dark nights of the soul—fear, depression, madness, trauma—are too often seen through the limiting lens of fear," observes psychologist Joan Borysenko (1993, 54). "In fear, we wish only to rid ourselves of apparent negativity rather than searching our souls for its gifts."

Psychotherapist Miriam Greenspan (2003, 7) has intensively studied the dark emotions and says, "Most adults have the entrenched idea that emotions like sorrow, despair, and fear are crippling, destructive and 'negative.' That last word says it all. … These emotions not only *feel* bad; we think they *are* bad—signs of emotional weakness, moral decay, spiritual inferiority, and personal inadequacy."

Fear is an issue, certainly: fear of the dark itself, fear that one may be swallowed by the experience, fear of death, of extinction, fear of the hidden parts of our own psyche which are all too real, fear of the judgment that is assumed to be represented by the experience.

Straight-out *disapproval* of this type of experience is sometimes a factor. When one believes that only positive thoughts and emotions are acceptable, anything uncomfortable is likely to be perceived as poor form, unclean, "negative." Disapproval is a hidden extension of fear, of alarm that one could be tainted by contact.

Then there's simple *avoidance,* a desire not to be inconvenienced. Perhaps we don't want to be bothered, weighed down, don't want to know about harsher realities. A narcissistic insularity says, "I am living in the light and I don't want to come out."

After thirty years as a psychotherapist, Greenspan (2003, 7) says of this, "A culture that insists on labeling suffering as pathology… inevitably ends up denying both the social and spiritual dimensions of our sorrows….[An] airy spiritual focus offers a healing path that often bypasses the reality of suffering on the ground—avoiding or denying the social roots of our pain and dissociating itself from the darkness in our world." This is not to disparage all of contemporary metaphysics, by any means, but merely to note that even spiritual systems have their shadow side.

To say it is time to start looking the monster in the eye is not an argument to romanticize suffering nor to embrace evil, not an invitation to wallow in bleakness nor to ignore the light; it is a call neither to Goths nor to Satanists—though they might learn some things quite interesting and applicable to themselves—nor an exaltation of the hysterical self-flagellation and rejoicing in pain of some medieval mystics. We are not to *dwell* in the disturbing NDE nor in any suffering once it is worked through but to deal with it as a storm: to recognize that storms exist, to have some understanding of what they are and how to prepare for them so that, when one arrives, we have a chance of getting through to clear skies.

In a time of terrible social crisis, it is imperative that we come, as a people, to recognize that it is the personal shadow, writ large, that creates the world shadow, that it is individual pride, greed, envy, wrath, lust, gluttony, and indifference that feed war, oppression, economic collapse, bigotry, child trafficking, spousal abuse, terrorism, and famine. The aggregate of the unattended personal negativity (what in a religious context is called sin) is the social evil. To continue ignoring or disapproving of the unpopular NDE—or one's own shadow or the homeless beggar or the neighbor we despise—is not only to deny and repress part of our own reality but to be unprepared and unprotected when meeting an unwelcome experience ourselves. The resulting spirituality is both thin and shallow, a desire with no substance. To run away from fear is itself fear.

Such acknowledgment does not weaken anyone's belief in the All, the Source, God as, in fact, the Good, the Light, the Ground— but it acknowledges that in reaching that awareness there may be tough questions, problems, experiences we would rather not have to deal with.

Greenspan again (26-27): "The world is in vital need of the truth that the dark emotions teach...When we master the art of staying fully awake in their presence, they move us through suffering. We discover that darkness has its own light."

What I am proposing is, in her words (6), that we make "personal odysseys through the dark emotions as a path of sacred power." By alienating our difficult emotions, we make ourselves timid. This denial of the difficult emotions, and of risk, is sabotaging not only our spiritual health but the psychological health of youngsters who are being taught to believe that any risk is too alarming to be tolerated and that they are too fragile to stand in the world on their own.

No Olympic gold medal winner has ever simply strolled to the podium without pain, without sacrifice. Siddartha did not find an end to suffering by sitting in the palace that was his birthright; Jesus did not remain in a small boat on the Sea of Galilee. In pain and darkness, in tragedy and struggle—there is where courage is found, and redemption. That is the path of sacred power. The least we can do is learn to deal with emotions we do not care for.

The life after death question

What is it about the classic light-filled near-death experiences that makes them so compelling? To people who are themselves dying, it is likely the indication that what is approaching may be, in fact, quite wonderful. (Steve Jobs' last words (Simpson, 2011): "Oh wow. Oh wow. Oh wow.") It may be reassurance that when those we love died, they experienced it as safe, as happy, as a joyful peace. And for those who are religious, or mystical, and perhaps for publishers and most of the media with an eye on marketability, the most significant thing about NDEs may lie in what they suggest about a life after death.

Many—perhaps most—human beings around the world believe in the survival of something about ourselves after the body has ceased to function. This is true of all cultures, so far as we know, and has been for as far back as human societies have left tokens in graves and marks on cave walls, though with no unanimity as to how this might work.

For the earliest traditional societies, life after death seems to have meant living on as one of the Ancestors, through one's children and their children or as an element of the communal memory. From this seemingly universal background grew a sense of a more tangible afterlife, though no two societies or sub-cultures share exactly the same view of what it might entail. The Egyptians began furnishing tombs for a comfortable post-mortem existence, at least for those who could afford the necessary embalming. Carol Zaleski (1996, 14) notes in *The Life of the World to Come* that the Spartan custom of using words like "immortal" and "deathless" as honorifics for fallen warriors foreshadowed the development of the Greek idea of "immortal soul," from which we now rejoice, "Elvis lives!"

From the sense of remembered existence to the idea of individuation after death, to the idea of a person's having an immortal soul, it must then have seemed only natural that a personal sense of self must accompany that immortal soul. The afterlife became the imagining of a continuation, somehow, of life on earth translated to a place most probably in the sky.

In religious communities, which traditionally link moral behavior with judgment at death or beyond, this produced the vision of being carried to Paradise to live with the angels, or perhaps to be judged as wanting and cast into an underground hell (which, as anyone who lives in volcano country knows, is where the fire is located). As

Zaleski also noted (1996, 36), "Those who flock to buy books on the near-death experience want to hear that they will not be robbed of the satisfaction of continued personal existence; they do not want to hear that they will be held accountable for sins."

Another observation on afterlife comes from transpersonal psychologist Charles Tart (1996, 321), whose work on states of consciousness has been foundational, and who knows better than most the persuasive evidence of some kind of continuation: "After 25 years of studying this, I have come to two conclusions. One is that, as I die, after a period of confusion and fear, I won't really be too surprised if I regain consciousness. On the other hand, I will be very surprised if 'I' regain consciousness."

Something about us, we believe, will continue somewhere, though the particulars differ. But do near-death experiences prove it to be true?

It would be impossible to cite all of the thousands of joyful claims that have been made since 1975 that near-death experiences "prove" an afterlife, all the tabloid headlines—"New PROOF of Life after Death!"—with their illustrations, badly Photoshopped, of surprisingly Middle Eastern-looking cities floating above the clouds. It would be equally impossible to list all the published arguments heatedly demonstrating that such a thing is impossible (the scathing comments in *The Skeptical Inquirer*, the frenzy of blogging disputes).

Despite the controversy, the very fact that near-death experiences exist, and that they so often occur in life-threatening circumstances, has persuasively worked to convince a good portion of the public and apparently most of the media that NDEs are conclusive evidence, even scientific evidence ("proof"), of an afterlife.

Strictly speaking, of course, there can be no such proof, for the simple reason that all NDEs are subjective experiences that cannot be observed by scientists or anyone else; they cannot be tested for accuracy, or quantified, or replicated in a laboratory setting. The only possible control group that could report accurately on whether NDEs are like afterlife would be a group of people who are unquestionably dead—and what scientist would believe *that* testimony? On the other hand, although no one can prove the argument, neither can anyone *disprove* the existence of an afterlife. It is entirely a matter of personal choice, what evidence one reads, and one's ability to accept ambiguity.

It is difficult to disagree with Carol Zaleski (1987, 187) that, "Those who testify to the transforming effect of near-death experience often say that their conviction that death is not the end gave them the freedom and energy to change their way of life. On the other hand, when the quest for immortality is isolated from other religious concerns…it can become something tawdry, egoistic, and this-worldly…The present danger is not that people will become convinced of immortality, but that the whole subject will be trivialized by a narrow focus on the case for or against survival."

Were They Really Dead?

The emphatic affirmations about life after death leave dangling a number of questions that will be pursued here briefly but not in any depth. One of them is vital: the pivotal question—were these people really dead? This is another one of those questions with passionate responses but no clear-cut answer.

Yes

For some individuals, their experience coincided with their having been declared clinically dead, without respiration or heartbeat. If final death is like clinical death, and if the experiencers were thus eye witnesses to the actual condition of being dead (as they report conscious experience during that time), then it must be true that they were, in fact, deceased. For many, this is self-evident. More than one person has declared emphatically, "I wasn't near death, I was dead. I was *dead* dead!" They will go to their final death convinced absolutely that it is a return trip and that recognizable life awaits on the other side as it did in their NDE. They *know* they were dead, and to them the NDE proves the reality of survival.

Maybe

A less enthusiastic view maintains that no one can say for certain that clinical death is identical to permanent death. If one defines "dead" as meaning *permanently* deceased, then those experiencers were not, strictly speaking, *really* dead, because they did not remain so. As gerontologist Robert Kastenbaum (1996, 258) has quipped, "If 'I' have survived to report the demise of 'Me,' then the report of Our death has been, in Mark Twain's words, 'greatly exaggerated.'" We cannot say that what the experiencers encountered was an accurate depiction of being truly dead, because they have come back to tell about it.

Probably not

The plot becomes even less clear when one considers that in the majority of what we know as near-death experience accounts, there was no medically confirmed clinical death. Although most of the individuals who have reported NDEs were in some kind of intense physical or emotional difficulty, it was not more than momentarily life-threatening. The experiences may exhibit the same characteristics as those of the "*dead* dead" type—but they occurred in people for whom "near-death" is a misnomer.

Not a bit

And finally, of course, there are the real puzzlers, the occasional look-like, act-like, sound-like experiences that pop up in a perfectly healthy person who is perhaps at the edge of sleep or in deep prayer or meditation. How do they indicate anything about death?

Along with Keats, here is Carol Zaleski (1996, 36): "Now we see in an enigma darkly, in the mirror of our culture. Only 'then,' when the veil is lifted, shall we see face to face. Now we must test the soundness of our images and symbols by practicing the traditional and modern arts of discernment, guided by both dogma and experience. Only then shall we know as we are known."

Until that veil is lifted, near-death studies will be a field that almost mandates ambiguity. Readers wanting more focus on survival are pointed to Gracia Fay Ellwood's (2001) thorough and insightful *The Uttermost Deep: The Challenge of Near-Death Experiences.*

Neither the question of "were they dead" nor of life after death will be settled here. The evidence can be read to support either a "yes" or "no" interpretation, and certainly a "maybe." For my part, just as I have little interest in the clinical dissection areas of near-death studies—the excited (and so far overblown) claims of "discovery of the cause of NDEs" in brain receptors or sleep disturbance, right temporal lobe seizure, endorphins, psychedelic substances, or conjectures about the dying brain—I am not much stirred about the proof-of-life-after-death debate. (It is my deep conviction that some answers are stored on a high shelf just out of our reach.) I assume that you and I will discover the truth all in good time—or if not, that that which once was "we" will no longer care. For now, I am content to think, and imagine, and hope, and to stand with the poet John Keats (2005, 135) and his respect for "Negative Capability," which is, in his words and punctuation, the necessity to be "in uncertainties, Mysteries, doubts without any irritable reaching after fact & reason."

My interest is in the varieties of near-death experience *itself* as a powerful shaper of lives here and now, and in how people go about interpreting and *living* with an NDE in a meaningful and useful way. Nevertheless, because that search for meaning is inextricably bound up, for many people, with the question of survival, and because even a hair-splitting author cannot ignore concerns about an afterlife following a difficult NDE, the next chapter looks at hell. How has the idea of hell shaped human thinking over the ages? How is it shaping ours? Most people find the history surprising.

7
Looking the Monster in the Eye: Hell

The earliest known account of a near-death experience comes from Plato, twenty-five centuries ago. The plot lines are so old, so pervasive world-wide, they are like seeds planted by the visionary experiences of our early family in the first seasons of human time. The power of those experiences—stories told and retold across who knows how many eons—rooted them in the very foundations of human beliefs across hundreds of generations. And with those tellings came their interpretations, variously told as Elysian fields, as happy hunting grounds, as green pastures, or as dim or ghastly territories where no one would wish to be.

Let us not mince words: Much of the powerful impact of near-death experiences comes from their reflecting the idea of heaven and hell somewhere beyond the ordinary world. A major reason for reluctance to look at distressing near-death experiences—and it is the source of terror for many experiencers—is a fear of discovering that the hell we hold in our minds may somehow actually exist. But despite the extent of that fear, or because of it, the subject is rarely discussed except in abstract theological terms or in religious circles that insist on a literal interpretation.

And so it remains the shadowy hulk at the back of our cave. It has been back there for so long… surely hell is outmoded. And yet, something about the idea is universal. And ancient. And for some individuals, it is as current as waking up *today* from an NDE.

A chapter's worth of history may clear up some questions and anxieties.

The hell of prehistory

In *The Life of the World to Come* (1996, 12), Zaleski has pointed out that a clear sense of what an afterlife might be is missing in the formative period of all the enduring religious traditions. This was still the case in the time of early Hinduism and the Classical period of Greece. The more imaginatively elaborated conceptions come later, as would be the case with Israel.

However, as simply a place for the dead, the idea of an underworld has existed as long as there have been societies. What most people do not realize is that although many of the underworlds look remarkably similar, their function as a place of punishment is a late development, and *eternal* punishment is a concept only within some sects of Christianity. (It is not my purpose to talk anyone out of a doctrinal conviction, only to demonstrate the evolutionary nature of hell's history and the range of other beliefs and cosmologies.)

The earliest known after-death landscapes—those of Bronze Age Mesopotamia—were visualized as shadowy places literally under the world, that functioned simply as the grave, the place of the dead. A warehouse, if you will.

The earliest intact story of a trip to the otherworld comes from Sumer, in Mesopotamia. Clay tablets inscribed about 2,500 years ago tell an even more ancient story, of how the goddess Inanna paid a visit to her sister in those shadowy regions of the dead. It is a soap opera of antiquity, full of personality conflicts, intrigue, jealousies, and narrow escapes. The Inanna story is worth mentioning not only because those clay tablets still exist, but because they mention details of the underworld that will recur again and again across the millennia in cultures around the world: a journey, overwhelming difficulties, barriers and monsters, bizarre turns, gifts.

Early Hinduism had a single eternal hell and, later, temporary hells—thousands of them, most not connected to earth. Buddhism also had multiple hells, as did lesser-known religions of powerful local charisma.

Most visualized hells have been earth-centered. In the Americas, even the loosely structured culture of the Arctic Inuit includes a frozen underworld in which the souls of the dead must be purified. A continent to the south, according to Mayan myth (Okeowo, 2008), the souls of the dead had to follow a dog with night vision on a horrific watery path and endure myriad challenges before they could rest in the afterlife.

As in Middle Eastern cosmology, the Aztec earth was believed to be a large disc surrounded by water. However, they must have been an executively talented people, because they envisioned thirteen levels of heaven and nine of the underworld—wheels within wheels, from the outermost void, the "black heaven," to Mictlan, the region of the dead, at the center. (Aztec) Destination after death depended upon what a person did on earth and how he or she died. Obviously they were a people of detail, the Aztecs, as their architecture also tells us.

The Judeo-Christian hell

If some readers find themselves surprised by how much variation there has been over time in Jewish and Christian ideas about the underworld, they are almost certain to be astonished to discover that today's conception of a demon-ridden hell is not biblical but a product of mistranslation and anachronism. As noted by Ziony Zevit (2001, 64), Distinguished Professor of Biblical Literature at University of California, Berkeley, "The idea that God is an angry figure who sends those He condemns to a place called Hell, where they spend eternity in torment separated from His presence, is missing from the

Bible and unknown in the early church. While heaven and Hell are decidedly real, they are experiential conditions rather than physical places, and both exist in the presence of God. In fact, nothing exists outside the presence of God."

BCE: Before the Common Era

For 2,000 years and more, the Israelite underworld was the previously-mentioned storage facility shared with the realm of Mot, the Canaanite god of death. It was Sheol, in the region of the dead; Yahweh (YHWH, the early Israelite deity) did not go there (Zevit, 2001, 64). Sheol had no particular religious significance to YHWH because, "In general, Yahwism as presented in extant biblical texts conceived of YHWH as lord of the living. Death was the ultimate contaminant of all that was particularly sacred to him...Yahwism... was concerned primarily with the middle level [of the cosmos], the level of life and creation."

During the nomadic period and through the Babylonian Captivity, (586-538 BCE) that is how it remained. The sense of Sheol's being a place of torment after death is never used by Moses or the early Prophets. Sheol was the destination of *everyone,* good or bad; thus it was possible to describe being dead as being "in Abraham's bosom," because of course the patriarch would be there. Says Ecclesiasticus 41:3-4, "Fear not death, whether it be ten or a hundred or a thousand years, there are no chastisements for life in Sheol" (Masumian, 2002, 32).

Further, Deuteronomy, chapter 28, gives an unambiguous look at the early Mosaic understanding of how YHWH's blessings and punishments would be apportioned—and they are entirely *in this world,* this life, not afterward. Here, from the New International Version (1993), is an excerpt of the blessings: "The fruit of your womb will be blessed, and the crops of your land and the young of your livestock—the calves of your herds and the lambs of your flocks. Your basket and your kneading trough will be blessed...everything you put your hand to."

The price for breaking the covenant is steep. There is no threat of eternal torment in an afterlife; but: "You will build a house, but you will not live in it. You will plant a vineyard, but you will not even begin to enjoy its fruit. Your ox will be slaughtered before your eyes, but you will eat none of it…Your sons and daughters will be given to another nation, and you will wear out your eyes watching for them day after day, powerless to lift a hand. A people that you do not know will eat what your land and labor produce, and you will have nothing but cruel oppression all your days."

This is clearly a people and a belief system grounded in *this* world.

It was a world of war and conquest, and the Israelite captivity ended when Cyrus, the Persian king, overran the Babylonians and allowed the people of Israel to return home if they wished. It was the beginning of exposure to the Persian religion Zoroastrianism with its colorful thought, including a rambunctious dualism.

What the Israelites who remained in Persia discovered, and what those who returned to their homeland under Persian rule would hear about, was the vibrant Zoroastrianism, claiming that everything in the cosmos is in eternal struggle between good and evil, light and dark, with good triumphing in the end. Zoroaster, who may have lived as early as 1,700 BCE—which would make him the first known prophet (Masumian, 16)—also introduced the idea of Apocalypse, a literary genre that became popular as escape literature.

Zoroastrian apocalyptic thought says that in the present days, evil people outnumber the good, but at the end of this age Ahura Mazda (the Wise Lord) will send a river of fire to cover the world and destroy everything, even Hell. There will be a Last Judgment which will separate the good from the evil, and a savior will come, and a new Golden Age will follow. Fire is a central element in Zoroastrian religious practice, a symbol of the sacred way, of wisdom and the "original light of God." (http://www.avesta.org/zfaq.html).

By the time Alexander and his Greek armies overran the Persians two hundred years later, a fire had been lighted in Sheol. Other Zoroastrian ideas—the dualism of good and evil, existence of a distinct heaven and a punishing hell, the return of a savior, and judgment in the End Time—had grown with the Children of Israel and flourished; they are first evident in the apocalyptic stories of Daniel and continue to the present day.

Somewhere around that time came the curious Book of Enoch, a Stephen King of the period. Enoch is not part of the Bible but was a popular tale of how a group of angels rebelled against God and led the people of Earth into wicked behaviors (including not only harlotry but eye shadow). It describes Sheol as divided into three areas: one for the righteous; a second for sinners who had been punished for their wrongdoings while on earth; and the third for the wicked who had received no earthly punishment. God bids the Archangel Michael to bind the fallen angels and looks to the future: "In those days they shall be led off to the abyss of fire: (and) to the torment and the prison in which they shall be confined for ever. And whosoever shall be condemned and destroyed will from thenceforth be bound together with them to the end of all generations." Enoch did not have to be accepted into the biblical canon to become part of popular thinking, for grisly stories have great sticking power.

For the Greeks, their Hades, like Sheol, was not a place of punishment but was simply the region of the grave. It was like a Sheol with neighborhoods: the righteous dead, wicked dead, and those in between, where there might still be conversations across the borders. Greek mythology told the tale of how Zeus overthrew the Titans and banished them to a place within Hades, called Tartarus, deep in the underworld, to keep them from harming the human race.

And so, Persian and Greek influences, as well as Egyptian, percolated through Hebrew thought after the return of the exiles to Jerusalem in 538 BC, becoming more colorful and involved as they went along for the next five hundred years.

With political upheavals and unrest, the jostling of cultures and tempers, abysmal poverty up against unimaginable wealth, the turn into what is now called the Common Era was a difficult time. The heavy hand of Roman rule had moved in. Apocalyptic thought was everywhere, with hints of revolution and expectations of the end of the world; a whisper of imminent revolt against tyrannical occupation forces might be well timed. Rumors of a Messiah coming to overthrow the oppressors were as common and feverish in the marketplace then as rumors of terrorists are in some quarters today. Itinerant healers and prophets roamed the countryside. Punishment for even minor wrongdoing was harsh and often hideous; so imagining judgment and terrible torments after life seemed plausible; it also provided ground-down ordinary people a satisfying way to think of getting back at all those who were doing them wrong—and that was just about everybody.

CE: The next two thousand years

First century
In that environment, Jesus, convicted of treason, was condemned to death in the year 33 CE for complex political and religious reasons and crucified by the Roman authorities—the shameful and horrifying execution of common criminals.

The first writings we have in what would become the Christian New Testament date from some twenty years after the death of Jesus. These are letters by the traveling missionary Paul, written from the early 50s until his martyrdom in 64. His letters to fledgling Jesus-following groups were concerned primarily with organizational matters and how members should be treating each other in light of what Paul has taught them. The letters make no mention of heaven, though he speaks of "living with the Lord forever" (Thessalonians 4) after the end of the world, which was assumed to be imminent. There is no mention of hell; non-believers simply die and disappear.

After Paul's letters came the four Gospels about Jesus' ministry—the documents known as Mark, Matthew, Luke, and John. A handful of additional letters by other writers, along with the dazzlingly apocalyptic vision known as Revelation, appeared late in the first century or early in the second. All are believed to have been written in Greek, the common language of the region.

The gospels of Mark, Matthew, and Luke are not biographies of Jesus but records of his activities; John is a spiritual reflection. The life of the world to come is mentioned only in passing, and then primarily regarding who would sit where. Jesus spent far less time talking about the final destiny of the wicked than one would think, considering the amount and vehemence of discussion since then.

Of the four Gospels, the chronology and shadings of eschatological (end times) thinking are like this:

The Gospel of Mark, written roughly 40 years after Jesus' death, circa 70 CE: heaven is for those who do good deeds. Mark makes a single mention (9:43-48) of the need to be wary of "the fire that never shall be quenched...where their worm dieth not" (it refers to the burning dump, Gehenna). In other words, for those who pay no attention to the needs of others, hell presents a real risk.

The Gospel of Matthew, c. 80-85 CE: Based almost entirely on Mark, Matthew was written after the madness of Nero, after Paul's martyrdom, after the destruction of the Temple and loss of Jerusalem, and in the midst of terrible persecutions. Not surprisingly, the work includes earnest moral teachings and understandable warnings of peril on all sides, with a definite awareness of suffering and all too real tortures. Heaven is for those who do good deeds. There is mention of Satan. Images are vivid but contradictory: For example, Matthew 25:30 refers to "the outer darkness" where "men will weep and gnash their teeth," but eleven verses later the description is of "the eternal fire prepared for the devil and his angels." Alice Turner (1993, 54) notes, "Matthew's great innovation was to attach eschatological (end time) warnings to the parables Mark attributed to Jesus. It is Matthew who establishes in the Christian mind that not to be saved is desperately perilous."

Gospel of Luke: 85-95 CE. Heaven is for those who do good deeds. Hell is a place of torment with heat and terrible thirst. In the New Testament's most vivid account of an afterlife, Luke tells the story of a rich man and the beggar Lazarus (not the Lazarus Jesus reportedly raised from the dead). This Lazarus, who has had a hard life, dies and is carried to Sheol by angels and finds himself "in Abraham's bosom." The rich man also dies but awakens in torment. He sees Abraham a distance away, with the beggar. He begs Abraham to "send Lazarus, that he may dip the tip of his finger in water, and cool my tongue; for I am tormented in this flame." Abraham's response in the King James translation, is, "Son, remember that thou in thy lifetime receivedst thy good things, and likewise Lazarus evil things: but now he is comforted, and thou art tormented." The devil, who is mentioned elsewhere in Luke, does not participate in this story.

Gospel of John: circa 100 CE. John never mentions hell. The word "heaven" is mentioned nineteen times, not as a place to which people are headed but as the source of spiritual good. For John, "eternal life" is an eternal now in which we all participate. (I am indebted to New Testament scholar Wayne Rollins for this observation, made in an email.)

No demons, no imps, no gargoyles with iron hooks in Jesus' teaching. Across Matthew, Mark, and Luke are eleven mentions of Gehenna, the burning garbage dump, addressed to Israel in a metaphorical sense to emphasize responsibility for helping to bring about the Kingdom of God *in this world*. The warning use of "Gehenna" is addressed to the nation, not to individuals (Dawson, 2004). An inferno of destruction would be the all-too-visible fate of an uncooperative Israel, as had happened before and as would in fact arrive catastrophically late in the first century with the fiery demolition of Jerusalem and the Second Temple, a massacre of the Jewish population, and what would be the beginning of a millennia-long diaspora. That was the vision. The judgment and punishment of *individuals* as interpreted by later theologians were never at the core of Jesus' teaching.

At the very end of the New Testament stands Revelation, the most overstated, under-understood, and misunderstood book of the entire Bible. Most probably written around 90 CE, at a time of massive oppression and a tyrannical emperor, Revelation is written in the style of an apocalypse, a popular style of escape literature, like futuristic science fiction today. Neither journalism (a factual account of physical-world events) nor a set of predictions about all of human history, apocalypse was an elaborately detailed literary form envisioning the end of the world, when God will balance the scales of justice. It was also a clever device to hide from the political powers a story of how they would be overthrown.

For sheer wonderment when taken literally, the book of Revelation reads like the Buzby Berkeley or Ziegfield Follies of End Times, with lavish details of color, demonic presences, crowds of angelic hosts, mythological populations, numerological predictions and symbolic pronouncements, mixed with meteorological fantasies and extravagant conclusions. Evil people are thrown into a lake of fire and gloatingly annihilated. Some are eternally punished. It would make a terrific video game.

However, its riot of "insider" symbols, images, and metaphors masks a treasonous political intrigue, at which level Revelation is clearly apocalyptic religious code intended as an encouragement to the Christian community to endure for a while the insupportable reign of the Emperor Domitian (or possibly Nero), because the Christ is returning momentarily to overthrow Rome and bring about the Kingdom of God.

Domitian's press has never been good and certainly never worse than in Revelation. At a spiritual level, the work encourages hope to the oppressed, and the assurance that God will "wipe away every tear."

The problem comes when a literary vision of the first century is read as if it were factual news reporting for the 21st century. Theologian Dennis Bratcher (2011) explains, "Its images and symbols are forms of fantasy rather than reality, and its language is cryptic, metaphorical, and highly symbolic…Strange multiheaded beasts, weird creatures, dragons, and odd combinations of normal images (locusts with scorpion's tails and human heads) are common ways of writing. It purposely presents a world that does not exist except as a means of communication."

When fantasy is concretized, the concept of a punitive hell takes on more weight.

Revelation was followed perhaps fifty years later by a vivid though sordid little piece known as the Apocalypse of Peter, a brief but potent work that was *not* included in the Bible but that, like Enoch, became popular for its sensationalism. It is obviously not by the disciple Peter, though using his name for prestige. The work set the stage for all later lurid depictions of hell. Gone are the quiet darkness of Sheol and its fires of the sacred, replaced by violence described with a particularly nasty, scatalogical, voyeuristic relish, as in this excerpt (Brashler):

> And some there were hanging by their tongues; and these were they that blasphemed the way of righteousness, and under them was laid fire flaming and tormenting them. 23 And there was a great lake full of flaming mire [excrement], wherein were certain men that turned away from righteousness; and angels, tormentors, were set over them.
>
> And there were also others, women, hanged by their hair above that mire which boiled up; and these were they that adorned themselves for adultery. And the men that were joined with them in the defilement of adultery were hanging by their feet, and had their heads hidden in the mire, and said: We believed not that we should come unto this place.
>
> And I saw the murderers and them that were consenting to them cast into a strait place full of evil, creeping things, and smitten by those beasts, and so turning themselves about in that torment. And upon them were set worms like clouds of darkness. And the souls of them that were murdered stood and looked upon the torment of those murderers and said: O God, righteous is thy judgment.

And on and on. Clearly, the psyche of the Middle East had suffered grievously during all the decades of upheaval, martyrdoms, social and military brutality, political oppression, and the harsh hand of near-psychotic emperors.

All in all, the Apocalypse of Peter marks the beginning of a sadistic bent in Christian theology that would persist to the present time. Although other world religions have hells of their own, "None of these hold a soul eternally, however, and no other religion ever raised hell to such importance as Christianity, under which it became a fantastic underground kingdom of cruelty, surrounded by dense strata of legend, myth, religious creed, and what, from a distance, we might call dubious psychology" (Turner, 3).

Augustine
For all his brilliance, Augustine (354-430 CE) contributed to that "dubious psychology." In working out his ideas about Original Sin and Free Will, Augustine arrived at concepts of hell and punishment that became inextricably linked with each other and with sex (about which he was seriously conflicted). For Augustine, hell is unavoidable, universal, everlasting, sensory, a bodily torture that punishes demons and humans alike. Punishment will be a lake of fire and brimstone—read, *never-ending* punishment. His influence was so great that 120 years after his death bishops meeting at the Synod of Constantinople considered an anathema (never ratified) that excommunication would come to anyone who openly disagreed that punishment in hell would be eternal and without the possibility of redemption (Synod, 2011).

Augustine remains a giant influence, particularly on the evangelical and conservative branches of Christian theology. Whether that is more for good or for ill is likely to be determined by your own perspective. At any rate, in his deductive reasoning Augustine offers a forecast of what would 700 years later be full-blown scholasticism—which is to say, *theoretical* rather than experiential descriptions of an afterlife. He has intellectualized them by carefully, structurally, analytically, taking into consideration Scripture, philosophy, prayer, and the writings of the early Church Fathers. His conclusions bear very little resemblance either to scripture as known by Jesus nor to today's NDEs. In the present day this can be problematic for people of faith who value the authority of doctrinal statements but disagree with such human conclusions as those of Augustine and others.

The medieval hell
Nine hundred years would pass, and then—Dante! Here they are, the illustrations of Dante's seven levels of hell, industriously exercising all the morbid implements of the human imagination—the machineries of torture, the pornographic, the scatological, the pathologically sadistic elements inherited from persecutions, and other mistreatment, the centuries of abuse and cruelty and despair that would be passed on to the Inquisition and other torture chambers. Here we see how the biblical fires have over time been embellished to satisfy the very understandable human desire for vengeance against the oppressor, now rationalized as an ambition shared by God—demons with instruments of torture, lots of pus, worms, excrement by the lake-full, whips, rack, eyes poked out with sharp and burning instruments, three-pronged fiery pitchforks, ferocious beasts, impalings, burning chains. And in the *abominable fancy*, the souls of the blessed perch overhead like so many ravens, sitting in smug self-righteousness, watching. It is imagination run wild in the service of theological doctrines of hell. Lots of projection going on. Lots.

In fairness to Christianity, it must be noted that there have always been other strains of thought that emphatically *do not* assume these ends. This is true today and has been true since the formative centuries of Christianity—in Origen, for instance, who taught that all souls ultimately return to God. These other strains have been a strong undercurrent throughout Christian history, less publicized because they are less titillating to the imagination. (Likewise, few graduate students write their dissertations about the God of Milton's *Paradise Lost* compared to those writing about his intriguing Satan.)

It is not comforting but at least fair to point out that the threat of hell is rationalized—consciously, at any rate—by those who defend fear as a means of saving sinners by frightening them into the protective arms of what they believe to be sure doctrine. In other words, horrific threat is justified as a presumed kindness, ostensibly leading to salvation. Here again is the conventional wisdom (not to mention projection), justifying the horror by a more humane impulse for fairness. Psychologically, it seems obvious that the gleeful recounting of threat and demonic torture bears strong resemblance to the same thrill moviegoers find in chainsaw murders. The impetus is more psychological than theological.

Hell in (mis)translation
With the destruction of the Jewish state and the rise of the Roman church, both the Tanakh and New Testament were translated from their original Hebrew and Greek into Latin. Jerome's translation, the Vulgate, was completed shortly after 400 CE and remained the standard for a thousand years before an English translation, Wycliffe's Bible, received Church approval. After the Reformation, in 1611, came the great Authorized King James Version of the Protestant Bible, translated not from the Latin but from the Hebrew and Greek.

In English Bibles, as scholars have long recognized, four words from the original languages have been translated as "hell": the words *Sheol, Hades, Tartarus,* and *Gehenna* (Orr, J. 1915, Hanson, 1888).

Tartarus appears only once, in a late letter to a Greek church, making a literary allusion that would have been familiar to that audience. In a mythological story, Zeus corralled the rebellious Titans in a dismal underworld called Tartarus to keep them from harming humans. Alluding to that story, the writer of 2 Peter says, "If God spared not the angels that sinned, but cast them down to [*Tartarosas*]…"

Sheol as a term seems to have confused the early English translators, who proved unwilling to understand it as meaning simply "the place of the dead." By the time of the King James version the idea of hell as a physical place of torment apart from the presence of God had taken such firm root that for a translator confronted by "Sheol," the translator's preconception produced "hell" in place of "grave" (Hanson, 1). The King James Old Testament translates Sheol

31 times as hell, in several places as "grave" or "pit," and once even as "dust" (Thayer, Orr).

The same fate came upon *Hades*, the Greek equivalent of the Hebrew *Sheol*. *Hades* was translated into the King James Version only once as "grave" but ten times as "hell." Although ordinary churchgoers have not understood the error, it has been abundantly clear to scholars. As far back as the mid-19th century a group of distinguished scholars wrote that the Greek *Hades* "ought never in Scripture to be rendered *hell*, at least in the sense wherein that word is universally understood by Christians. In the Old Testament the corresponding word is *Sheol*, which signifies the state of the dead in general, without regard to the goodness or badness of the persons, their happiness or misery." (Thayer) And yet the misleading translations keep coming.

The word *Gehenna* is a Greek translation of the Hebrew "Ge Henna," referring to a seriously foul, ever-burning dump outside Jerusalem, where the bodies of executed criminals were thrown to be burned along with dead animals and other more hideous refuse of the city. Gehenna came to represent anything that was foul and repulsive, deserving of severe judgment or condemnation. Common usage indicated a severity of punishment rather than a duration of time; there was no sense of "forever" about the word. That is the sense in which Jesus used it to warn the nation of Israel of the consequence of their inattention to God. The site was considered accursed because it had been a place of fiery child sacrifice in earlier times; so as the concept of a punitive hell grew, "Gehenna" became its equivalent.

These mistranslations make hell (in its later meaning) appear far more prevalent in the English translations of the Bible than it is in either the original Hebrew Bible or Greek New Testament. That same group of scholars quoted above concluded, "It is very plain that neither in the Septuagint version of the Old Testament, nor in the New, does the word *hades* convey the meaning which the present English word *hell*, in the Christian usage, always conveys to our minds." Modern readers are clearly misled by anachronistic translations.

The modern hell
Since the Enlightenment, hell has evolved into several clearly identifiable strands, in addition to the view that it is nonexistent.

Mainstream religious views
Many Jews and virtually all secularists would agree that the question of hell is moot: there is no afterlife to worry about, except as we are remembered and continue to influence our offspring and society. Because there is a variety of opinion in Judaism about an afterlife, this is by no means a settled issue, except that there is no belief in hell on the order of the visualizations just described.

The Eastern Orthodox Christian perspective is that, although hell is not physical, "the Bible indicates that everyone comes before God in the next life, and it is because of being in God's presence that they either suffer eternally, or experience eternal joy" (Chopelas).

With a different twist, today's Catechism of the Catholic Church (paragraph 1033) defines hell as: "To die in mortal sin without repenting and accepting God's merciful love means remaining separated from him for ever by our own free choice. This state of definitive self-exclusion from communion with God and the blessed is called 'hell.'"

The Anglican-based Episcopal Church of the United States generally agrees with Rome's approach, seeing hell as a choice made by an individual to separate from God. Hell is understood as a state of being or a state of mind rather than as a physical location. Most liberal to moderate Protestant denominations concur, if they believe in hell at all.

Most mainstream theologians seem to recognize that there is no clear, consistent biblical teaching about the afterlife and that there has been little consistency as it evolved; however, in many churches, the subject of hell so rarely comes up that parishioners are likely to have no idea what the Bible says or their church advocates.

The conservative Christian view
Conservative evangelical denominations do not agree with any of the above positions, and some combat those notions furiously. The

Hollywood version of hell generally represents the conservative Christian view, which they believe to be biblical.

By evangelical I mean the almost 2,000 faith groups and denominations representing some 35% of the North American adult population, that hold strongly to some variant of Protestant Christian doctrines, beliefs, and practices. (http://www.religioustolerance.org/chr_evan.htm)

> *Note:* Conservative Christian readers may be distressed by the contents of this section. I regret that but cannot avoid it. The fundamentalist position is discussed here because of its disproportionate influence on popular culture and the public's concept of both hell and Christianity itself. In no way do I intend the following discussion to suggest that the sincere beliefs of fundamentalist Christians are anything other than their right. In the words of the organization Religious Tolerance, I can "believe that members of another religion are hopelessly deluded, and still support their right to enjoy religious freedom" (http://www.religioustolerance.org/evan_dis.htm). Fundamentalist views are so far from my own that they are like different religions entirely; yet both stand under the Christian umbrella (though the conservative view does not acknowledge this).

The central focus of all groups within the evangelical movement rests on fervent protection of doctrine (Enns, 2011) and trust in a literal reading of the Bible, which is considered to be without error (not only the Word of God but *the words of God*). Along with that belief come varying degrees of discomfort with the values of the modern world, whether science or social mores. As the degree of conservatism intensifies, convictions become increasingly tightly structured, typically emphasizing biblical passages and church doctrines that teach divine wrath. The result is a heavily fear-based and uniquely punitive perspective.

The view is not a throw-back to medievalism but is, like all the world's fundamentalisms, a complex reaction to the modern age with religious, social, and political implications, mixed at its radical extreme with a strong current of paranoia and conspiracy theory.

Fundamentalism's global nature today belies its origins in Western thought after the Enlightenment, as described in *Strong Religion: The Rise of Fundamentalisms around the World* (Almond, 20).

> A 'culture of progress' celebrated the spreading confident belief that humanity, through the power of reason, the triumphant discoveries of science, the magnificent inventions of technology, and the secular transformation of traditional institutions, was on a clear course toward the mastery of the evils of the human situation. Religious communities and elites were put on the defensive…Fundamentalist movements are the historical counterattacks mounted from these threatened religious traditions, seeking to hold ground against this spreading secular 'contamination' and even to regain ground by taking advantage of the weaknesses of modernization."

In its secular appearance, the fundamentalist attitude includes absolutisms such as Marxism and extreme materialism. Its religious mode has been described (Almond, 2003, 14) as "a reactive, selective, absolutist, comprehensive mode of antisecular religious activism… skilled in manipulating sacred texts and traditional teachings to serve political ends."

Overall, the trend is global and includes Christian, Jewish, and Islamic fundamentalism as well as some radical elements in Buddhism and Hinduism, though they differ in their particular approaches. In the United States, Christian fundamentalism includes many conservative denominations and independent congregations, all of which not only accept but promote the existence of an actual, physical hell very much in the medieval mode.

A particularly vivid illustration of this proliferating trend comes by way of Jason C. Bivins (2008) at North Carolina State University, in his book *Religion of Fear: The Politics of Horror in Conservative Evangelicalism.* In an earlier article, Bivins documented the parallels visible between evangelicalism's emotional discourses and those of genre horror. He says (2007, 82), "The cultural politics of recent decades have…given birth to a particularly rich and powerful fear regime, which I call the Religion of Fear, situated at the intersection of popular entertainment, conservative politics, and evangelicalism's complicated negotiation of its own identity."

His book looks specifically at the popular *Left Behind* novels of Tim LaHaye, the doctrinaire comic books of Jack Chick, anti-rock and -rap censorship, and the recent church-sponsored Halloween Hell Houses.

A descendent of the old "houses of horror," Hell Houses have now spread to hundreds of churches and are enthusiastically promoted to the entire community. A Hell House is a religious "haunted house," scripted and stage managed around themes of fear, evil, and damnation, often with sophisticated sound and light shows. "Demons" (tour guides) escort visitors to view scenes in which actors play out graphic (even gross) enactments of "mustn'ts" such as violent date rape, a botched late-term abortion, bloody drunk driving fatality, death by AIDS, illustrating for each scene the grisly hell that must be its consequence. The final scene portrays heaven, asking visitors, "Which would you choose?" Visitors are encouraged to accept salvation by repenting of their sins on the spot and committing their life to Christ.

Bivins comments (2008, 95), "A typical Hell House experience is…energized by the conviction, shared with many practitioners and participants, that evil, demonology, and Hell are very real. The supernatural dwells in American society, frequently manifesting in behaviors such as premarital sex, drug use, school shootings, and so forth." As reported by the Canadian website ReligiousTolerance.org, prominent Hell House promoter the Rev. Keenan Roberts told the *Denver Post* that the exhibit was designed to "show young people that they can go to hell for abortion, adultery, homosexuality, drinking and other things unless they repent and end the behavior." (http://www.religioustolerance.org/hallo_he.htm)

As Bivins concludes (2008, 95), "The sins and causes of damnation are quite clearly linked to the hot-button moral and political issues that have for over three decades been at the heart of [New Christian Right] culture and activism. This is not to downplay the Hell Houses' and their sponsors' intentions to proselytize and save souls they believe are at risk. But it is crucial to understand that the risks envisioned and narrated are those which conservative evangelicals have long attributed to post-WWII American liberalism as well."

The reason for pointing out so much detail about issues with Christian fundamentalism is that they wield great influence culturally as well as theologically. It is not the sense of hell as states of consciousness that make headlines, but modes of "entertainment" modeled on Hell Houses and their lurid theatrics, becoming embedded in national consciousness and private terror. And it is in large part the implications of a politicized evangelicanism that make matters so difficult for near-death experiencers when they try to find someone to talk with about their experience.

The modern NDE hell

In contrast to the deliberately imagined grotesqueries of the medieval religious fantasy and modern Hell House, most actual accounts of today's hellish near-death experiences seem remarkably sedate, though they are no less terrifying. The horror and fear are deep and genuine, but their descriptions are primarily emotional rather than visual, internal rather than external. YouTube examples notwithstanding, most people describe not demonic populations but landscapes—barren and sterile, to be sure, or terrifyingly fiery, but rarely grotesque. The traditional guide is often still present. Although fire may be seen, it is typically not felt; monsters, demons, or graphic tortures seem infrequent. This distancing does not lessen the emotional intensity of the experience, only makes it less populous.

There is, however, a powerful sense of threat and often an oceanic fear. In fact, fewer people report actually *seeing* a hellish landscape than those who say they saw something that made them think they *might be about to see* hell ("...large rusty doors with a rusty lock and chain, people sitting outside on benches. He was so afraid of what he saw he was in a panic and knew he was at the very doors of hell...") What is there about rusty doors and people sitting on benches that inspires such an immediate panicked assumption of hell?

When other people are encountered, they are generally understood as being lost, wandering, and bewildered; if they are perceived as being in torment, it seems to arise from the ugliness of their surroundings and their inner state rather than from the malevolence of perceptible demonic beings. For the most part, they are like the group reported by a woman as having "sad depressed looks; they seemed to shuffle, as someone would on a chain gang...they looked washed out, dull, gray. And they seemed to be forever shuffling and moving around, not knowing where they were going, not knowing who to follow or what to look for" (Moody, 1977, 19).

Although sounds of wailing or discordance are commonly reported, it is background noise; the experiencer does not actually see the source of the sound:

"They chattered like blackbirds."

"I was moving along as part of a river of sound—a constant babble of human noise...I felt myself sinking into and becoming part of the stream and slowly being submerged by it. A great fear possessed me as if I knew that once overcome by this ever growing mass of noise that I would be lost (Gray, 51).

"Demons were all around me. I could hear them but could not see them."

I admit to being at a loss to explain why I have seen descriptions of monsters only in conservative Christian hellish accounts, for instance, in Wiese's *23 Minutes in Hell* (Wiese, 2006). Perhaps it is a vividness of expectation—though why expectation should work only in these circumstances and not in others is beyond my ability to explain.

As for the differences between the medieval and literary versions of hell and today's NDEs, it seems possible that waking consciousness has more lurid visual potential than many experiences of hell itself. The medieval depictions and Hell Houses, like some Christian revival sermons, are like the graphics of today's movies—sadistic, gross, violent (think Jonathan Edwards or the 19th century missionary priest John Furniss). By contrast, as Turner and this study indicate, with rare exceptions, modern NDEs strongly tend to be visually less violent and significantly less vindictively cruel, though they have lost none of their horrifying emotional power.

A similar observation has been made by Michael W. Cuneo (2001, 274), who spent two years of intensive investigation for his book *American Exorcism*. He reports:

> The truth is, I don't know about the demons. I've personally witnessed more than fifty exorcisms—and this isn't even counting the occasions where I've seen dozens of people undergoing exorcism all at once. And I still don't know…At the exorcisms I attended, there were no spinning heads, no levitating bodies, no voices from beyond the grave. (There was plenty of vomiting, no question about it, but nothing more impressive than what you'd probably catch most Saturday nights out behind your local bar.) I wasn't counting on demonic fireworks, but neither was I counting them out. After all was said and done, more than fifty exorcisms—no fireworks at all.

This seeming mildness of modern NDEs brings condemnation from those of the devout who relish Augustine's teachings about eternal torment for the unbaptized and unsaved, especially those whose beliefs differ from their own. There are still plenty of hellfire sermons being preached to support that view, and the expectation still carries enormous cultural weight, even among people with no religious belief.

Commentary on hell

The point of this lengthy discussion of the varied views of hell is, first, to establish an awareness that hell has never been a constant; its description shifts and changes over time, whether as a type of experiential awareness or as an imagined place. One is not initially less frightening than another, although the notion of falling into a cultural idea seems likelier to be a healable condition than falling into an immovable doctrine. This will be explored at greater length in Chapter 12. Secondly, although the data do not support the idea that people get what they expect, what we believe about heaven and hell indicates what we believe about God—or perhaps, for a secularist, whether the universe is friendly. And that underlying belief may guide everything.

Experiences similar to a disturbing NDE

Deathbed vision

From our vantage point, distressing deathbed visions and distressing NDEs seem identical, except, of course, that the person having an NDE can return to waking consciousness and may describe the experience later. We have no objective way of knowing the status of deathbed visions except what we are told before the individual dies. Anything beyond that is a matter of subjective belief, whether scientific, religious or spiritual, rather than objective fact.

UFO abduction

Curiously, as the presence of demonic entities has faded from near-death experience accounts and exorcisms, they seem to be appearing in a neighboring type of event. In stories of UFO abductions, what may be yesterday's demons are now constituted as more culturally familiar space aliens. The torments are perceived not as punishment for sin but as quasi-medical procedures. There is an interesting topic lurking here for someone's graduate thesis.

An extended discussion of this subject appears in psychotherapist

John Ryan Houle's excellent study, *Perils of the Soul: Ancient Wisdom and the New Age* (Haule, 1999). Haule is extraordinarily sensitive to the way in which the effect of a distressing NDE, like that of a UFO abduction, is likely to conflict with the great underlying American myth of personal control and materiality:

> [These experiencers and abductees] have been dragged out of the fleshly world kicking and screaming, have been forced to examine the unthinkable, to face the terror and dread that the public pseudo-myth strives to tame. They have confronted the Being-toward-death that structures our fleshly existence far more ultimately than any tame pursuit of happiness. [They] have been thrust into a no-man's land where the stories we tell ourselves publicly have been rendered meaningless. Unless they seriously grapple with monumental shocks of radical otherness, they will remain suspended between the chimeras enshrined in our public consensus and the madness of the unthinkable" (Haule, 186).

Misinterpretation and hallucination

In the blurry areas between sleep and waking, the hypnogogic state of consciousness, there is plenty of room for misinterpretation. Anyone who has worked in a clinical setting knows of situations in which hallucinations occur, or actual physical circumstances are misinterpreted by a disoriented patient.

One man told me at some length of having an anaphylactic reaction in his doctor's office and his vivid memory of what followed. He recalls shouting and confusion, being attacked and then tied to a cart by four demons who loomed over him screaming, as they rushed with him toward a set of double doors leading to Eternity. Abruptly, he says, he fell into a deep pit, dashing himself against the side as he fell. He said he awakened in the carriage of Death, speeding toward everlasting torment. He could hear the howls of chanting devils.

The actual physical circumstances of the event, he said, were that as he went into shock, his physician shouted to the nurse to come and assist, and to the secretary to call the ambulance squad from next door. Three emergency medical technicians rushed in and struggled—he was evidently a big man—to lift him onto the gurney, where he was strapped to keep him from falling off. The three EMTs and the physician (the four "demons") rushed him, on the gurney ("tied to a cart"), down a crowded corridor and through a set of double doors out of the building; but as they did so, the gurney tipped on a step and flipped over, knocking him momentarily unconscious ("falling into a deep pit, dashing himself against the side"). The EMTs got him into the ambulance and raced for the hospital, siren screaming (the "carriage of Death, with demons wailing").

Item by item, the physical circumstances of that experience are paralleled by the man's shock-fueled misapprehension of those events. It is easy to recognize the source of his misconceptions and to wish that his clinicians might help him to see them as misinterpretations of actual physical circumstances rather than as divine judgment or an NDE.

Few experience accounts so closely parallel actual physical circumstances, and this kind of semantic distinction is guaranteed to be of greater interest to researchers than to the person who carries the memory of such an experience. It will be extremely helpful when health care professionals, psychotherapists, and clergy are able to help an individual deal with *whatever* the experience was, no matter what academics name it. (The difference is rather like telling a child there is nothing to cry about because he was stung by a wasp and not a hornet—the problem is the pain, not the label.)

Shamanic initiation

The experience of dismemberment and restoration described by Howard Storm (Chapter 2) is a dramatic example of the type of event known as the "shamanic initiation." A significant difference is that while a shaman-in-training would have known what to expect,

Storm had no such advantage, as his cultural background provided no context for what he experienced.

In tribal societies, the functions of priest, magician, physician, pharmacist, and psychotherapist are traditionally filled by a psychically gifted shaman, the so-called "medicine man." The individual, male or female, is often identified early in adolescence as being especially intuitive, likely to be emotionally volatile, a loner who might be subject to frequent ailments, "on the edge." It is this very quality of fluidity between worlds—the ability to move between the material world everyone sees and the "someplace else" of illness, sometimes madness, and profound spiritual insight—that makes the true shaman effective.

This is serious business, not the romanticized shamanism of weekend workshops. The actual call to the shamanic vocation, as described by Mircia Eliade (1964, *xii*), "is manifested by a crisis, a temporary derangement of the future shaman's spiritual equilibrium. All the observations and analyses that have been made on this point… show us, in actual process as it were, *the repercussions, within the psyche, of…the radical separation between profane and sacred and the resultant splitting of the world.*" (Emphasis added.)

The "splitting of the world" is that rupture between physical reality and psychic/spiritual reality that mark the deepest NDEs.

Entry to the shaman's vocation will be marked by ecstatic experiences involving the traditional and seemingly universal pattern of initiation: suffering, death, and resurrection. As Eliade describes it (1964, 34), "The content of these first ecstatic experiences…almost always includes one or more of the following themes: dismemberment of the body, followed by a renewal of the internal organs and viscera; ascent to the sky and dialogue with the gods or spirits; descent to the underworld and conversations with spirits and the souls of dead shamans; various revelations."

Storm's spontaneous experience vividly reconstructs this pattern of suffering-death-resurrection, with dismemberment and the "splitting of the world." His eventual move to a religious vocation is not surprising.

Lucid nightmare

A phenomenon sharing many resemblances with the distressing near-death experience is the lucid nightmare. A lucid dream is one in which the dreamer is aware of dreaming and can consciously interact with the dream material. This control is not always possible within a lucid nightmare. Writer and dream educator Ryan Hurd says of this: (Personal communication)

> The dreamer/visionary does not necessarily have volitional control of the dream content. Sometimes the imagery just "does its thing" regardless of the dreamer's desires: including witnessing horrific acts, titanic feelings and sensations, terrible noises, etc. In some lucid nightmares, if the dreamer can get a handle on fear/expectation, the dream can change. Other times, not so much: the vision is stronger than the dreamer's wish. In dream research, there's a distinction between lucidity (self-awareness, or metacognition) and volition, even though they overlap.

Hurd's *Dreamstudies.org* website provides more information about both lucid dreaming and sleep paralysis and the mysterious figures that populate both types of experiences (Hurd, 2011).

Interesting threads run between near-death experience, lucid dreaming, and the rapid eye movement (REM) of deep sleep states. Although NDEs seem to have the most enduring memory and effects, lucid dreams are remembered after awakening with a much higher frequency than nonlucid dreams, probably due to the presence of a *mental set to remember* (La Berge, 2000). For information about techniques of working with lucid dreams and nightmares, which can also be helpful with NDEs, see Chapter 13, "Bringing the NDE Home."

What use is hell?

Featureless warehouse, highly elaborated fantasies, fiery underworld, or mostly bleak scenarios—it is clear that there is no universal understanding of hell. For every strong conviction and determined theory there is at least one complementary doubt or disagreement. Even the biblical descriptions range from a vague underground "somewhere" to Matthew's conflicting depictions (hot or cold, underground or in space), and on to the fantastical apocalyptic literary images of Revelation. Clearly, we cannot describe hell with the unanimity that could be granted, say, to the Chicago skyline. Hell cannot be empirically proven to be a literal "place."

However, although we may be unable to locate hell geographically, it clearly serves a useful psychological and spiritual function and therefore has found its place within human moral psychology. There is an entire literature on this topic, which I am breaking out into three aspects for brief discussion. First, the concepts of heaven and hell exist because fairness and justice, with reciprocity, are innate features of our moral functioning. Second, heaven and hell exist as responses to our naturally intense death anxiety. Third, to be dealt with in a later chapter, heaven and hell are very real as part of the makeup of human consciousness itself.

Fairness/justice

It takes only an afternoon with young children to recognize how early in life the demand for fairness sets in, whether in the distribution of cookies or the assignment of nap times. As experimental psychologist Richard Beck (2006) has noted, "Our brains are wired as fairness and reciprocity engines." Hell is a product of that moral imperative.

Our hunger for justice is universal. Mythologies everywhere have provided with ways of believing that although bullying and greed, unfairness and cruelty may flourish now, there will come a time when justice will triumph, decency will be rewarded, and the wicked will get what they deserve. The gods—or God—will see to it.

The idea of hell satisfies the reward/punishment imperative, but it is not without problems. First, when interpreted stringently it violates reciprocity, that basic criterion of justice, that punishment should fit the crime. The sense of reciprocity, of balance, is so deeply ingrained in our consciousness, it may be instinctual. More than a thousand years before Zoroastrian fire moved into Sheol, the Babylonian Code of Hammurabi decreed that payback for a crime should be not more serious than the crime itself. That principle would be echoed later in the Law of Leviticus and Deuteronomy, instituting "eye for eye, tooth for tooth" reciprocity rather than limitless vengeance.

And there's the problem with a conventional notion of hell. Let's say that a teen shoplifts a valuable collection of CDs. Or that a mom lies when police ask if she knows where her criminal son is hiding. Their crimes, or sins, have a finite value. Yet according to a narrow slice of theological thought, the wrath of God demands that they will undergo limitless agony for a limitless duration of time for a finite cause Reciprocity has vanished. Or say that entire nations of children are born where they will never hear what a group across the planet considers true teachings, and are thus consigned by that group to suffer eternally. As illustrated schematically by psychologist Richard Beck (Beck, 2006b):

$$\text{Infinite punishment} > \text{finite offense} = \text{Unjust}$$

I leave it to the reader to decide whether this actually proves that God is unjust or suggests that this says more about the psychology of those who hold to this view than it does about God. For a wonderfully readable exploration of this entire issue, see Richard Beck's blog *Experimental Theology*, especially his post on "The Gift of Hell."

Death anxiety

Animals, we assume, don't spend much time sitting around wondering about themselves and death. We assume they don't worry about the "when" or what it will mean for them. At some point, they simply die. We know, though, from archeological findings about burial practices, that once human consciousness emerged—that is, when we developed language enough to think about ourselves—even very early people began worrying about death. Death anxiety has been with us ever since. Unlike cocker spaniels and trout and elk, we live in the awareness that each of us will die. And therefore, as Ernest Becker (1974, 15) has said, "Underneath all appearances the fear of death is universally present."

In fact, cultural anthropologist Becker, who won a Pulitzer Prize for his book *The Denial of Death*, presents a compelling argument that death anxiety is the covert fuel of every worldview. It is all around us, hidden in what every culture teaches its children is important, in the strivings we believe are for worldly achievement but that may more authentically be to build our own memorial, a kind of continuing life on earth—a fortune to leave the family, a sports trophy or hand-sewn quilt to recall our skill, a college building bearing our name testifying to our success and importance, a notebook of best-ever recipes that will keep our name alive for well-fed generations.

Salvation means being rescued from that anxiety/terror. (I will not really die but will transition to something else. I will not die but will live on in these home movies…this garden…these holiday rituals…this reputation.) We don't recognize the anxiety for what it is, for as Becker (20) points out, "'Repression takes care of the complex symbol of death for most people."

Ironically, hell affords one way of dealing with this overwhelming anxiety by prompting the setting of boundaries. Psychologist Richard Beck (2007a) explains:

> "Death is a terrifying prospect. This is exacerbated if one also believes there is a hell of never-ending torment. Thus, faith, belief and doctrine begin to cluster around defining the Saved versus the Lost…If my faith is thanatocentric [death-centered] then faith becomes fundamentally about where I stand at the moment of death. Am I with the saved or with the lost? How can I tell? Well, you can tell by drawing ecclesial lines in the sand and then check—self-verify—where you stand. And you keep checking, almost daily, because death can come at any

moment. Faith becomes a kind of obsessive-compulsive salvation check: Am I in? Yes, I'm in. Am I in? Yes, I'm in. Am I in? Yes, I'm in. Doctrine becomes about existential self-soothing.

In his following post, Beck (2007b) continues: "And if ... the clarity of the boundary is what is so reassuring, then it stands to reason that we need, for existential soothing, a group of people to be clearly on the other side of the line. A clearly defined saved group by necessity creates a clearly defined damned group. And the more clearly defined the better. In short, many Christians *need* a clearly defined damned group to reap existential solace."

The issue is not Christianity but human psychology. It is not *Christianity* that is dependent on that view but a segment of its people whose psychological makeup leads them to take that interpretation. The fear engendered universally by that minority view has great power and quickly goes viral, precisely because of the underlying death anxiety in all of us.

Even for secularists, hell provides a conceptual edge. It is the ultimate edge at which we are forced to define whatever it is to which we give ultimate worth. God, if you are religious—but what kind of God? And if not God, the question shows us to ourselves. What characteristics, what qualities, do I honor? What has true value? What measures are essential for respect? Whatever those qualities of worth are, there is our sense of ultimate value, the springboards of our decision-making and responses to the world. That is who we are.

Says the author of a thoughtful blog (Liminality), "So I guess I have come to a conclusion in a way, and in the end I find that it's not about hell or losing one's salvation, it's about the way I live my life. That's where it begins, and that's where it ends."

8
Personal Filters

When near-death experiences were first being investigated in the 1970s, the key question was on the order of, "What was that?" The second question, at least for researchers, was "Where did it come from?" For experiencers, the question is almost always, "What does this mean?"

The three types of response described earlier—conversion, reductionism, and unresolved despair—rest on the answer to "What does this mean?" Life rests on interpretation. In most cases, the initial interpretation, the one that seems self-evident, is the literal reading of the NDE, as if it were a news report or historical text. It is like describing a trip to the Grand Canyon: I went to a place and saw these things, met these people, brought back these souvenir memories. For all experiencers, it seems, the "face value" reading, the literal one, will be synonymous with the *first interpretation;* for many, it will be the *only* interpretation they ever come to. This is the level at which it presents as a narrative, a story.

There is something about the way the human mind works that, given a wheelbarrow full of parts, a person will instantly begin to make it into something recognizable. We are patterning creatures, seeing faces in cloud formations and creatures in the shapes of trees at night, linking individuals and events into stories. As every family or class reunion testifies, humans are by nature story-tellers, building meaning out of the narratives of our individual lives and cultural histories. We are introduced to religion by stories, not by doctrines of belief; we first meet national and tribal history in tales of heroes and ancestors, of achievements and sorrows. Stories are the baskets in which we carry our meanings.

And yet, in telling our stories, we cannot convey an experience itself; we can only translate it into another medium. This is the same problem artists have, or dreamers, trying to describe their inner experience to an audience in the outer world. As a Swedish student of the history of ideas once wrote (in a blog that has disappeared), "Dreams are pure dreams only as long as they are not retold in any way—when they are, they become interpretations of dreams, representations of them, but not dreams at all…What cannot be translated into [an understandable concept] is simply not presented. It either leaves a gap, or it is ignored, or it is substituted by something socially recognizable… There is no word for something that people are unable to recognize."

It is the same with near-death experiences. They seem to have a beginning, middle, and an end, like a plot line; they are described as having settings, and many have characters. So, an NDE—that staggeringly powerful assortment of sensations, images, and emotions, will later, in waking consciousness, be translated into a narrative, a story. In the process, the inner event will be taken out of its original context as experience and forced into words, filtered and shaped by whatever pre-existing concepts are in the person's mind—or, if there are no concepts that fit, a story whose meaning will be adapted to the first reasonable-sounding explanation the individual encounters when awake. A later chapter will discuss how a person can examine alternative explanations, but first come the immediate impressions and their translations into words.

Many of the inner experiences may be similar, even close to identical. But because of the influence of those pre-existing ideas in each individual, there is no single "literal interpretation." Here, for example, are some typical filters found among experiencers in the Judeo-Christian West; they are culturally limited because it is wise for an author to speak only of what she knows.

The secular filter
The first words of a phone call: "I hope you won't think I'm crazy, but…" or, "This is going to sound really nuts, but…" As Kenneth Ring has repeatedly quipped, the people who have the hardest time with an NDE are whose who don't know what it was they encountered, they just know it wasn't supposed to be there.

A secular response—that is, one based on flat-out disbelief in the possibility of any religious or spiritual reality—is almost guaranteed to be that the NDE was a psychotic episode. When one believes that only physical reality can be genuine, anything else is, as one physician said bluntly, "Bunk, hokum, and poppycock!"

From that literal, materially-based logic, activities such as being outside of one's body, flying through space, or encountering mysterious entities "out there" are all manifestly impossible. When that impossible happens, however, and takes up residence in memory where it is demanding an explanation, the likeliest answer has to do with psychosis and hallucinations. "My mind is playing tricks. I can't be sane and have such an experience!"

Inversely, a similar confusion of NDE as psychotic episode may also be the response when the experience contradicts a devoutly religious person's doctrinal expectations or imagery. ("This isn't like what my religion says is true, so it must mean I'm crazy." An alternative may be, "It must be satanic.")

In fact, NDEs are *not* hallucinations, *not* the sign of mental illness or a drug gone wrong; thy are clinically quite different from those aberrations, with different effects. As indicated by repeated research, the person's mental health is most probably just fine, though badly shaken. Whether the cognitive dissonance is secular or religious, the person will go through a period of major adjustment in worldview or a flight into militant repression.

The blank slate filter

Sometimes, especially with a particularly vivid and powerful NDE, the experiencer has no vocabulary with which to interpret it and will have to wait for input from others.

A Canadian man with no religious background or symbolic vocabulary had no idea what to make of his glorious NDE and was deeply troubled by that inability. Then he met a group of people devoted to the Order of Melchidizek, a sect promoting a particularly complex understanding of a fragment of Biblical text that has somehow acquired a vigorously symbolic interpretation. His new acquaintances were excited to hear that my friend's NDE sounded rather like their beliefs. Perhaps because of the very elaborations of their conversation, their theological explanations coincided with the sense my friend had of the complexity, glory, and cosmic importance conveyed by his NDE. To the end of his life he was obsessed by what he saw as correlations and intricate interrelationships between his NDE and the Malchidizek scenario, and could (and did) proselytize to friends for hours at a time, almost, alas, unceasingly.

What the group provided him was a narrative basket in which he could carry the meanings of his experience. Could a different vocabulary have answered his need? Very possibly so; but his relief at finding a sympathetic point of view was greater than his curiosity to know what other explanations might be found. The same is also true for the many people who find a vocabulary for a frightening NDE in hell-fire-and-damnation religious sects. Sometimes the need for a sense of certainty outweighs all other considerations.

The non-fundamentalist religious filter

For anyone coming from a religious tradition, that will be the likeliest filter through which an NDE arrives in waking consciousness. A middle-aged woman, devoutly Catholic, was not surprised to find she had a guide with her during a pleasant NDE: "Oh, it was Saint Jude," she said confidently. "I pray to him all the time, so he knows me best." She had no difficulty retuning to her church and devotional life with a deepened sense of its validity. The messages in the majority of NDEs, of unconditional love, service to others, and a lessening of materialism, support many religious teachings and can easily be understood in those terms.

For those whose experience does not easily mesh with their religious tradition, the situation is murkier. In my own case, I awoke from an NDE knowing beyond question that there is—call it *an unquestionably real way of being out there* where, in otherwise emptiness, mysterious and impersonal but knowledgeable entities are able to announce with authority that one has been wiped out of existence entirely and for all time, past as well as future, along with everyone and every thing on earth. Poof—*gone*.

Nothing about that NDE fit with the the narrative background of my faith, the loving God of my religious teachings or my cultural understandings: not the out-of-body experience or the rocketing into space, not the impersonal entities that I did not recognize as being symbols from outside my own religious tradition, not their message, not the utter emptiness, and certainly not the perceived absence of God. This was clearly an other-worldly event, and though not the conventional hell, it was certainly nothing recognizable. Nothing about the event was on my radar or in my conscious storehouse of concepts.

But we are patterning creatures, looking for coherence. My memory bank took the pieces of the experience and put them together with a scrap of information about doctrine that I had heard about (but had not believed as fact), and came up with—the Calvinist doctrine of predestination, the idea that God has decided beforehand who will be saved and who will be, if not damned to hell, at least booted away from the presence of God. Quite obviously, in my conclusion, I was on the wrong side of the deal. God had decreed that I be blotted out.

Was this the only possible interpretation of that NDE? No. Decades later, I know that. But it was the only one then in my pantry of possibilities, so to speak; it was the only one *available*. Had the doctrinal perspective won out, it would have destroyed my sanity. But... You remember our instincts for justice? Ironically, it was my protest against injustice and a stubborn resistance to that doctrinal interpretation that led me, eventually, to a far deeper, better informed, and more nuanced faith within that same tradition (though without predestination).

For people who find themselves in an NDE moving—or being pulled—downward, and perceiving a reddish glow, the theological filter is likely to render it, as one man said in shaking horror, "a reflection of the fires at the gates of hell." Greater familiarity with the entire range of symbolic functions of fire would provide a more complete way of understanding that experience and putting it to productive use in the rest of life. (More on this later.) Until then, the man is left with only his terror and the perceived prospect of his concept of hell, both the fruit of a strictly literal interpretation.

One of the oddities of this type of experience is the appearance in an NDE (and sometimes in a dream) of an image from a different cultural tradition. The result, as in my case, may be a predictable lack of recognition, or bewilderment, like that of the young Jewish woman who identified the guide in her NDE as "a Jesus look-like." With only a literal reading of the event, there will be a great possibility for confusion and misunderstanding of the full meaning of the experience.

The fundamentalist religious filter

"It's about this deep desire for certainty," Bernard Haykel, a leading Salafi expert at Princeton University, has said (2011). "They are responding to a kind of disenchantment with the modern world."

He was speaking about the deeply conservative Salafi element of Islam, but the statement is true of any fundamentalist position. Fundamentalism is an attitude, not a religious system. Secular fundamentalisms such as scientism or pure Marxism firmly deny that anything beyond the material world can have reality. Religious or secular, the fundamentalist search always points to a deep longing for a "safe harbor" and changeless certainties. Any fundamentalism meets the need for cognitive closure, which Arie Kruglanski (2004, 6), Distinguished Professor at the University of Maryland, has defined as an individual's "need for a firm answer to a question, *any* firm answer as opposed to confusion and/or ambiguity."

The genuinely fundamentalist position in any tradition is a relatively recent (20th century) phenomenon. It is a pushing back against the revolutions brought about by modernism in the past four centuries—the shifting beliefs that have been typical since the Enlightenment, the culture-shattering social upheavals of the Industrial Revolution, the social/sexual turmoil of the past sixty years, the explosive globalization that threatens a secure sense of "who's who" and "what's right," the plunge into the ambiguities of quantum mechanics and multiverses.

Because fundamentalism looks to its foundational writings as absolute truth and takes an uncompromisingly defensive mode to protect its beliefs and values, it is neither ecumenical nor flexible. For those of any fundamentalist group believing that their text is inerrant—that it *must be factually true*—there is the added weight of conviction that beliefs based on that source must also be without error. In short, anyone who believes otherwise—who is not part of the believing cohort—is without hope of salvation, however that may be defined.

This bears on the interpretation to be made of an NDE.

When a member on the in-side of the sect experiences a blissful NDE, the experience can be viewed as a realistic affirmation of what is waiting at death and beyond *as long as it confirms approved doctrine*. If it does not confirm doctrine, it is a Satanic delusion, which the person will have a difficult time explaining.

If that same blissful NDE is reported by someone on the out-side of the sect, it will be considered a Satanic delusion to lure that person into hell by giving the idea that heaven is possible for an unbeliever.

A distressing NDE will be a sign that an individual is "not right" with God, and that great effort must be made to align the person with the beliefs and practices of the group. A hellish NDE, as described in the Rawlings books, is internalized as a glimpse of an actual place, a graphic warning to live by the group's teachings; for otherwise, when the person dies, that hell will be literal, conscious, and eternal. Period, no discussion.

That worldview *is* the meaning. The answer has been provided. The question for the individual becomes how to identify which behaviors have caused an upsetting NDE, and to change them. As long as the cognitive and psychological structure remains intact, a fundamentalist system offers believers security and reassurance. For those who don't fit the model, or who see or need a different interpretation, the pain of being within the community will be extreme. The fundamentalist approach is straightforward but has driven more than a few away.

The metaphysical filter

The first modern accounts of near-death experiences burst onto the scene in the mid-1970s, the very heart of the New Age movement. Talk about timing! NDEs emerged into a ferment of cultural change and overturning traditions, when established religious traditions were struggling yet "spirituality" was being rediscovered, when people's minds—and evidently their unconscious—were opening and available for what seemed like new information. Arriving when it did, *Life After Life* was a cultural equivalent to the dream of every children's librarian: "The right book for the right child at the right time." Perfect.

In *Megatrends 2000*, futurist author John Naisbitt (1990, 227) observed, "In turbulent times, in times of great change, people head for the two extremes: fundamentalism and personal, spiritual experience…[In the 1970s and 1980s] in every major U.S. and European city, thousands who seek insight and personal growth cluster around a metaphysical bookstore, a spiritual teacher, or an education center."

Although the terms "metaphysical" and "New Age" are not identical, and a half-century later the latter term has moved out of favor, there are enough commonalities between them that the terms are often used together. Despite the implications of *"New* Age," metaphysics is far from new. Rooted in philosophical and religious traditions that have surfaced repeatedly over thousands of years, metaphysics is now a potpourri of Christianity, Eastern mysticism, Gnosticism, Theosophy and New Thought, modern psychology, particle physics, and contemporary cosmology, with a strong strain of alternative medicine.

Religion and metaphysics share a common passion for what lies beyond the physical world, for answers to question like, "Who's in charge?" and "How are we to live?" and "What does it mean?" The heart of the differences between them lies in that distinction mentioned by Naisbitt: religion lives in community, whereas metaphysics lives in the individual search.

A postmodern metaphysical journey, no less than an organized religious tradition, is based on beliefs and understandings, and has its own fundamentalism; a principle difference, is that whereas for most people religion is a search for the *answers* to questions, metaphysics looks for personal *experience* around the questions. Here lies perhaps the deepest heart of the contemporary life pattern: the desire for individual search and personal experience, the push away from organization, authority, and community to "I can do it myself!"

And so, as Edgar Cayce biographer Harmon Bro observed (1993, 178), we find such disparate persons as seer Edgar Cayce, psychic Jane Roberts, medium Arthur Ford, journalist Ruth Montgomery, actress Shirley MacLaine, and the latest stars of the spirituality talk show circuits, all sharing the same bookstore space with, sometimes, the Dalai Lama. "What do all these have in common to make a marketing category," asked Bro, "not only in bookstores but in hotel conferences and living room study groups? Surely, it is their espousal of private authority for truth, bypassing critical norms of disciplined inquiry."

For near-death experiencers making a postmodern or metaphysical interpretation, the temptations to literalize are no different than for anyone else. Here, no less than with any organized religion, discernment is absolutely essential. For example, how much truth is there in the idea that we create our own reality?

Harmon Bro (1993, 179) puts the challenge of discernment this way: "As William James long ago warned, it is ever tempting to validate truth by roots rather than by fruits. If a teaching or practice can be shown to come from a trance or automatic writing, or is presented as from an evolved master on another plane, that makes it fascinating to the mind vulnerable to the brewing unconscious, and to a life searching for shortcuts in an age of canned entertainment and politics of expediency."

With a blissful NDE, so manifestly an experience on a higher plane, it is tempting to believe that one has oneself become an evolved master. The metaphysical approach is very apt to encourage a tendency to concretize "creating one's own reality" into a conviction that a pleasurable NDE has been manifested out of the goodness of oneself, or that one has instantaneously "evolved" or been chosen (ego) by God/the universe to do something heroic or special (ego-building) because of one's "higher plane" (ego inflation). After a glorious NDE, it has been too often the case that literalism in this tradition has led to disastrous grandiosity and corruption of personality.

Conversely, with a distressing NDE, the risk is to take at face value that same "Law of Attraction" which leads to internalizing the idea that all of one's life events are one's own doing. The belief that an individual acted, however inadvertently, as a magnet to attract a terrifying NDE may suggest something evil inherent in that person's life and self. From the perspective of karma, a hellish NDE may lead to an interpretation surprisingly like that of fundamentalism—that torment is what one has asked for and deserves, whether one understands it or not.

In fact, because contemporary metaphysical thought has so strongly emphasized the belief (or certainly the hope) that only the light is real and has value, it has by and large denied or ignored the "dark night" aspects of spirituality. Groups with a metaphysical inclination have been known not to welcome individuals with such an experience.

Late in the 20th century, theologian Matthew Fox (1993, 197) looked at the people he had been meeting on the New Age circuit and noticed something about them:

> Many…have given up on the religious tradition of their birth which, they often feel, has failed to teach them mystical practice and a mystical inheritance. Many of these persons are angry at their religious tradition (they may be Jewish, Roman Catholic, Anglican, or Protestant), and New Age allows them to let go of what they perceive as the failure of their religious heritage. Many of them may be 'recovering' Catholics, Baptists, Presbyterians, Jews, and so on. It is because of the failure they perceive in the current religious practice of the West that they are drawn to what David Spangler picturesquely calls the "county fair" of … attractions which, because of their common denominator of promising some spiritual experience, become a kind of oasis to religious seekers who are feeling a call to experience Divinity instead of just hearing about God or about God's commandments. It is my experience that there is much pain [among them] (as there is within our whole culture), but that much of that pain is so deep…that it rarely gets exorcised or dealt with. This is why many of them overindulge in the "light" energies they are offered and tend to shy away from the wounds, the darkness, the suffering of others brought about by realities of injustice in society. It is because they have not been able to deal with their own suffering that this denial of the dark often holds appeal.

This issue is very real for many experiencers who have found few resources and little helpful vocabulary in popular metaphysics with which to get beyond a literal interpretation of a distressing NDE.

These are examples of what a literal filter may look like; there may be more. Such an understanding may serve an individual for a brief while or for a long time but is almost certain to need deepening for integration to be complete. Deepening is the topic of the next chapters.

9
Widening the Horizon

The essential question goes deeper than how to describe a disturbing near-death experience, or a pleasurable one, for that matter. What does it *mean*? How can it be explained in terms that make sense in the world…and if The Way Things Are is not the way I thought, what then? What follows is an exploration.

The cosmos
The cosmos used to be so simple. For thousands of years it could be described as a snow globe.

The snow globe universe
Imagine a snow globe at the very center of a large crystal globe, the latter marking the extent of the universe. In the snow-globe cosmos, the fixed stars were attached to the inside of that crystal sphere, as far as anything could go from earth. Below them were the high heavens, home to God and his light-beings, the archangels, angels, seraphim, and cherubim.

The rounded cover of the snow globe represents the firmament, which was believed to be a hollow shell holding the winds, snow, rain and hail, with places for the sun, moon, and planets, each traveling an individual celestial path. The inner side of the shell was conveniently fitted with windows through which God and the angels could look down at the earth and its inhabitants.

Below the firmament, the inside of the snow globe, were the earthly sky—shaped like a dome, as the eye can plainly see—and then Earth, a flat disk surrounded on all sides by the great World Ocean. Below the Earth, somewhere underground were the regions of the dead, and, in some views, a fiery place. And below them all were the great waters of the deep and gigantic pillars, like bridge casings, that supported the firmament.

The cosmos was orderly. It was understandable. It was secure. And so, in the small part of the planet that is Europe, in that part of time we know as the end of the Middle Ages, the dominant religion and culture happily understood that God had deliberately created Earth to be the center of the universe. Human beings were the very purpose of that Creation, each individual with a secure niche of status and function.

Like the physical cosmos, the organization of its inhabitants was orderly and stable, described as a Great Chain of Being. At the very top, God reigned over all the universe, and closest below him were the orders of heavenly host made of pure light, the spirit-beings, ranked in order of power and importance. Just below them in the hierarchy were humans, constituted of both spirit and flesh, their orders also arranged by importance—first kings, princes, courtiers and warriors, the commoners and then peasants. Next in order came creatures, animated but without a soul, all of them ranked (dogs above sheep, butterflies above grubs, fish with bones above eels and squid); then plants (edible plants ranked above poison ivy). Lowest on the Great Chain was the inanimate material world of minerals and rocks and dirt.

The system was orderly and understandable; it was *permanent*. Moreover, it was psychologically and spiritually reassuring: God's in His heaven; all's right with the world; I am who and where God wants me to be.

Copernicus

That safe and stable universe of the Judeo-Christian imagination cracked midway through the 1500s, when the astronomer Copernicus demonstrated the possibility that the sun, not Earth, was the center of our galaxy. His discovery, and the work of scientific giants like Kepler and Newton, began two hundred years of reformulating astronomy that would ultimately dismantle the entire cosmology. Humanity was about to be eased toward the door and then evicted from that secure old home place represented by the Great Chain of Being in the snow globe universe.

It was the onset of the Scientific Revolution, leading directly to the Industrial Revolution, in which accomplishments built so swiftly and so compellingly that science began to replace religion as the prime authority—for some people the only authority—for truth. The ultimate result was the rising powerful philosophy of materialism, claiming that only the physical world has anything of value to say, that metaphysics and God-talk and the world of the spirit are illusory.

The implications of a heliocentric universe and its byproducts of rationalistic philosophy were so extreme for Western thinking that it would take centuries before their truth began to be understood. What was triumph for science became a psychological catastrophe for humans, the implications of which we are still feeling. After thousands of years of stability, within a handful of generations Earth would be reduced to being one among countless other circling orbs in an unimaginably vast space in which there was no sign of heaven.

But there would be more. Darwin came, with evidence that God's creatures great and small had not originated in the single divine week of the Genesis story. Humanity was not the proud result of a single act of God but had developed step by infinitesimal step from earlier life forms, the landward progress of a Devonian fish that, as Loren Eiseley put it, had cunningly managed "to end as a two-legged character with a straw hat" (1959, 47).

Confusion

Today's cosmos is not so homelike nor theology so immediate as in snow globe times. Our universe is enormous, as we know from Hubble telescope photos of space and the digital mapping of our social networks. There is not one religion, or even two or three but tens of thousands, competing worldviews with differing interpretations of reality. (The Google "List of religions and spiritual traditions" can be quite a shock.)

And as if that weren't enough, the insistence of the past 300 years that what is factual must be countable and only the physical is real, has diminished our ability to respect the world of symbol and sense, of image and imagination. We think all prose is journalism. We have to a significant extent lost our story and our imagination.

Says Shunyamurti (2011), "Once we have lost touch with wonderment and delight, replaced by the dull vulcan submission to the rules of reason, we have left the eternal home of the gods and entered history, the long, boring descent into totalitarian anti-life, and its ultimate demise, that is now occurring, in mounting waves of chaos and conflagration."

And so we find, at one pole, groups so traumatized by the barrage of change and instability and by impersonality and perceived wickedness that they are attempting to concretize the present into their dream of a past that never was. Fundamentalisms are sweeping the world. At the opposite pole are the futurist folk who thrive on open structure and kaleidoscopic worldview, who adroitly manage without dizziness a perpetual shifting of planes, happy to believe that their own psyches are all they need to comprehend what used to be called sacred.

Further, we are split, pulled in turn by the materialist view with its rational explanations and practical applications that surround us, and then by persisting questions about everything that hangs outside the box that scientism provides—the mysteries and phenomena and visions for which materialism has neither room nor patience. We see this conflict in the dislocation between reductionist neuroscientific explanations of NDEs and the feet-not-touching-the-ground dreaminess of many experiencers. It takes hard work to be clear about the context in which we are living.

East and West: thinking the way we do

"Where we are," for the purposes of this book, is early in the 21st century, in a developed Western society, which means that as a culture we have a Judeo-Christian heritage. Having this perspective shapes everything about our understanding of what is going on in the world and in ourselves, and what it means to be human; and although the tradition is undergoing drastic change, it remains foundational.

Every society over time, both consciously and unconsciously, explores the myriad of its human and social potentials, and those which seem most compatible drift upward in importance until they seem natural and inevitable in that society. Together with the stories that have grown out of the communal experience, those elements will become the mental picture by which that society understands The Way Things Are and How Things Work, and defines what (if anything) is sacred and what it is to be human. Within that picture, every individual then develops his or her own model of reality.

Each of these mental pictures, whether designed by a society or an individual person, contains a basic "recipe" for being human: an assumption as to what constitutes the *basic social unit*; some construct to explain the underpinnings of *human nature*; and a more or less systematic model of whatever we consider to be ultimately important—a *faith model*. Until a century or so ago in the West, this almost invariably meant a Judeo-Christian religious perspective. Today's faith model will be religious for some; for increasing numbers, it will be secular, or a personalized spirituality. In any case, the faith model will build our mythology, what we hold to be true and of value.

Charles T. Tart is among the pioneers of scientifically-based research into human consciousness. Commenting on the conventional wisdom of any culture, he has observed that ". . . we believe certain things simply because we were trained to believe them." (1975, 40) He goes on:

"By the simple fact of being born human, having a certain type of body and nervous system, existing in the environmental conditions of planet earth, a large (but certainly not infinite) number of potentials are *possible* for you. Because you are born into a *particular* culture, existing at a *particular* time and place on the surface of the planet, however, only a small (perhaps a very small) number of those potentials will ever be realized and become *actualities*...defined as the essence of being human...

"Most of us know how to do arithmetic, speak English, write a check, drive an automobile; and most of us know about things, like eating with our hands, which are repellent to us (naturally or through training?) Not many of us, though, were trained early in childhood to enter [a state of consciousness] where we can be, for example, possessed by a friendly spirit that will teach us songs and dances, as is done by some cultures. Nor were most of us trained to gain control over our dreams and acquire spirit guides in those dreams who will teach us useful things, as the Senoi of Malaysia are. Each of us is simultaneously the beneficiary of his cultural heritage and the victim and slave of his culture's narrowness. What I believe is worse is that few of us have any realization of this situation. Like almost all people in all cultures at all times, we think our *own* local culture is the best and other peoples are uncivilized or savages."

A note about God-talk

In much of what follows, there will be mention of God. Let me be quite clear: I do not use the word here in a doctrinal sense, and there is a vast theological range in the quoted authors who employ it. Although I will not be using the word to mean "an old white man in the sky," I have no quarrel with those who find meaning in that sense, provided they allow me the same courtesy to mean it differently. For those whose blood pressure rises at sight of the word, I suggest thinking of "God" as a metaphor for "whatever mystery is behind it all." And for neo-atheists who decry any acceptance of spirituality, I suggest reading a different book.

In the West: up close and personal

What is authentically Western is becoming blurred by the great social upheaval of the present age, the merging of cultures and the stirring of their ideas into new traditions. However, the power of millennia of cultural history cannot be erased in a single lifetime, or even a single century, and so the general pattern of our past remains for the most part intact.

The family of Western monotheism—Judaism, Christianity, and Islam—has a unique temperament among the world's spiritual traditions. It could be called *gregarious*, with "I/Thou" at its center, directed toward relationship with God, with the self and others, and from those relationships to service—to other people, nature, the arts, something beyond the personal boundary. It begins, though, with the identification of that self.

Self

The very name of the Western god translates roughly as a thunder of identity: "*I Am That I Am*," as the ancient Yahweh announced to Moses. Western tradition began in relationship with that *I Am*. Many centuries later, emphasis on the individual, on our personal "I am" has developed to high art. The United States, especially, has lived for three centuries with the great and largely unquestioned myth of the individual: that the very essence of being human is one's individuality, to be one's self, to be unique in the here-and-now. We speak of self-realization and self-actualization, of being "authentic" and becoming "who we really are." Parents say proudly of a strong-minded toddler, "She's her own person, all right!" We honor superstars more than teams. In economic life we strive for self-sufficiency, abhor dependency, accumulate private property. In short, each of us is *saturated* with the sense of individuality, personhood, specialness, selfhood. The strength of this myth exceeds our ability to carry it out; but we live and dream and vote as if it were true.

Ego is the core of the everyday self. It is the Walter Cronkite of our internal personal communication network, the anchorperson, the one we think we know: the center around which an individual organizes, the broadcasting 'on-air' component of the self, the self-image, the "me." Ego tells us who we think we are. Babies and toddlers are virtually all ego, with no regard for anyone else. "Me! Me!" *"Mine!"* "I do it."

In order to function in the world, everyone needs that sturdy sense of self as a base, and the development of a healthy ego is the task of the early years. Its adequate functioning makes life in society possible. Without ego, a person has all the psychological stability of Jell-O, or, as psychiatrist Bruce Greyson once commented, "Without ego—there's schizophrenia."

Eventually, of course, psychologically healthy children do discover that other people have needs and feelings, and learn to take them into account as they develop empathy and other social skills. Psychological development is a *process*, into ego and beyond, moving outward from that first ancient sense of oneness to encompass greater inclusion. Its goal is a mature arrival, eventually, at a "second naïveté," a stage beyond ego absorption that recognizes again a shared essence, a partnership with the universe, with God, but without the toddler's arrogance. The trajectory takes time; forcibly giving one's ego over prematurely will have emotionally catastrophic results.

From his professional career devoted to psychiatry and spiritual direction, Gerald May (1982, 124) observes:

> A common misinterpretation of spiritual teachings assumes that self-image is 'bad' because it seems to pose such an obstacle to spiritual realization and results in so many distortions and paradoxes. Especially in some popularizations of Eastern thought, the self-image is seen as the primary human defect, a malady that must be overcome and extinguished before life can be lived in fullness. Nothing could be further from the truth. The alternative to total entrapment by self-image is not necessarily total alienation from it; self-image and self-definition do have their purposes. They are absolutely necessary for expedient functioning on the face of this planet. One

does need to know where one's self stops and something 'other' begins in order to do the business of the world. Many contemplative theologies maintain that self-image is the proper instrument of divine will. It is God's workhorse, needing not to be eradicated but only to find its proper perspective. On a personal level, it is only because we feel separate and self-identified that we are able to appreciate our existence.

World and relationship

The monotheistic genealogy goes back to the wealthy Bronze Age herdsman Abraham, who made a covenant—not merely an agreement but a binding *relationship*—with his God, the YHWH whose name is too sacred to be spoken. In all three of these monotheistic traditions, the Almighty—whether called Elohim, Adonai, HaShem, Yahweh, God, Allah—is perceived as a living presence with which there is, inescapably, personal and/or national encounter. This is the perceived God which (or who), through the interactions of humanity, creates history; this God which (or who) is beyond human imagining, yet who creates, empowers, provides, rescues, instructs, demands, chastises, supports, punishes, heals, loves, and at last takes home.

Whether one is personally religious is irrelevant. Built on that ancient and enduring legacy of covenant, of bondedness with God and each other, Western psychology and spiritual practice look for relationship, not detachment. The ideal is to attach not to the things of the world but to God and love—and not for oneself, but as a gift for others (Mother Teresa of Calcutta, Martin Luther King, Jr.). The goal of Western disciplines is to lead, as Richard Foster has said (1978, 14) "to the inner wholeness necessary to give ourselves to God freely, and to the spiritual perception necessary to attack social evils."

Hear Elie Wiesel's (1972, 5) shining description of the Hasidic movement in Judaism: "The fervent waiting, the longing for redemption; the erratic wanderings over untraveled roads; the link between man and his Creator, between the individual act and its repercussions in the celestial spheres; the importance of ordinary words;

the accent on fervor and on friendship too; the concept of miracles performed by man for man."

Or the great 20th century Jewish theologian Martin Buber (1947, 4):

> The world, in which you live, just as it is and not otherwise, affords you that association with God, which will redeem you and whatever divine aspect of the world you have been entrusted with. And your own character, the very qualities which make you what you are, constitutes your special approach to God, your special potential use for Him. Do not be vexed at your delight in creatures and things! But do not let it shackle itself to creatures and things; through these, press on to God. . . You shall not stifle your surging powers, but let them work at holy work, and rest a holy rest in God.

Finally, from the great religious historian Huston Smith (1958, 279), a Christian:

> The Semitically originated religions emerge as exceptional in insisting that human beings are ineradicably body as well as spirit and that this coupling is not a liability. From this basic premise three corollaries follow: (1) that the material aspects of life are important (hence the strong emphasis in the West on humanitarianism and social service); (2) that matter can participate in the condition of salvation itself (affirmed by the doctrine of the Resurrection of the Body); and that nature can host the Divine (the Kingdom of God is to come 'on Earth,' to which Christianity adds its doctrine of the Incarnation).

It is out of this drive for relationship, for care of others, that these became the traditions famous for founding hospitals and universities, orphanages and asylums. The Western traditions may yearn for a return to Paradise, but—except for some extremes of Augustine and

Calvin and the Gnostics—they also take Creation and life on earth both seriously and joyfully.

In the East: detachment

A quite different perspective exists in Eastern traditions, especially those which arose in India: Hinduism and its offshoot Buddhism in its many variations. Whereas Western traditions lean to the gregarious, the Eastern are more *introverted*, dedicated to the inner spiritual life. Here the essence of belief is an awareness of life as suffering, and a consequent desire to move beyond the physical world in which that suffering occurs. The task in Hinduism and Buddhism is to recognize that the 'realities' of the physical world are ultimately illusory, and to let go of identification with them. In Huston Smith's words (1991, 278), "Salvation in such contexts involves freeing the soul from its material container."

In contrast to the United States, some societies hold the group to be the basic social unit. Japan does, for one. These are the societies in which, as Carol Zaleski (1987, 196) notes, "the individual feels his identity securely only when merged with the community…purging himself of idiosyncrasy."

The great Romanian mythologist Mircea Eliade (1954, 4) has observed that in archaic societies, which follow this model, "Neither the things of the world nor human acts, properly speaking, have any autonomous intrinsic value. Objects or acts acquire value, and in so doing become real, because they participate…in a reality which transcends them…Their meaning, their value, are…connected with their property of reproducing a mythical example…[They] are repeated because they were consecrated in the beginning by gods, ancestors, or heroes."

It is not the individual who matters, but the individual's connectedness to the whole. Some music directors and sports coaches train to this model, prizing a flawless functioning of the whole over dazzling individual performances.

The potentials developed within these societies and organizations enhance the shared values of cooperation, teamwork, modesty, fitting in, not sticking out in a crowd. Bonded by tradition and the security of knowing what is expected, these societies and the people who live in them tend to feel uncomfortable with innovation.

What is real, if it is not the physical world? *Nirvana* is real. Nirvana as a precise concept does not exist in Western traditions, though it is close to what is meant by *Godhead*, that indescribable *Something* which towers over and behind the objective universe and which goes beyond any idea of God's having personality.

Nirvana is associated in Buddhist writings with a variety of attributes: "Nirvana is permanent, stable, imperishable, immovable, ageless, deathless, unborn and unbecome…power, bliss and happiness, the secure refuge, the shelter, and the place of unassailable safety; that it is the real Truth and the supreme Reality; that it is the Good, the supreme goal and the one and only consummation of our life, the eternal, hidden and incomprehensible Peace." (Conze, 1981).

This is the language of mysticism. In Western secular terms, psychology notwithstanding, this may sound like nonsense. In religious terms, it sounds more like certain of the Psalms than it does like the anthropomorphism of the first chapters of Genesis. In a similar vein, the Montreal Zen Center website includes a quote from the Buddha: "There is that sphere wherein is neither earth nor water, fire nor air: it is not the infinity of space, nor the infinity of perception; it is not nothingness, nor is it neither idea nor non-idea; it is neither this world nor the next, nor is it both; it is neither the sun nor the moon. It neither comes nor goes, it neither abides nor passes away; it is not caused, established, begun, supported; it is the end of suffering."

What Buddhism considers real, then, is not the physical aspect of life but that object-less wholeness which is beyond definition or articulation, beyond space and time. It is not God the Creator in any Western sense because a Creator God has personality, and personality is a limitation, and Nirvana, or the Godhead, is beyond limiting.

The ultimate goal in Buddhism is the letting go of all attachments to the objective world and self, to be like an individual raindrop losing itself in the ocean of Cosmic Mind. It is the spiritual equivalent of the Christian concept of salvation, albeit with entirely different aims and understandings, its destination being more like the Void (properly understood) than heaven.

Harmonizing

What if the Void and heaven are not opposites but differing perspectives of whatever is ultimate?

Harmon Bro (1993, 192-193) noted "the tension between *obedience* and *gnosis*, which runs deep in faith traditions…Put in stark terms, biblical faith has stressed obedience, while those springing from Hindu roots… have stressed overcoming ignorance in favor of salvific illumination, which is the basic meaning of gnosis. It is possible that obedience and gnosis always need each other, lest keeping the commandments becomes legalism and seeking transcendent wisdom becomes morally bankrupt."

Likewise, Lionel Corbett has suggested that similar journeys may follow different routes, (1996, 159):

> Even the most sublime wisdom is of no value if it is given at the wrong time, to the wrong person or in the wrong manner… We may need to make a personal choice between Buddhism's assertion that there is no self in the sense of an entity (anatman), and the Judaeo-Christian and psychological assumption that such an entity exists…[In Buddhism] there is no self as a separate entity distinct from the totality of consciousness.… and each experience must be allowed to fall away as a stage towards realizing the illusory nature of ego-Self separation. Or, if one prefers the idea of relationship, one may choose to savour each numinous experience as a way of deepening the ego's relationship to our true centre and identity.

In short, no road is the *only* road, though to reach any destination it is advisable to travel one road at a time. As will be more thoroughly discussed in the next chapter, many roads are lined with the images described in near-death and similar spiritual experiences and can help carry us to a way of dealing with them. People with an Eastern understanding or a particular temperament may find fewer conceptual hurdles in "letting go" than the majority of Westerners, but the either road guides travelers home.

The Void

Western culture is not prepared to deal easily with the Void. The entire concept, which is so basic to Buddhism, is virtually unknown in the Abrahamic religions, with their binding, enduring *relationship* between humanity and God. Further, between the religious reverence for covenant and the capitalist reverence for things, *we are trained into objects*. Our self-identity depends on objects, whether persons or things, which become our landmarks.

Here it becomes clear why experiences of the Void create such havoc for those who have grown up in Western ways of thinking. Where ego is too suddenly challenged, there is neither self nor Other, and therefore no possibility of relationship, and without relationship, we have no existence; we are simply obliterated.

Any NDE is a mystical experience, but with few exceptions, Western people are not educated mystics. The fear in experiences of the Void rises out of profound, fathomless detachment from self and other, for which most of us are totally unprepared.

In addressing the fear produced by the Void, Gerald May quoted the fourteenth century spiritual guide, *Theologica Germanica*: "Nothing burns in hell but self-will." May commented (1982, 103) that "Notions of giving up and self-surrender rub harshly against the grain of modern society, but the contemplatives go even further. They proclaim, with a conviction that can be absolutely frightening, that self-image must truly die...A dying image of self, or a dying belief in such an image, must be accompanied by a dying of one's images of the world as well. It is not an easy business."

By contrast, the Montreal Zen Center director can say with utter serenity, "We can come to see that we are not a thing, a body, a soul, a person, or even a spirit. Fundamentally we are beyond all forms and ideas." That freedom is, in fact, Nirvana. It is, in fact, the Void.

It is not possible to discuss Nirvana without discussing the Void, and it is not possible to discuss either of them adequately today without mentioning astrophysics. For our purposes, one of the clearest explanations comes from Columbia University physicist Brian Greene, whose PBS special and book are titled *The Fabric of the Cosmos.*

Suppose, says Greene, suppose we took away everything in the physical universe—what would be left? We would say "Nothing." If we took its picture, it would be empty. And as Greene agrees, we would be right; but we would also be wrong. He asks, "How do you make sense of something that looks like nothing?" At this point, experiencers of the Void sit up and take notice.

"As it turns out," he tells us, "empty space is not nothing; it's *something*."

(Buddhists are nodding and smiling.)

"Empty space is not nothing; it's something with hidden characteristics as real as all the stuff in our everyday lives. In fact, space is so real it can bend; it can twist; and it can ripple—so real that empty space itself helped shape everything in the world around us and forms the very fabric of the cosmos."

In the book, he summarizes (32): "Space is unavoidably suffused with what are called quantum fields and possibly a diffuse uniform energy called a cosmological constant—modern echoes of the old and discredited notion of a space-filling aether."

There's a lot going on, beyond our ability to see it with our own eyes. I am not suggesting that Nirvana is outer space, nor that it is located in outer space, nor that an experience of the Void is an actual trip into outer space any more than a blissful NDE is a voyage to a physical heaven. However, there is this curious resemblance among Godhead, space, the Void, and Nirvana—that what seems so empty may be full of everything there is. It suggests an archetypal connection. We are all describing the same universe, after all, whether scientists, psychologists, mystics, theologians, or plumbers and the kid with a homemade telescope; the language will differ, but it is the same universe.

There are no answers here, but intimations of likenesses suggesting that there may be more to this whole business of spirituality than the doctrinally strict accept or confirmed skeptics admit.

10
The Janus Self

Janus, you will recall, was the Roman god with two faces, one looking into the future, the other into the past; he was the god of gateways, of transition and beginnings and development. Who better to represent the psyche and spirit in our search for meaning in the NDE?

In situ

In 1981, three young researchers from Washington State (Lindley *et al*, 113) defined a "negative" NDE as "one that contains extreme fear, panic, or anger. It may also contain visions of demonic creatures that threaten or taunt the subject…Most negative experiences begin with a rush of fear and panic or with a vision of wrathful or fearful creatures…[but are] usually transformed, at some point, into a positive experience in which all negativity vanishes and the first stage of death [peacefulness] is achieved."

Right there, with no more information than that, a person with a broad knowledge of depth psychology or the history of indigenous religions should have been able to discuss what was going on with near-death experiences. Jungian and New Testament scholar Wayne

Rollins saw it immediately: "Whether personified with gaping throat and jaws, devouring, or as emptiness—these experiences...are signposts of invitation to true maturity, the promise of integration precipitated by despair: Erikson's 'ego integrity.'" (His quote, in its entirety, appears in the discussion of symbolic language in Chapter 13.)

The evidence would be obvious to an ordinary citizen of any shamanic culture, now or at other times throughout history; yet for the typical person in the Americas or Europe today, finding a reasonable way to understand frightening near-death experiences has been very difficult. That so many bright and well-educated people have had to struggle for so long to get a glimmer of understanding—well, it should keep our scientific arrogance in check. Now, after decades of study, we can begin to put frightening near-death experiences into a context that can help us fathom their place and possible purpose.

Whether we observe our own small children or read the record of the earliest known tribal societies, we can see the outlines of an answer. Three themes appear again and again:

1) First, children and early people in general accept *the psychological reality of non-physical presences*. These may be perceived as nature spirits, playmates only they can see, monsters in the closet, or simply mysterious *powers*. Whatever they are named, the presence of non-physical realities is as real in the experience of today's child as it has always been to shamanic peoples. That world, the experiential but non-physical, is taken with as much seriousness as the physical world. Only our blindly materialist culture denies this as truth.

2) Second, some of those realities will be perceived as frightening. Children whose protective parents hide the fairy tale books nonetheless know there are monsters in the closet and Things under the bed.

3) Third, the child, like most societies, will develop some kind of technique, some ritual, for acknowledging and interacting with those realities. A protective ritual may be as simple as pulling a binkie over one's head at night, hugging a stuffed rabbit, or saying a magical word, or as complex as a week-long ceremonial involving an entire community.

These three themes—the non-physical understood as psychologically real, acknowledgment of the existence of frightening non-physical realities, and the development of strategies for dealing with them—offer a perspective for exploring distressing near-death experiences.

As a cultural stance, then, the technological West is comfortable with physical reality, disdainful of the idea of non-physical reality, and downright hostile to any such inbreaking *presence*. Even in the recent rage for angels, it was hard to escape noticing a self-consciousness about the interest, a giddy sensationalism or hyper-sentimentality suggesting that although angels might be fashionable and their actions perhaps demonstrable, something about them isn't quite…*normal*.

This is the cultural stance, the conventional wisdom of what "everyone knows." Yet to repeat part of a quote from Charles Tart (1989, 5): "Each of us is simultaneously the beneficiary of his cultural heritage and the victim and slave of his culture's narrowness…Like almost all people in all cultures at all times, we think our *own* local culture is the best and other peoples are uncivilized or savages."

Our own cultural uneasiness with non-physical experience plays into the invisibility of frightening NDEs. We tend to fall in line behind the conventional wisdom, taking positions without really thinking about them.

For one thing, we are unsurprised when near-death experiences are *pathologized*. It is often useful to remind ourselves of word origins: in this case, that the prefix *path-*means "diseased, disordered," which is what our conventional wisdom tends to think of non-physical experiences. Again and again and again, the first words from any near-death experiencer are, "I know you're going to think I'm crazy, but…" "This is probably just nuts, but…" "My story may sound insane, but…" In the emphatic words of a letter from a 29-year-old New England housewife and mother, "Please understand before I go any further that I am an everyday *normal* housewife, even a little conservative, but am definitely *not* a weirdo."

The Catch-22 for many individuals after an NDE is that they *know* what they experienced but they *can't believe* what they experienced; they think their minds must be disordered; something must be wrong. "Everyone knows" experiences like NDEs can't happen. "Everyone knows" that people can't have any sensations or experiences when they're unconscious. "Everyone knows" your consciousness is *in* your physical body; it can't possibly leave and go wandering off. "That's crazy." In the mainstream of Western thought, the physical world is the only possible *real* world, and therefore the only sane one.

This narrowing of our sense of reality to physical-only shows in even the simplest use of language. A child insists there are monsters under the bed, or in the closet. No, there are no monsters, says a frazzled parent. "It's all in your mind." Meaning: it isn't real. The implications are really astonishing. The phrase is absolutely clear: Something which exists in your mind—in other words, anything that is thought, imagined, felt as true—does not have equal validity with a physical object. A physical monster would bring a parent running; the child's fear is merely exasperating.

As psychiatrist Stanislav Grof and Christina Grof (1989, 5) put it, "Experiences of deities and demons, mythical heroes and landscapes, or celestial and infernal regions have no logical place in the world as it is understood by Western science. Therefore it seems obvious to suggest, as the medical perspective does, that they must be products of some unknown physical process of disease. The mystical nature of many experiences...puts them automatically into the category of pathology, since spirituality is not seen as a legitimate dimension in the exclusively material universe of traditional science."

A second way in which NDEs can be dismissed is by *trivializing* them, minimizing their importance, as reductionist arguments do. The more I can automatically put down an experience that doesn't fit my world view, dismiss it as meaningless or absurd, the less chance that I will have to take it seriously. It becomes simply trivial. Trivializing is frequently accompanied by a phrase such as

"It's nothing but…" or "It's only…" So you had a near-death experience? "It's nothing but" the byproduct of a response to medication, or a lack of oxygen, an effect of coming out of anesthesia, or a spurt of activity in the temporal lobe. "It's only" a play of hallucinations, or a wishful attempt of the mind to attach importance to random images. "It's only…"

Reductionist arguments, which are most often phrased in clinical or scientific language, seem to provide the security of objectivity. In reality, they say very little except about a possible physical process. Limiting our understanding of human experience only to laboratory measures is like accepting the joking news bulletin that reports the value of a person in terms of the market price of the chemical components of the body. It used to be seventy-five cents.

Even if a physiological cause of NDEs were identified—so what? Identification of a biological *process* that may accompany an event likely contributes no useful information about the event's emotional or psychological *effects*. And it is those effects with which a person lives, day to day, after a profound experience. Writing for the *Journal of Nervous and Mental Disease,* Bruce Greyson (1983, 376) observed, "Regardless of the physiological and eschatological significance of the NDE, the experience, its recollection, and its recounting are profound psychological events with identifiable and meaningful precipitants and sequelae."

In other words, the labels that begin "It's only…" may be of no use at all in any non-clinical, practical sense.

Religion, spirituality, psychology

Like Janus, we see in two directions: psychologically, into ourselves, and spiritually, into the transcendent; when structured and organized, this becomes religion. Just as some conservative religious sects refuse to take psychology seriously, confining their attention to spirit and dogma alone, some secular persons, believing spirituality to be at best questionable, dogmatically confine their questions to psychology alone. (Interestingly enough, that is where a new religious energy is rising.)

Just to be clear, I believe both those positions are like blinders to a horse and need clarification. For the following discussion, here is my very brief definition of terms:

Psyche: all of the forces in an individual that influence the person's thought, behavior, and personality.

Psychology: the study of the psyche: how we perceive, understand, and act within the world. From the personal perspective, it involves understanding how and why we feel, think, respond, and behave as we do both internally and socially.

Spirituality: anything having to do with a sensed ultimate reality or transcendent dimension; it may include recognition of a force/power/energy/ spirit/God that may be considered divine. In recent popular usage, the word "spirituality" typically contrasts with "religion" and refers to a personal practice by an individual in recognition of that transcendent dimension; it may be outside of any religious tradition or be a "cookbook" mixing of selected elements from two or more traditions. There are many different types of spirituality, such as private or public, disciplined or unstructured, focusing on nature and/or doctrinal statements, reclusive to communal.

Religion

The following three definitions of *transcendent, religion,* and *ideology* are from Professor of Religion Leonard Swidler (2000, 6), an expert on dialogue across belief systems, now retired from Temple University:

> The transcendent, as the roots of the word indicate, means 'that which goes beyond' the everyday, the ordinary, the surface experience of reality. It can refer to spirits, gods, a personal God, an impersonal God, Emptiness, etc.
>
> Religion is an explanation of the ultimate meaning of life, based on a notion of the transcendent, and how to live accordingly. Organized religion normally contains the four 'C's': *creed*, cognitive aspect, beliefs, everything that goes into the

"explanation" of the ultimate meaning of life; *code*, teachings about behavior or ethics; *cult*, ritual activities that relate the follower to the transcendent; and *community*—structure, organization, relationship among the followers, which can be anything from egalitarian to monarchical. Especially in modern times there have developed 'explanations of the ultimate meaning of life, and how to live accordingly' which are not based on a notion of the transcendent, for example atheistic Marxism and secular humanism. Although in every respect these "explanations" function as religions traditionally have in human life, because they omit the idea of the transcendent it is best to give these 'explanations' a separate name. The name often used is *ideology*.

As a term, then, *religion* includes both formal religious traditions and spirituality generally, whereas *a religion* means one of the organized associations; to be *religious* has come to mean that a person is affiliated with one of those traditions.

It is worth emphasizing that the enduring religious traditions of Judaism, Christianity, Islam, and Buddhism originated not as deliberate "inventions"; but grew from the profoundly transforming spiritual experiences and teachings of four dynamic individuals—Moses, Jesus, Muhammed, and Siddhartha Gautama—together with the writings and traditions of their followers, codified over time into a way of life and an approach to the transcendent.

In purely practical terms, there is always an overlap between psychology and religion/spirituality. What may be acknowledged as sin or spiritual failing in a religious context (a jealous rage, selfishness, a theft, infidelity, a lie with unfortunate consequences) can also be addressed psychologically in a therapist's office in an effort to understand and modify the behavior. Experientially, an encounter with transcendence may be described either religiously or psychologically. A recent trend in some quarters is the psychological approach *to* religion, of which more will be said later.

Because the terminologies of psychology and theology differ when they describe archetypal experiences, Western thought has come to have the sense that religious and psychological vocabularies are describing different factors of the person. This split, which clearly grows out of the division between science and religion, has partitioned off religious experience as if it had nothing to do with normal human development. Lionel Corbett (1996, 60), speaking for an influential contemporary view of this issue, says, "We are not used to the idea that *elements of the divine are important in forming the very structure of the mind.*" (Emphasis in original. The idea contains an echo of the Genesis concept that the breath of God is inherent in the human makeup.)

In Jung's work, the word "Self" (capital "s") refers to a person's entire non-physical being—consciousness, the ego, personal unconscious, collective unconscious—the whole package that is that person's perceptual being. It could be considered the individual *daimon*, the point at which we perhaps touch Godhead. That is the sense in which Jungian therapist and scholar Edinger (1972, 9) makes the following observation:

> There is in the unconscious a transpersonal center of latent consciousness and obscure intentionality. The discovery of this center, which Jung called the Self, is like the discovery of extraterrestrial intelligence. Man is now no longer alone in the psyche and in the cosmos. The vicissitudes of life take on new and enlarged meaning. Dreams, fantasies, illness, accident and coincidence become potential messages from the unseen Partner with whom we share our life. At first, the encounter with the Self is indeed a defeat for the ego; but with perseverance, Deo volente, light is born from the darkness. One meets the 'Immortal One' who wounds and heals, who casts down and raises up, who makes small and makes large—in a word, the One who makes one whole.

Some will call this God (though Jung himself did not; he called it the Self, believing God to be beyond the Self). Some will take it to be the Christ, or Allah; others will not know what to call it. In any case, it is that wholeness we are after.

Spirit

Individuals who find themselves in distressing NDEs that involve a sense of transcendence with feelings of awe and terror may be encountering what the German scholar Rudolf Otto (1958, 12) termed the "numinosum," the Holy. Such an encounter may be interpreted from within a religious tradition or as a generalized spirituality; it occurs across all traditions. This is not the tamed "walking in the garden with God" kind of holy but the original *holy terror*, "the fear of God" so expertly captured by Old Testament writers as a sense of overpowering awe. Otto describes the forms and responses of such meetings with the overpowering sacred in the encounter he calls the *mysterium tremendum*:

> It may burst in sudden eruption up from the depths of the soul with spasms and convulsions, or lead to the strangest excitements, to intoxicated frenzy, to transport, and to ecstasy. It has its wild and demonic forms and can sink to an almost grisly horror and shuddering. It has its crude, barbaric antecedents and early manifestations, and again it may be developed into something beautiful and pure and glorious. It may become the hushed, trembling and speechless humility of the creature in the presence of—whom or what? In the presence of that which is a mystery inexpressible and above all creatures.

Psyche

In the quote above, Otto was describing the ranges of feeling that have been associated with profound spiritual experience. From the psychological perspective, here is psychiatrist Stanislav Grof, (1994, 21) describing the range of feeling from encounters that people may have with the depths of their psyche:

> Modern research brought unexpected new insights...[that] people can encounter an entire spectrum of unusual experiences, including sequences of agony and dying, passing through hell, facing divine judgment, being reborn, reaching the celestial realms, and confronting memories from previous incarnations. These states were strikingly similar to those described in the eschatological texts of ancient and pre-industrial cultures...[S]tudies of near-death states...showed that the experiences associated with life-threatening situations bear a deep resemblance to the descriptions from the ancient books of the dead, as well as those reported by subjects in psychedelic sessions and modern experiential psychotherapy. It has thus become clear that *the ancient eschatological texts are actually maps of the inner territories of the psyche encountered in profound [non-ordinary states of consciousness]*, including those associated with biological dying. [Emphasis added.]

What Otto describes in terms of *spirit*, Grof discusses as experiences of the *psyche*. Phenomenologically, there is no difference between them; they are describing the same experiences. Two vocabularies, one universe. The similarities are obvious. "The psyche," says Corbett (2), "is the essential medium for religious experience."

With the psyche as that essential medium, our psychology obviously plays a part in spirituality, and not only at its innermost territories. Whatever problems, issues, and blind spots we have in ordinary life will affect the way in which we enter, understand, and respond to a near-death (or any other) experience that arises from those deepest sources. Unresolved, problems with the way we think and feel will mark the health of our spiritual life—a troubled resentment toward parents, difficulty maintaining relationships, hostile conditions with neighbors and co-workers, addictions (from ingested chemicals to money or sex), eating disorders, low self-esteem or, conversely, narcissism. That is the work of psychology.

With or without an event as powerful as an NDE in our lives, it is not enough to think that spirituality alone will fix everything—though it is tempting to try. Editor Connie Zweig (1991, *xiv*) illustrates a pervasive contemporary belief:

> I had believed, with a kind of spiritual hubris, that a deep and committed inner life would protect me from human suffering, that I could somehow deflate the power of the shadow with my metaphysical practices and beliefs. I had assumed, in effect, that it was managed, as I managed my moods and my diet, with the discipline of self-control… Seekers are often led to believe that, with the right teacher or the right practice, they can transcend to higher levels of awareness without dealing with their more petty vices or ugly emotional attachments.

It doesn't work. It doesn't work in any belief setting. I have often told audiences in my public talks, "If there is an eleventh Commandment, it is, 'Thou shalt do thy inner work.'" That's where we become our own household help and begin to clean up after ourselves. The only way to clear the floor is to begin picking up clutter and putting things where they belong. With or without professional help, it is imperative to figure out what the issues and questions are and begin to work on clearing them up.

We know very little about how people actually cope after a distressing NDE. Some use denial or withdraw into a long-term defensiveness; some attempt to paper over their issues with stringent theology; many flounder; depression seems common. While a few work through to a kind of compassionate intersubjectivity, this may take decades. In any event, it is self-evident that any deep spiritual event cannot be adequately understood and integrated if it cannot be seen clearly because of all the personal baggage cluttering the mind.

Doing one's inner work does not mean obsessing about it, which is also unhealthy, particularly when simultaneously attempting to follow a spiritual path. David Spangler, one of the most notable voices of the New Age movement, has said about this (1993, 94), "The psychologizing of spirituality leads to two general phenomena, both of which interfere with the movement toward the divine. The first is to turn one's attention away from the world and into the never-ending realms of the psyche." Like dusting a house in a windy desert town, he says, the process of this cleaning is never ending, for there is always new dust: "Healing our inner being is important, but if that is made the object of our spiritual journey, we may find ourselves on an endless quest, perpetually self-absorbed to the detriment of my connections with the larger society and world of which we are a part."

Spangler's entire statement is so helpful, here is the rest of it (97-98):

> The other extreme is to locate divinity within the self, so that if I go deep enough or high enough within myself, I will find God. In this perspective, we each create our own reality, since that ultimate creative power that we call God is the essential nature of the psyche. This is an attractive idea with a certain resonance, unfortunate in the American predilection for the self-sufficient individual who makes his own way, takes care of herself in all circumstances, exhibits no weakness (often little compassion) and expects others to do the same. Horatio Alger turned into a spiritual as well as an economic myth. 'If everyone creates a personal reality, then I don't have to bother with the poor, the disadvantaged, the oppressed; after all, they are creating that reality for themselves and if they don't like it, then they can change it. And if they don't change it, why, it must be because they don't choose to.'
>
> Needless to say, such self-divinization is a prescription for selfishness and a withdrawal from the world. It ignores social justice and closes itself to the real pain of others and to the ways in which we are all responsible for creating the conditions that contribute to that pain. While certain New Age teachings may have wrapped it up in a spiritual glitter ('I can find my divinity, but if you can't find yours, that's your

problem!...), we find the underlying attitude rampant in modern economics, politics, and religion: 'I'm all right, Jack, and if you're not, then it's your own fault. If you can't make a decent life for yourself, perhaps you're just too lazy!'

I have included Spangler's entire quote because the attitudes he parodies will be so recognizable to those with a distressing NDE who have found themselves marginalized or outright excluded because of their experience by some of the "enlightened" in recent years.

Spangler's comments about social justice are not isolated. The British author and religious scholar Paul Heelas (1996, 25) has commented that "People working at [a charity in the UK] were not prepared to support Ethiopian charities. To do so, it was felt, would simply serve to perpetuate Ethiopian dependency-habits."

In a popular vein, a well-known syndicated advice columnist (Yoffe, 2010) heard from a reader who had been experiencing recurring unemployment, had to move twice, had lost a sibling, and was having trouble keeping his/her chin up. The reason for writing to the column:

Reader: I have a friend who asked if I was feeling a little down, and when I admitted it (something that is hard for me), she basically said it was my fault, and my negative energy was attracting negative events...What should I have said?

Emily Yoffe: *The Secret* and other garbage of that ilk suggests people abandon friends with problems so that they don't get 'infected' by their negativity. So you could have said you understand her new set of beliefs mean you two have to keep your distance and that you wish her all the best."

Clearly, contemporary spiritual views about the bounds (and bonds) of friendship are wildly divergent.

The challenge, it seems, is to recognize the validity of both psychology and spirituality. Neither holds all the cards. Rather, says theologian J. Harold Ellens (1981, 318), "It might be better to conceive of the relationship of psychology and spirituality as a genuine *dialogue*. Neither is to be subordinated to each other, nor are they to be seen as identical. Instead of attempting a full integration of the two, it would be more valuable to pay attention to the *points of intersection* between them, asking how they inform and critique each other." This will be discussed in greater detail in the following chapter.

Ego resistance
Where the Western (especially U.S.) psychology of individualism meets the demands of spirituality, there is a significant collision: Donald Trump meets Gandhi; Rush Limbaugh encounters the Dalai Lama; any of us encounters a near-death or similar experience. Life lived within the myth of the self comes up against the spiritual demand for surrender. We are aghast. What's worse, we are unprepared.

A basic argument in the spiritual and psychological literature is that a frightening experience reflects the failure of an individual ego to yield to the experience. Grof (1980, 15) has pointed out, about the range of experiences described earlier, "It is now understood… that these are experiential states of quite regular occurrence when one is facing biological death. Instead of useless pieces of knowledge, the data about the hells and heavens can prove to be invaluable cartographies of strange experiential worlds which each of us will have to enter at some point in the future…Avoidance and reluctance to surrender are considered two major dangers."

And yes, the ego does refuse to yield; succumbing contradicts everything we know from a Western background. Other cultures at other times, as well as the contemplative Western religious orders, have developed ways of preparing people for such demands, and how to respond to them. The relatively well-known *Bardo Thodol (Book of the Dead)* serves as a textbook of rituals for what Tibetan Buddhists can expect at death and how to navigate the process; the Egyptian

Book of the Dead did likewise. Similarly, the Christian *Ars Moriendi* (*Art of Dying*) in 15th century Europe served much the same function, suggesting that one would be met by demons and angels and how to make a successful passage through to heaven.

The purpose of any of those rituals was, in Grof's words (1980, 15), "not to allow the dying to use denial and die unprepared [but to] allow the deceased to recognize as opportunities for liberation the states with which he has already become acquainted during his [spiritual] practice."

As there is precious little in the West to serve this purpose today, it is no wonder that when an ordinary individual walks around a corner of life and drops into the Void, there is only despair; or that those who encounter visions of demons should feel themselves defenseless.

The difficulty is clear. On the one hand we have an entire culture devoted either to unhelpful religious practices or to the sacredness of personal identity, everyone ignorant of spiritual practices related to death and knowing nothing of what to expect in such experiences. Frightening NDEs and similar experiences are shunned and dismissed, making their "invaluable cartographies" unavailable and unrespected.

And yet, on the other hand, in the near-death literature it is common to find the view that some experiences are terrifying because the individual "should have" given in to it, should have surrendered. This assumes not only that the person knows this beforehand but that the response can be somehow both imagined and volitional from within the experience. This is a cultural dilemma. It also ignores the real possibility that sometimes one may be well advised not to be taken in by the terrifying vision, not to go with it but to find a different way around.

Ego death
A parallel issue running through much of the literature is the question of what is often called (erroneously enough) "ego death." In normal human development, as we have seen, the movement is from infantile narcissism and self-absorption to the development of an ego identity sturdy enough to navigate through the demands and challenges of living, eventually broadening to discover that the

boundaries of a life extend well beyond one's ego identity. From this perspective, the objective is to recognize the ego and its demands and bring them under observation and control. This is not the death of ego but the maturing of one's understanding of it.

The hazard, it seems to me, in the contemporary romance of "ego death" as a destination is the tendency to believe that such an attainment would bestow a moral superiority, a kind of spirituality-climbing. When that notion is coupled with the conviction that having a transformative NDE means an effortless arrival at ego death, the results can be socially devastating and even sometimes hilarious. It is well to keep in mind the fabled case of the telegenic near-death experiencer who, after several major TV appearances, announced to a startled IANDS staff person that the NDEr's opinions should be given precedence in any discussion because "my consciousness is higher than your consciousness." So much for ego death.

Left brain/right brain

Based on a considerable literature about the "sidedness" of brain function—the left hemisphere governing cognition and organizing functions and the right hemisphere governing creativity—a popular myth has emerged suggesting that to be "left brained" is to be rigidly abstract, logical, authoritarian, rule-bound, and (by frequent inference) probably unsmiling, while living in the "right brain" leads to an enlightened life of joyful creativity, serenity, and wellbeing. I have even heard it suggested that if only people with distressing NDEs had "lived more in their right brain," their experiences would have been blissful rather than traumatic. Time to regroup.

In the words of psychiatrist Bruce Greyson, in an email:

> I'm not aware of any evidence for a link between brain laterality and emotional valence [whether emotions are positive or negative]. Generally speaking, the left brain is associated with dispassionate linear reasoning (e.g., language) and the right brain with nonlinear pattern recognition (e.g., music) and

with biasing outcomes by applying emotional significance to the decisions of the left brain. So fright and revulsion would be associated with the right brain just as are love and peace... The whole laterality question is more up in the air now than it was a few decades ago... With increasing evidence of the remarkable degree of brain plasticity, it no longer is accurate to say that any cortical function is inextricably linked to one particular part of the cortex. There may be one cortical area that usually handles, say, spoken language, but if that area is damaged, other areas can in time learn to take on the function of the damaged piece.

In short, the right hemisphere of the brain typically processes *all* emotions, not only pleasant ones. We do well to remind ourselves that without structure (left hemisphere), we would be like so much mental custard. Without language (left hemisphere), we would undo the work of our being human. Without discernment and common sense (left hemisphere), we become easy marks for spiritual charlatans and crooks. Two halves make a whole brain and a whole person.

Mysticism

It is probably evident, now, that one great difference marks the distinction between the Eastern traditions of Hinduism and Buddhism and the Western monotheistic religions of Judaism, Christianity and Islam. The difference is that Hinduism and Buddhism are at heart mystical and the Western traditions are not. Walter Stace (1960, 124) has noted that Hinduism and Buddhism "are rooted in mysticism, have mysticism at their core, and would not be what they are without it."

Christianity has its mystics, of course, as do Judaism and Islam; but the pursuit of mystical experience is not central as it is in the Eastern disciplines. (That includes Eastern Orthodox Christianity, which is more mystical than its sisters.) Theologian Richard J. Foster (1978, 15) has said, "Eastern meditation is an attempt to empty the mind; Christian meditation is an attempt to empty the mind in order to fill it. The two ideas are radically different." Foster's reference to Christian practice applies as well to the other Western traditions.

So, although Western religious traditions have also known the Void, that knowledge has existed principally within isolated communities such as cloistered Orders, not in the open air of pulpit and religious education. It often comes as a surprise to Christians that contemplative religious orders for many years followed a type of meditational practice which advocated what Morton Kelsey (1976, 72) called "mental communion in an imageless void. In fact, the Void joins the Bridegroom as one of the common interpretations of the mystical encounter."

How to describe the Holy from an encounter that is very much like being in a sensory deprivation chamber? In one of his sermons, the 12th century St. Bernard said of his contacts with the Absolute:

"It is not by the eyes that He enters, for He is without form or color that they can discern; nor by the ears, for His coming is without sound; nor by the nostrils, for it is not with the air but with the mind that He is blended. By what avenue then has He entered? Or perhaps the fact may be that He has not entered at all, nor indeed come at all from outside; for not one of these things belongs to outside. Yet it has not come from within me." (Bernard, in Underhill, 244)

What are we to make of *that*? What are we to make of what Meister Eckhart calls "the still wilderness where no one is at home"? What are we to do with an imageless Reality? That is what the Void is, imageless. As white is the presence of all colors and black is the absence of all colors, the Void is both of them, and transparent as well. Talk about it is invariably nonsense, because it cannot be described. This Absolute is God, but not as God is known from the stories of Western tradition—and to a person who encounters the Void unaware that God wears no face as well as many faces, then the God/Absolute of the Void may feel like no God at all—like abandonment. This is not the Creator of the Sistine Chapel, gloriously made in the image of Man; not the Creator of Genesis, walking in a garden in the cool of the evening; not the familiar old white man with a beard, alternating between Santa Claus and Darth Vader. This is encounter with something unknown to us.

In the 6th century Dionysius the Areopagite called it the "Divine Darkness" in which God is said to dwell (Treatise on Divine Names). Six hundred years later, Blessed John Ruysbroeck (The Book of Supreme Truth), struggling to disentangle anthropomorphic images from his knowledge of the Absolute said, "Divine Abyss": "And the bare, uplifted will is transformed and drenched through by abysmal love, even as iron is by fire. And the bare, uplifted memory feels itself enwrapped and established in an abysmal Absence of Image. And thereby the created image is united above reason in a threefold way with its Eternal Image, which is the origin of its being and its life; and this origin is preserved and possessed, essentially and eternally, through a simple seeing in an imageless void."

Still another almost-six-hundred years, and the great Reb Menahem-Mendl, a disciple of the Baal Shem Tov's successor, said, "My mission on earth is to recognize the void—inside and outside me— and fill it." (Wiesel, 1972, 84)

Not for the first time, here is Evelyn Underhill (2010, 349) to the rescue:

> What, then, do those who use this image of the 'dark' really mean by it? They mean this: that God in His absolute Reality is unknowable—is dark—to man's intellect, which is adapted to other purposes than those of divine intuition. When...the whole personality...comes into contact with that Reality, it enters a plane of experience to which none of the categories of the intellect apply. Reason finds itself, in a most actual sense, 'in the dark'—immersed in the Cloud of Unknowing...He who enters into the 'nothingness' or 'ground of the soul,' enters also into the 'Dark': a statement which seems simple enough until we try to realize what it means.

In short, we are on our own and will understand as best we are able.

11
The Cultural Milieu

A new Axial Age
"It's all too hard, too confused. How can I make sense out of this experience…my life…*anything?*" Here is a true fact to keep in mind: You have every right to feel bewildered. We're *all* bewildered. The world really *is* chaotic in a way that has occurred only twice before in all of human history. At the same time that we bring the just-described East/West cultural attributes into our understanding, 3,000 years of Western culture are restructuring around us at a pace faster than we can comprehend. In trying to make sense of our times and our lives—much less our NDEs—we are piecing together our puzzle on a background that won't hold still.

The first such radical shift came perhaps 10,000 years ago, when the morphing of nomadic, hunter-gathering cultures began the shift to agriculture and life in towns. We hear echoes of that turmoil in the stories of Eden and Cain and Abel: the conflict of values between the hunter and the tiller of fields. Nothing would ever be the same.

Some 9,000 years would pass before another shift of that magnitude. And then, in roughly the years between 800 and 200 BCE, something fundamental happened in the thinking and even in the very nature, of people around the world. Humanity discovered morality. Cultures thousands of miles apart developed a version of the Golden Rule and laid a foundation of philosophical, legal, and spiritual understanding that underlies everything we know, even today. German philosopher Karl Jaspers (Jaspers), who coined the term "Axial Age," said of the period, "Fundamental ideas rose everywhere in the Axial Age…Extraordinary events are crowded into this period."

The great religious traditions emerged in that age. In China there were Confucius and Lao Tzu and the foundations of Chinese philosophy; from India, the Buddha, the Upanishads, and all the varieties of philosophical thought; in Palestine it was the age of the Hebrew prophets, stirring the rise of social conscience and an intense sense of justice; Greece produced Homer, Socrates, Plato, Aristotle, Archimedes, Alexander the Great, and developed the first Olympic games (the earliest public recognition of what was at the time globalism). It was the age of great empires: the Persian, Macedonian, Thracian, Roman, whose venturings roughly shoved parochial cultures into contact with each other, creating a diffusion of ideas and customs and a blurring of tribal and ethnic boundaries, with resulting economic upheavals. We should recognize the pattern.

In the words of historian John C. Plott (1977, 19), from the Mediterranean to India and China, "virtually the same problems were dealt with almost simultaneously: the nature of the world, soul, and God; the distinction of matter and mind and/or spirit…and the setting up of rules of conduct."

That same kind of turmoil is with us today, on a larger scale but with the same elements: stunningly new ideas, radical shifts in religion, globalism and a jostling of cultures, and economic upheavals. What is different is the pace. We, too, have moved poignantly but irrevocably from a world of coherent but insular worldviews to one that pushes past our emotional and conceptual borders, disturbing our ways of thinking and living. in which we are overwhelmed by a multiplicity of peoples and belief systems, and a sense that nothing feels secure.

Interviewed for the online magazine *EnlightenNext*, Karen Armstrong (2005), author of *A History of God*, said:

> Today we are amid a second Axial Age and are undergoing a period of transition similar to that of the first Axial Age. Its roots lie in the sixteenth and seventeenth centuries of the modern era, when the people of Western Europe began to evolve a different type of society. Since that time, Western civilization has transformed the world. The economic changes of the last four hundred years have been accompanied by immense social, political, and intellectual revolutions, with the development of an entirely different scientific and rational concept of the nature of truth. But despite the cult of rationality, modern history has been punctuated by witch hunts and world wars which have been explosions of unreason (http://is.gd/5SchsF).

Leonard Swidler (2008), has said of the 20th century's wars, "In fact, however, those vast world conflagrations were manifestations of the dark side of the unique breakthrough in the history of humankind [of] the modern development of Christendom-become-Western Civilization, now becoming Global Civilization. Never before had there been world wars; likewise, never before had there been world political organizations (League of Nations, United Nations). Never before did humanity possess the real possibility of destroying all human life—whether through nuclear or ecological catastrophe. These unique negative realities/potentialities were possible, however, only because of the correspondingly unique accomplishments of Christendom/Western/ Global Civilization—the like of which the world has never before seen."

Ewert Cousins (1994, 4), renowned pioneer in interfaith dialogue, has also commented on the price of a broader consciousness. He observed that although the first Axial Age brought the sense of individual identity "as distinct from the tribe and from nature...it brought loss as well. Axial persons were in possession of their own identity, it is true, but they had lost their organic relation to nature and community. They now ran the risk of being alienated from the matrix of being and life." And that is precisely where we find ourselves, floundering to recover a matrix of being and life.

As discussed in Chapter 1, the loss of the secure Ptolemaic cosmology has been so culturally traumatic that it is taking centuries to sink in. While the technological aspects of scientific discoveries may be tolerated, their philosophical implications are harder and take longer to accept. (Think of the seemingly endless furor over evolution!) This way to fundamentalisms.

Further, spurred by wars, economic necessity, and technological advances in travel, a great migration of peoples is again happening: Home towns that a generation ago were monocultural, with a single religion, maybe one diner, everyone speaking one language and working for the same company, now find themselves with a half-dozen religions in town, and Indian, Mexican, Chinese, Japanese, Peruvian, and Italian restaurants right around the corner, at the same time the Internet is pumping more and more new information into their awareness. Once-secure jobs have been outsourced to places never heard of before. Homogeneity is gone: the school district where my children grew up now draws from families speaking any of 66 different languages. (Courant)

Faced by the dislocations resulting from such sweeping change, swelling waves of people have succumbed to a rage that is fueling political and social uprisings, with verbal and physical attacks against newcomers and any who represent difference. People may not recognize the source of their anger, but from a dispassionate distance it is unmistakable. And still the change continues, and the pace quickens.

What this means is that in human terms, Western culture—what we have known in our local identities as, for instance, Uncle Sam, John Bull, "the maple leaf forever," or simply "the way we do things"—has lost its coherence. (Though note that "coherence" is no guarantee of "peacefulness.")

For example, it is obvious from the text of this book that my life experience is embedded in the Judeo-Christian stories of the Creation, Eden, Cain and Abel, Easter, the loving God—it is the ground of my language and allusions, the symbolic connections I make, the references I assume readers will understand. That mythos provides the context for my conscious life, including its emotional tie to a five-times-great-grandfather who first translated the Bible into Welsh. At the same time, in this developing Second Axial Age I am now aware that for some readers, my language and context are likely to be alienating. Although I know no other way to speak, there is a constant awareness of the need to write so that secularists, Buddhists, Hindus, Muslims, Wiccans, "recovering Christians," and who knows how many others will also be able to relate to the text. Tricky! And for many people, a devastating loss of security.

There was such a shock of recognition, the first time I heard Jean Houston say we are the "people of the parentheses," living between two great narratives. We in the Americas and Europe stand between the time when the Judeo-Christian story with all its pre-Copernican, pre-Newtonian assumptions was simply the air we breathed, and the time of a sweeping new story—whatever it will be—that is still to come. So now, here we are, half a world of people with no central, shaping cultural myth, adrift in a storm of belief systems, looking for home. So many personal stories, yet no shared story. No wonder we find ourselves confused! In that absence, we go as loners, no longer part of a common community identity with an inherent sense of meaning.

It is a new thing, and inescapable, this radical individualism within globalism, that has the potential to bring the social and economic world as we know it to its knees. Jung (1933) said he thought that finding a new myth could take 600 years. Two hundred or so to go.

But what of religion?

Where does religion fit into understanding near-death experiences? Or does it fit at all in a time of enthusiastic atheism and rebellion against organized religion? The majority of near-death experiences impart messages basic to Judeo-Christian tradition—particularly love of the sacred and of others, and service to those in need—but they are not necessarily described in the language that is expected by those traditions. Are they religious?

Terms

Historian of religion Ann Taves (2009, 162) has observed that when people use the adjectives 'magical,' 'religious,' 'superstitious,' 'spiritual,' 'mystical,' 'secular' or 'ideological' to apply to such an experience, it is the pre-existing belief of the speaker rather than the experience itself that determines which word will be chosen.

This linguistic sophistication is, by the way, a perfect illustration of how a postmodern understanding creates a dilemma when trying to determine the meaning of our experiences, as to a post-modernist all statements refer meaning back to the individual speaker rather than to a stable and foundational cultural system of shared truths. This is exactly what is meant by being "between stories." At any rate, an individual NDE might be categorized and interpreted as any of those terms—yet whether religious, mystical, magical, superstitious, spiritual, ideological, or secular, it is the same individual experience. Life is not necessarily clearer in an Axial Age.

Is a near-death experience a religious experience? Certainly some experiencers have found them profoundly religious. For the man who excitedly tries to tell his family and nurses that he has just been with Jesus, or the woman happy at having being met by Saint Jude, or the four-year-old whose story of seeing Jesus in heaven creates a mega-bestseller, there is no question: this is an event saturated with meaning as perceived in a specific religious context. For the man who believed he saw the gates of hell, or for any of Maurice Rawlings' patients who awoke terrified, as for the now-evangelizing author (Wiese) of *23 Minutes in Hell*, these were appallingly, shiveringly real experiences with a religious explanation. Inversely, there are powerful religious implications for the people who actively perceived

God as absent, like the woman who said, "God wasn't there. That's what scared me."

"Religion is an explanation of the ultimate meaning of life, based on a notion of the transcendent, and how to live accordingly" (Leonard Swidler, 2000, 6). Someone once said to me that the purpose of religion is "to chart that level of reality at which physical science becomes ineffective." Any experience that deals with "the beyond"—with the *more*—might be considered by some a religious experience.

Certainly visionary experiences, whether NDEs or something similar, lie at the heart of all the enduring religious traditions. For each of these traditions, the origin point has been a single individual with one or more powerful experiences: Moses, Confucius, Lao Tse, Siddhartha Gautama, Jesus, Mohammed. Spiritually gifted, highly charismatic, they were teachers and leaders around whom people gathered. Over time and shared experiences, their teachings became accepted as a moral and spiritual path, and when the number of followers became great enough—as with any group—organization followed, a body of writings developed, with eventual codification of teachings and practice.

Contrary to a good deal of secular and especially neo-atheist opinion, it is highly unlikely that religion *originated* in a political desire for control or manipulation with pasted-on spiritual attributes. In all the enduring traditions, religion has grown, always, out of transfiguring experience and the resulting mission to share a body of overwhelmingly perceived truth. The assumption of control comes much later, with growth and the potential for power, not before it.

Mainstream struggle: decline, adapt, reinterpret

The French sociologist of religion Yves Lambert (1999, 302), who considers the centuries of modernity to be a new Axial Age, points out that "Modernity appears to have four principal types of religious effects: decline, adaptation and reinterpretation, conservative reaction, and innovation. It produces secularization as well as new religious forms, in particular: worldliness, dehier-archization of the human and the divine, self-spirituality, parascientificity, pluralism, amid mobility."

It is all of these trends which have been swirling through the time period during which near-death experiences were becoming known.

Secularization and decline
It is not only human experience that may be trivialized by reductionist thinking. God, too, has had a tough time of it for the better part of 300 years. As the development of scientific method made high technology possible, revelations of natural cause whittled away at the Western concept of God as the answer to all questions. Didn't Genesis say that humans had dominion over the earth?—with industrialization we could *really* have it, and with each new technology, humans moved faster, dug deeper, produced more, took more control. Only God could make a tree when Joyce Kilmer wrote his poem, but tissue culture enables a botanist to produce one in a greenhouse, and to modify its genetic structure while he's at it.

Drip, drip, drip…and with every discovery, the role that had been allocated to the sacred in Western culture eroded a fraction. As it seemed that the domain of God grew smaller while human accomplishment increased, the material world became the center of attention, until after a time it became, for many people, the sole reality. Science became the god.

Within only a few generations, the educated Western population had been trained to become a literal-minded society, to think in terms of fact, proof, authentication, objectivity. Materialist thinking tossed out fairy tales as unrealistic and dismissed dreams as essentially without importance in the 'real' world. It misunderstood and pooh-poohed religious mythologies as merely primitive attempts to explain the natural world and condescended to intense spiritual experience as the meaningless excess of a disordered brain. It rarely occurred to anyone in the materialist community that they were missing the point.

By now even the most devoutly religious people are so saturated by the values and expectations of materialism that those measures have spilled over into the understanding of what religion is and is about. If facts, proof, authentication, and objectivity are good things in science, should they not also be good in all areas of human concern?

And so, religion, too, moved bit by bit from its natural concerns toward an expectation that it, too, would produce facts, proof, authentication, an objective view—although these are precisely the qualities that spiritual experience cannot provide. It cannot provide them because *by its very nature*, spiritual experience looks not straight ahead but out of the corners of its eyes; it deals with symbol, suggestion, and a *subjective* view—in short, with Mystery.

We are faced with the present epidemic of flat-out ignorance about spiritual life, whether the source is militant atheism or a rigidly intellectualized religious doctrine. Every near-death experiencer knows this who has tried to find someone to talk to, someone who genuinely understands what is going on with NDEs.

Experiencers have told many sad stories of going to a professional for help in understanding their NDE, only to find themselves caught up in the medical model, pathologized by a diagnostic label and the NDE dismissed as meaningless. (R.D. Laing (1979), the sometimes radical Scottish psychiatrist, has called this "the blind leading the half-blind.") People have also told of being dismissed by their rabbi or pastor as well, for in a secular society much awareness of deep spiritual process is lost or distorted, even within religious institutions themselves. Rigid doctrine produces a still different type of misunderstanding. The problem is, of course, that not every religious professional or every religious congregation is equal to the task. Many are, in fact, unprepared to deal with in-breaking spiritual experience that does not follow the rules or the dogma.

It is not unusual to find that the religious implications of NDEs are highlighted by what in the experience is *un*expected, which may be anything—an out-of-body event, encounter with presences, the message, and more. Such a disconnect can be traumatic, whether it conflicts with the person's religious teachings or lacks any resemblance to them. The challenge is shared by clergy and experiencers alike, and for the clergy it may threaten an entire career. For what seems to be the only published discussion of the "deafening silence" surrounding clergy and NDEs, see Mark Fox, *Religion, Spirituality, and the Near-Death Experience* (2002).

A great many experiencers have observed, often with dismay at their religious institution, that the message of their NDE was far more open, more universalizing and inclusive than what their tradition teaches. Which is true, this overwhelming, "realer than real" experience or the dogma? When this is the case, the weight of truth often falls to the felt experience rather than to the tradition, leading to a sometimes lengthy period of intense doubt, spiritual struggle, guilt and fear, perhaps a falling-away from association with the former faith. The more doctrinally rigid the background, the more difficult this period will be, especially for those who must somehow come to terms with the notion that NDEs are satanic deception, tempting people away from orthodox belief. Experiencers who move from intensely dogmatic religion to a more open belief community commonly mention the universalizing message as their reason for change; but the move, while freeing, is difficult.

For most religious institutions, individual spiritual experience has historically been difficult to deal with; private revelation rarely accords perfectly with established teachings, and a choir of soloists, so to speak, destroys congregational harmony. Further, today's traditionally trained clergy are likely to have few resources for dealing pastorally with the issues presented by near-death or similar experience and the kind of passion it is likely to inspire. They may believe the experiencer is making up a good tale to get attention; or they may disapprove of the whole idea of individual spiritual revelation; they may simply not know how to talk about such a direct in-breaking of spirit; it is almost certain that they have no alternative ideas to doctrinal consistency. Further, like most other professionals, very few clergy will know how to recognize or handle a full-blown spiritual emergency; many have never heard of such a thing.

During the 1980s, a 230-year-old Congregational parish in New England (the liberal United Church of Christ) was deeply involved with efforts to feed the hungry, house the homeless, reject oppression. True to the passion of their denomination, members worked for love of God, justice in the world, and compassion in their parish; mysticism has never been a strong suit for this denomination, whose forerunners include the pragmatic Pilgrims themselves. Yet as described by author Gary Dorsey (1995, 99), their pastors were deeply perplexed by a rise in reports of mystical occurrences in the congregation.

> "Parishioners claimed to be seeing visions. They yammered at ghosts, experienced private conversions, and discovered illumination through dreams. Increasingly, as [the ministers] went on their rounds, they heard astonishing tales and drew a blank. What do you say when a woman insists she has seen her deceased husband lumbering silently around the living room at night? ('Don't worry,' Van [the senior pastor] told her, 'Rudolph never did have much to say!') Or someone claims he died and came back to life? Sometimes Van wanted to laugh out loud. But these were not the visions of lunatics. These were earnest, sophisticated, college-educated adults with graduate degrees and grown children; older, traditional, long-rooted grandparents with pensions and ever-present travel plans; single and divorced professional men and women with impossible schedules. He heard from people of all kinds. Sometimes, he thought, it seemed as if they were all emerging from three hundred years of solitude, but he still did not know what it meant or exactly how to respond."

The parishioners of that church were unusually fortunate, because their church added to the staff a part-time spiritual director—a person with experience and special training which few seminaries have offered until very recently.

Even when clergy and congregations at the local level are inadequate to the needs of experiencers, however, the major traditions in their broad structures of narrative, symbol, liturgy, and process still represent finely balanced networks of commentary on spiritual realities and techniques for living safely with them. The resources are there to be reclaimed. Stanislav Grof and Christina Grof (1979, 7) put it this way: "Various spiritual disciplines and mystical traditions...represent rich repositories of invaluable knowledge with regard to these deeper domains of the mind. It has been known for centuries that many dramatic and difficult episodes can occur during spiritual practice and that the road to enlightenment can be rough and stormy."

Psychiatrist Gerald G. May (1982, 110) has the last word here: "As arid as theology may seem in our modern experience-oriented world, it remains one of the best human protections against spiritual distortions. It is somewhat ironic that as our culture probes into the realms of spiritual experience as a reaction against too much dry theology, we are ever more in need of that theology to keep our explorations sane."

Taking those insights seriously, it is all the more disturbing that there has been so little public commentary, other than fundamentalist warnings about deception, about how to interpret near-death experience from a Christian, Jewish, or Islamic worldview. In the absence of leadership from their tradition, inquirers wanting to know about NDEs from a faith perspective have been pretty much on their own.

Into this theological absence came the New Age movement, which greeted NDEs with more open enthusiasm than has been evidenced by the mainstream religions. For many searching experiencers from a religious background, the metaphysical community and their bookstores, workshops, monthly meetings, and publications have become *the* source of information and opinion.

Adaptation and reinterpretation

The American quest
A recurring and intoxicating impulse throughout American history has been its perpetual ferment of religious belief and spiritual practice. Something in the water, the air, the sheer size of the continent

seems to have suggested filling all that open space with new thinking, new visions, new religions and belief systems, incorporating ancient doctrine and the latest science along with private visions and, yes, occasional crackpot theorizing. The nation has popped with Transcendentalism, Shakerism, Spiritualism, Christian Science, Theosophy, Oneida Community, Hutterites, Pentecostalism, Mormonism, Seventh-day Adventism, Jehovah's Witnesses, Eckankar, Scientology, and more. More recent additions include Neo-Calvinism, the Emerging and movement, and a flourish of atheism. According to the Watchman's Fellowship's index of cults and religions, more than 1,200 unique religions and belief systems were recognized in the United States in 2001 (Watchman). Alongside them, of course, has come the deepening materialism of popular thought.

In a Zurich lecture in 1931, Carl Jung, the great psychiatrist and theorist, presented a blazingly perceptive lecture on "The Spiritual Problem of Modern Man." (Jung, 1933) After almost four centuries of deepening materialism and the dimming or outright loss of the West's major religious and philosophical symbols, he said, the energies of the psyche had begun saying, "enough"; they would begin calling back their own. In his lecture, he looked to a coming tide of interest in Eastern religions, theosophy, the esoteric, parapsychology, and a re-envisioning of the roles of matter, the feminine, the psyche, and the divine.

He spoke fifty years before the gender-neutralizing of congregational hymns and school textbooks, forty before Greenpeace and Gaia; yet Jung recognized a stirring in the depths of the collective unconscious. Unfortunately, it was Wotan and the warrior gods and heroes of Norse mythology that would rise first and overtake Germany and the world under Hitler's Third Reich. A more benign mythos would have to wait.

The latest New Age
What Jung forecast was delayed but not squashed. Far from it: From the 1960s through the 1980s, the New Age movement marked the visible onset of an emerging cultural consciousness that we are, in

fact and like it or not, living in a time of profound, inescapable cultural transformation.

It was generational volcano, a sociopolitical, sociospiritual convulsion (which many of its elders thought sociopathic) loudly and vigorously protesting an unpopular war and creating political mayhem and a moral shake-up. It defied authority of all kinds, spat in the face of parental conformity, and in general played havoc with social expectations. It was a political, psychological, and spiritual Perfect Storm, a wave of hunger for a sense of connection with mystery and meaning, a fever to remake the world that split the nation's loyalties and woke the spirits of the Neo-Platonists from their long sleep. To the religious conservative, the radical changes—perceived as a stunning "decline of values"—would set the stage for the strong backlash that is marking the beginning of the 21st century.

Despite conservative alarm, the spiritual aspect of the New Age movement manifested in an explosion of interest—or at least an explosion of snippets of interest—in Jesus, First Nation North American beliefs, Hinduism, Buddhism, Sufism, Kabbalah, Gnosticism, spirit guides, panentheism, theosophy, Wicca, neopaganism, the Goddess, shamanism, sacred sites, human divinization, evolutionary human divinization, some spiritualism and metaphysics, not to mention vibrational energies, crystals, aromatherapy, drumming, massage, communicating with whales, and a lot of tie-dying. It overflowed with what P.M.H. Atwater (private communication) has described as "states of consciousness, psychic phenomena, open sexual and partnering relationships, mind-altering substances, and the shallow embrace of anything that even seems based on the freedom to flow with whatever feels right"—and with the tsunami of books and workshops on what one might call 'generic spirituality.' Over much of the same period came all "the books with 'light' in their title," the near-death experience literature.

Along with Eastern religious and philosophic traditions, which seemed refreshingly exotic to the often-lapsed Christians and Jews of the New Age community (very little has been heard from Islam), much of what burst into view came from the ancient Hermetic tradition that has run like an underground river through Western thought for more than two thousand years.

Nicholas Goodrick-Clarke (1985, 17), Director of the Centre for the Study of Esotericism at Britain's University of Exeter, describes the tradition as "having its basis in a religious way of thinking, the roots of which stretch back into antiquity and which may be described as the Western esoteric tradition. Its principal ingredients have been identified as Gnosticism, the Hermetic treatises on alchemy and magic, Neo-Platonism, and the Kabbalah, all originating in the eastern Mediterranean area during the first few centuries AD." (The magi, astrologers who carried gifts to the infant Jesus, came from the esoteric tradition within Zoroastrianism.)

Like many a modern spiritual adventurer, the Apostle Paul himself (1 Corinthians 12) rejoiced in the effects that may come to those who have been transformed in spirit: wisdom, knowledge, the ability to heal, work miracles, discern spirits, speak in diverse tongues, interpret the speaking in tongues, prophesy. Within the shelter and structure of a religious tradition, these will be observed and tested as genuine or illusory. By contrast, in both the newly Christianizing groups to which Paul wrote and the New Age movement, religious naïveté and high enthusiasm could provide few such safeguards or tests of discernment.

Never mind the fine points for the moment. The New Age movement was fertile. In politics, ethics, and spirituality, it contributed positive-thinking, experience-fostering, optimistic views that looked for affirmation rather than condemnatory judgment and that encouraged exploration rather than mere observance of authoritarian laws and commands. Further, in ways that the Abrahamic traditions could not or did not wish to, theosophy and its cousin philosophies embraced a non-exclusivist point of view which complemented the newfound interest in Eastern tradition—an attractive idea for young people singing, "We are the world."

Third, whether in Theosophy itself, or New Thought, Unity, or Science of Mind, or the Neoplatonic and Hermetic tradition that had such influence on medieval Christianity and Judaism, here was a loving God with little resemblance to the wrathful Jehovah of proof-text tradition. This ancient view of God was of an all-embracing One, the All, the ancient, creating Source. And so came both the Jesus Movement and resonance with the Force of the iconic *Star Wars*—and that in no disrespectful sense whatsoever.

And fourth, in the belief systems that were converging in the new broth, there was—not pantheism, "nature worship"—but pan*en*theism, the conviction that God permeates all of creation, that God is in all and all are in God—which means that in some measure each individual person is directly connected not only to every other individual person and the universe itself but is connected to that One, that All...and is in some measure divine. (This is clearly problematic when that "in some measure" becomes confused with the ego.)

David Spangler (1993, 101-102) summarizes the desire:

> The spirituality [that is being sought] lies not in discerning a particular path to the divine but in asking the question, What is the nature of an ecological God contrasted to a cathedral God? That is, what kind of god, goddess, or sacredness can encompass and embrace a Christian, a Buddhist, a scientist, a psychologist, a Jew, a Muslim, a neopagan, a mystic, a human being, a tree, a river, a mountain, a planet? What kind of God lives in the connections between things and in the wholeness of life rather than at the end of a particular religious path? ...This may seem 'new' to many folk, but in fact this aspect is also present in the best of our historical spiritual paths, particularly in the mystical traditions of our great religions.

NDErs who could connect to that mystical tradition tended to remain in their home faith. Others moved on. For experiencers struggling to reconcile an old belief structure with a new one that has been thrust upon them, the conflict can seem world-shaking. It may be helpful to know that their struggle is part of a long history.

Eugene Taylor (1999, 12), author of *Shadow Culture: Psychology and Spirituality in America* has neatly and reassuringly captured the distinction between mainstream and alternative (shadow) cultures:

> [I]n the larger view, while the Judeo-Christian, Greco-Roman, Western European, and Anglo-American definition of reality continues to dominate Western civilization, throughout its history the West has…also fostered a shadow culture that is distinctly visionary in character. Beyond the religious law of the Jewish Pharisees, the mystical Essenes flourished. Beside Aristotle's logic was Plato's analogy of the cave. Alongside early Christianity were Gnosticism and Neoplatonism. Behind the Talmud was the Kabbalah. As a counterpoint to the religion of the Mullahs was Sufism. In the shadow of Catholicism and the Protestant Reformation were the Rosicrucians and the Freemasons. Next to astronomy was astrology; alongside chemistry was alchemy; and beside mathematics was numerology …As opposed to the dominant culture, which has been outward, rational, reductionistic, dominated by the senses, and driven by the letter of the law, this alternative reality tradition has been inner, contemplative, ascetic, and mystical, believing itself to be the true aristocracy of the spirit from which the letter of the law was derived.

The signal mark of the New Age period, as has often been remarked, may be the elevation of self-discovery as the ultimate pursuit. In part this coincided nicely with the all-American myth of individualism, mentioned earlier, the sense of the entitled self now elevated to divinity. The role of psychology has also played a part, given its influence in the culture generally, especially with the development of the Human Potential movement and its encouragement of dawning possibilities. These are precisely the characteristics toward which evangelical Christianity turns its most hostile attacks, as they perceive correctly that they are the root of so much change and movement away from traditional social and denominational religious structure.

However much it appears that tradition of all sorts is losing its footing, Taylor further observes (10) that the counterculture movement just described has been "a profoundly Caucasian phenomenon. Asian cultures are already steeped in alternative views of transcendent reality; Latinos hold a deep native spirituality behind the symbols of traditional Christianity; African Americans have an ethnic religious tradition that has remained intact and have created uniquely American churches; Native Americans already have an integrated view of the physical and spiritual world. They are hardly surprised when white authors on the New York *Times* best-seller list proclaim that there is, in fact, a spiritual world!"

PART III
Dancing Past The Dark

12
Narrowing the Focus

All this background! We know some facts, we know some history; but we still don't know how to talk about harrowing experiences as anything other than hell or abandonment. My intent in this section is to shift focus for a while, to move from a strictly death-focused understanding of NDEs to consider their importance in the here-and-now.

The focus problem
Two issues have tended to keep blurring the lens through which we look at near-death experiences: bliss and death.

Attention to near-death experience has focused overwhelmingly on bliss—on ecstatic feelings, beautiful scenes, loving encounters, rapturous spirituality. When people talk about NDEs they generally focus on three aspects of bliss:

- the blissful NDE's association with death, in which every story has a happy ending and death itself essentially disappears;
- the blissful conviction that experiencers return to life as spiritually evolved beings who embrace the world with unconditional

love, lose interest in material gain, and want only to learn and serve others;
- the blissful reports that experiencers return from an NDE with sudden gifts for healing, psychic talents, electrical sensitivity that can control street lamps, or other effects that include a rumor (untested) of increased IQ, but which prove they are special.

In this exclusively pleasant focus, which P.M.H. Atwater (1994) was the first to call "the myth of the NDE," every NDE is radiant and every story has a happy ending. These have been the headline-getters, the topics of talk show fascination. Yet although this desire for the good news is fully, wrenchingly understandable, it distorts the whole picture.

This brings us to several dilemmas. For one thing, expectations are inflated because very few talk show hosts have asked if those changes aren't difficult to manage, and few have remarked on the depression, confusion and social alienation that commonly follow even the happiest NDE.

More broadly, if one makes the assumption of the "myth of the NDE"—that true near-death experience equates to true death, that all death is happy death, and that all effects are blissful—then, despite the shared pattern and elements, either a distressing experience cannot be an NDE, or the reported news of near-death experience has been skewed and partial, and only *some* people have a happy ending.

This is not what anyone wants to hear. Conversation stops.

Furthermore, the term "near-death experience" was coined by Raymond Moody because the accounts he collected for his epochal book came from people who had been very close to physical death, resuscitated from clinical death, or had actually died after telling their experience to someone (1975, 16). In addition to the "bliss dilemma," then, we must deal with the "death issue" that NDEs are often viewed only as doorways to an afterlife.

This emphasis means confronting the inevitable conceptions of heaven and hell—which can be construed either as a theological response or as a pair of ingrown cultural suppositions—but which in any case muddy the waters and lead to the previously-discussed judgments about characterological defects in some experiencers, not to mention ego-inflation in others, plus all the anxieties about hell that have marked the past two thousand years. And because of these distractions, there is still no close examination of pleasant near-death experience as anything but a gateway to heaven, no attention whatever to the distressing experiences, and no help for those who are left alone to deal with them.

At this point, the field is too cluttered for clear thinking.

These distractions have had the effect of leading even people within the field of near-death studies away from exploring the *experience itself*. The NDE has been interminably *described* but rarely *examined*. The result is a kind of flatness, a literalness, an assumption that the experience consists solely of heavenly "places to go and people to see," as if their primary significance were their landscapes and encounters and possibly their evolutionary potential.

What my friend said

I had been bothered by this for a long time, so I asked a gifted spiritual and psychic friend—also a near-death experiencer—"How can we get people to think about distressing NDEs when all they want to hear are the radiant stories about the other side?"

Her response snapped back: "An NDE isn't *about* the other side! It's about *here*! It's about going deep and mining inside ourselves until we understand."

I remembered a question posed by philosopher Mishka Jambor (1997, 164): "What kinds of beings are we, that we can feel in such a profound way that the *feeling alone makes for heaven and hell?*"

And that led me to consider, what more is there to an NDE than the literal surface? What may it mean, not about death or dying or an afterlife, but about now? I found myself deeply wondering about the idea that "we can feel in such a profound way that *the feeling alone makes for heaven and hell.*"

What is there about these experiences that they should *by design* remain so durable and so vivid in a person's life? There is evidence in the consciousness literature that memory and emotional intensity are bound together, and that consciousness is grounded in emotion rather than in higher-level processes like language. This being the case, it becomes clear that the emotional intensity of the NDE ensures that it will be stabilized in memory throughout a person's entire life. Why? Like those blessings in Deuteronomy, whatever these gifts may indicate ultimately, they are to be kept and lived out first in *this* world.

What is the experience about, what purpose does it serve, that it must be saved in the memory and life of an experiencer? If these experiences are important here, now, while we can work with them in life…what then?

In that spirit, this next section sets to one side the usual questions about death-related phenomena. It will look only at the near-death experience itself, which is to say its themes and images, and the emotions they arouse in people inside the experience. In the words of Jungian scholar and philosopher Michael Grosso (1983, 5), "Instead of trying to figure out whether it is an illusion or a defense mechanism or a phantasm conjured by some brain mechanism, let us enter into the mythic near-death journey and see where it leads us."

Unpacking the experience

The shock

Psychotherapist and author Alex Lukeman (1998), himself a near-death experiencer who has made a specialty of helping clients deal with nightmares, has said of events like NDEs that they are "…the ego's encounter with the underlying unconscious and transcendent dynamics of the [Holy], and the accompanying destruction of traditional and habitual patterns of perception and understanding, including religious belief structures and socially accepted concepts of the nature of human existence and behavior."

Reread that. He is talking about *the destruction of all one's understandings about reality.* The shock of that destruction is central to near-death and similar experiences. Here it is described by Jungian psychotherapist John Ryan Haule (1999, 63) as a common response to out-of-body experience:

> We will never understand the nature of out-of-body journeys until we grasp the emotional power of that shock. To see that body is to know that it is not me. Such knowledge disrupts everything I have known about myself from earliest childhood until now. We all take it for granted that we are the person we remember and perceive ourselves to be…[yet] to stand outside my body and know my vision is real, is to be exposed to the unthinkable. The world cannot be as I have constructed it; it is unimaginably different. It constitutes the death of everything I have come to know and depend upon. I am not who I thought I was and the world is not as I assembled it. I have entered a realm that is Wholly Other, and I have not the faintest idea what it is or how to negotiate it. I have lost all certainties. Nothing is dependable. Anything can happen. I am a powerless mote blown willy-nilly in an endless ether…I do not know how to be a soul.

It is as if we suddenly see a rip in the fabric of the universe. Haule (64) describes an event from a fishing trip to a favorite, idyllic lake in New England. For days of warm weather and blue sky he and his son had fished the clear waters of the much-loved lake, watching the fish deep down, seeing the familiar play of light and shadow in the reeds and grasses underwater. Late in the week, Haule hooked a large bass that began a lengthy fight and eventually disappeared into a patch of seaweed with the line taut behind him. Nothing budged, and Haule became angry, thinking he had misunderstood what he had on his line; perhaps he had hooked an underwater rock or was tangled in the reeds. He pulled harder. And suddenly, out of unsuspected depths beneath the grasses, the enraged bass exploded from a hidden underworld, rocketing toward the boat like a demonic creature, shattering Haule's sense of the lake's proportions and tranquility and revealing to him a wild, deeper underwater realm of "demons and cannibalism." Here was a previously secret world that existed beneath the tranquil floor of the lake he thought he knew so well. Reality had torn before his eyes, and the encounter shook him to the core.

An NDE or abruptly dislocating psychic experience shatters our sense of physical reality and with it our sense of security. The same is true of many UFO abduction experiences and shamanic initiations, as described in Chapter 6. Whether the events are literally, physically, materially real or not is irrelevant; they are real *experiences*, profoundly real in the *imaginal* sense, a sudden, shocking revelation of truths previously unrecognized about the world we thought we knew. They share the characteristics described by Joseph Campbell (1986, 55) of things understood "as *meta*physically grounded in a dreamlike mythological realm beyond space and time, which, since it is physically invisible, can be known only to the mind." (His emphasis.)

We should memorize it: *Things which, since they are physically invisible, can be known only to the mind.*

Haule, the fisherman at the lake, says of them (187):

> As long as we can avoid the dreadful enchanted world beneath our everyday lake, we surely will. For the evidence is unmistakable. When they come oozing or rushing through the gaps, the first representatives of the greater cosmos appear abusive, humiliating, even satanic. Our terror schematizes them as Archons, "small grays," and demons. As long as the water sprite is nothing more than a smallmouth bass, everything is in its place…But the more we accept the possibility that that silvery being bashing through the rug of seaweed down below us might very well be *more* than a fish, anything can happen. The world is suddenly devoid of dependable rules. We know not where we stand.

One is left with an absolute certainty: *"There's more!"* This is sometimes worded, *"Something is going on!"* Whatever the precipitant, whatever the explanatory theory, and whether or not the NDE is about survival after death, this destruction of one's previous understandings about reality is vitally, profoundly meaningful.

The remembered experience remains embedded, a vivid aspect of everyday functioning in *this life,* in the here-and-now, and must be dealt with in those terms. The pragmatic question is whether it will be dealt with well or badly, and that depends largely on the information and resources available. Information *is* available, though not without effort, as it must be chiseled out of other disciplines like trilobites out of rock. It is a task of mythological proportions. We begin with a close look at the elements within a disturbing NDE.

The elements

The basic components of near-death experiences have been corroborated by virtually every researcher since Moody—by Ring, Sabom, Greyson, Gallup, and others. With only percentages changing from study to study, these are the interchangeable elements of that pattern that makes them recognizable as near-death experiences: out-of-body event, movement through darkness, intense emotional response, ineffability, noetic quality, presence or absence of light, encounters with entities, transiency, and so on.

As mentioned in Chapter 5, it was Margot Grey in her 1985 British study who first observed that frightening NDEs include the same basic elements as blissful experiences but with differing details and emotions. As Ring and others detailed blissful experiences, she noted the distinctive features of disturbing ones (58):

> …a feeling of extreme fear or panic…emotional and mental anguish, extending to states of the utmost desperation… a great sense of desolation. … the brink of a pit…the edge of an abyss…being tricked into death and [needing] to keep their wits about them to prevent this from happening.

> The hell-like experience ... includes all [those] elements ... often a definite sense of being dragged down by some evil force... visions of wrathful or demonic creatures ...[or] unseen beings or figures which are often faceless or hooded.... intensely cold or unbearably hot. ...sounds that resemble the wailing of 'souls' in torment, ...a fearsome noise

In getting beneath the surface of these NDEs, it is not enough to look at their external features. What is it, specifically, that makes them so bone-deeply upsetting? Here is where the examination of these NDEs becomes more than simple description.

Sounds

As mentioned in Chapter 2 on hellish experiences, distressing NDEs often feature uncanny or jarring sounds (wails, moans, buzzing, shrieking): "The noise was fearsome, with snarling and crashing like maddened wild animals, gnashing their teeth." (Gray, 70)

"Sudden sound," says a Franklin Institute (2004) article titled "Noise and Stress," "is an urgent wake-up call that alerts and activates the stress response — a biological alarm that affects the brain in powerful ways. Because loud noise often heralds bad news, animals and humans have evolved a rapid response to audio stressors."

From the outset, then, a disturbing NDE may involve the kind of sound guaranteed biologically to suggest crisis, even in an unconscious state.

Odors

Just as sound can generate instant emotional response, so does the sense of smell. David B. Givens (undated), of the Center for Nonverbal Studies, says, "The olfactory sense evolved as an 'early warning' system to detect food, mates, and dangers (e.g., predators) from a distance. ... aroma cues are taken very seriously by the brain. ... Few changes have been made in aroma receptors since the time of the jawless fishes (circa. 500 million years ago), making smell a conservative, compelling, and trusted sense...More than any other sense, smell evokes strong emotional tendencies to approach or avoid."

As might be expected, blissful NDEs are often said to smell like flowers, whereas less pleasant NDEs include distasteful, sometimes putrid odors. Howard Storm mentions smelling like rotting chicken.

Movement

Most NDEs include a definite sense of movement, suggesting that like the apocalyptic voyages of medieval times, these are journeys; one is "going somewhere." When that sensed movement is downward, it may trigger the instinctual fear of falling, like the sudden jerk of a baby who feels unsure of his stability.

Interestingly enough, the very word *emotion* derives from *e- (out) + movere (to move)*, so, "to move out," implies moving as out of one state into another, such as from calm into agitation or disturbance. Brent Dean Robbins (1999) of Duquesne University has observed that "[E]motions are characterized by various potential movements away or toward an actual or implicit other or entity." In other words, one's instinctive response to an emotional situation is either to extend toward it or contract from it. It is no surprise, then, that mentions of "backpedaling" appear in accounts of distressing, not blissful, NDEs.

The images

What are the constituent images within distressing near-death experiences, and are they unique to NDEs or can they be found elsewhere? What might they mean—or are they simply arbitrary images without meaning—as the now-disappeared blog of a schizophrenic once put it, "suffering before the incomprehensible"?

The first generation of professional near-death studies dealt largely (and necessarily) with descriptive reports of near-death experiences. As a result, with little comparative work going on, there has been in much of the literature a sense of uniqueness in near-death experiences, as though they were a floating island to themselves with few or no moorings in the broader bed of other scholarship or social witness. With few exceptions, it is as if near-death experiences were a Columbus-like discovery of a new world beyond anything else in human awareness. There has been little "archaeology" of the images reported in NDEs. (Among the exceptions I think of the work of sociologist Allan Kellehear (1996), with philosopher Michael Grosso (1986) and religious scholar Carol Zaleski (1987).)

Theoretical images
What I am calling *theoretical* images are those from the imaginations of people who, in ordinary waking states of consciousness, ancient, medieval and modern, were *thinking* about what hell (or heaven) might be like rather than *experiencing* it. These are the images of conscious imagination that populate literature and film, and all types of art and sacred iconography, what a scholar of Kabbalah (Green, 2004, 3) calls "sacred fantasies." Because they are public, they are what we expect to see in hell.

Hindu iconography provides a genuine festival of hellish images going back some thousands of years — imaginatively detailed and horrible demons, imps, monsters, wraiths, lakes of fire, pits, devouring animals, often engaged in torments, viciousness, malevolence, violence.

Such images are by no means only death-related. The 1997 conference of the Association for Asian Studies included two presentations pertinent here. From the University of Alabama, historian Haruko Wakabayashi (1997) pointed out that images of demons and hells are found in great abundance in medieval Japan, not only as a product of people's imaginations, but as reflections of their views of the real world. For instance, a description of hell and the kinds of people who fall into it may be read as a social critique. Demons in *Noh* dramas may be interpreted as an expression of madness which lies hidden in human nature. Demons in literature and scroll paintings, portrayed in Chinese-style costumes, reveal the perceptions of "other" and the growth of nationalism in medieval Japan. The notion of "others" as demons created the demonic image of the enemy during World War II (on both sides).

Professor Soho K. Machida (1997) of Hiroshima University observed that in the oldest surviving Japanese dramatic form, the highly stylized *Noh* plays, one mask, which appears in only three *Noh* plays, depicts the intense anger, shame, or jealousy of its wearer. It is the most horrific, demonic face, complete with horns and fangs; yet its name, the *han'nya* mask, derives from the Sanskrit word meaning wisdom, which is required to achieve Buddhahood. Why would such a positive term as "wisdom" be applied to the most demonic of Noh masks? Machida suggests that the nature of salvation in those *Noh* plays reveals that *sanity and insanity, salvation and despair* are inextricably intertwined and can be expressed in the same facial expression. Here is a corollary to the idea of the wisdom and power within the dark emotions.

The incorporation of opposites, as in the *han'nya* mask, has been echoed in Western thought by the currently unfashionable concept of the *daimonic* as an operating force.

In *Anger, Madness, and the Daimonic: The Psychological Genesis of Violence, Evil, and Creativity* psychotherapist Stephen A. Diamond (1999) devotes an entire chapter to a discussion of the *daimones* (pronounced *day*-muns). As originally conceived, *daimones* were considered the source of emotions both good and bad, functioning as mediators between the physical world and spirit, between humans and gods. They could be called daemons or angels or simply "spirits." Daimons were understood to be potentially both good and evil; but eventually the good gods *and their destructive qualities* were divided from the evil demons *and their potential for good*, shifting constructive qualities to the gods and destructive qualities onto the demons. It was one of the prices of monotheism, that loss of complexity. And so began the gradual degradation of the daimon into our modern misunderstanding of the *demon* as exclusively evil, and the ascendancy of the Judeo-Christian conception of the *devil* as evil incarnate.

Existentialist psychologist Rollo May (1969, 123) described the *daimonic* as "any natural function which has the power to take over the whole person." This points to the existence of demons as a mysterious force that feels like an external, independent influence in a person's life. They are, in the medieval sense, forces (including angels) at the threshold between this world and the macrocosm. (It was this sense of objectifying that finally enabled me to give up smoking, when I began to think of my addiction as an entity, a demon, and refused to continue giving it power over me.)

That role of demons is similar to that attributed to monsters: The word comes from the Latin *monstrum*, "that which is shown forth or revealed" (as in the English word *demonstrate*. Says James Greer (2001, 1), "In the original sense of the word, a monster is a revelation, something shown forth…The myth, the terror, and the strangeness all have their roots in the nature of the realm of…revelations, where the hidden and the unknown show furtive glimpses of themselves. If we pay attention to them, monsters reveal the reality of the impossible, or of those things we label impossible; they point out that *the world we think we live in, and the world we actually inhabit, may not be the same place at all.*" (Emphasis added.)

The almost universal dragon character appears in Chinese script around 1,600 BC, roughly the time of the Hebrew patriarchs. Chinese dragons are potent and benevolent creatures. Unlike their European counterparts, which are aggressive and suggest chaos and destruction, Chinese dragons bring good luck. They do not devour maidens.

Shinzen Young (2005), an American Buddhist teacher of mindfulness meditation, has noted that terrifying images—insectoid, grotesquely otherworldly, demonic—may appear in advanced meditation. He teaches that they are:

> best interpreted as part of a natural process of release from the deep archetypal levels of the mind. Such upwelling visionary material is a natural function of human consciousness and should not be cause for the slightest concern: You are not going crazy. You are not going to get weird. You are not going to be possessed by devils, assailed by Satanists, or devoured by

monsters. You are not going to be sucked into another world. However, if you have a history of prior mental illness, you should discuss these phenomena both with your meditation teacher and a therapist.

From a naturalistic perspective, such images would be related to the claim of neuroscientist Rick Strassman (2000) that the psychedelic substance abbreviated DMT may account for this type of event. Almost half of Strassman's research subjects who had taken DMT reported encountering otherworldly beings they described as clowns, elves, robots, insects, E.T.-like humanoids, or indescribable "entities." One of the subjects claimed to have been eaten alive by insectoid creatures (Horgan, 2006). Perhaps unfortunately, Strassman had not heard Shinzen Young's analysis, for the research project was promptly scrapped.

Observing the consistency of frightening images across time and space, from ancient Mesopotamia and traditional Asia through early modern Europe and modern Africa, anthropologist Rodney Needham (1978) concludes, there may be some kind of "psychic constant," some "autonomous image to which the human mind is naturally predisposed." For Needham, the primary factors of human experience present as what he calls "semantic units" manifesting what might be called the psychic unity of humankind. The semantic units are "elementary constituents of culture — independent of the will and nonsystematic, but that can be combined into symbolic complexes, such as the image of the witch or forms of myth." (Think *memes,* think archetypes, think the next chapter.)

Religious historian David Frankfurter (2008), in his much-referenced *Evil Incarnate: Rumors of Demonic Conspiracy and Satanic Abuse in History,* asks, "Are we 'hardwired' to believe in monsters or demonic enemies? There is a depth, a universality and fascinated horror that surrounds them that seems to correspond to what psychoanalysts call 'primary process' thinking. These are ways of thinking about Otherness, of imagining an upside-down world that inverts our own, of encountering local malevolence suddenly in universal scope, and of sensing the collapse of vital boundaries between 'us' and those monstrous 'others.'"

"Throughout history," writes author and editor Connie Zweig (2001, *xvi*), "the shadow [the dark side of human nature] has appeared via the human imagination as a monster, a dragon, a Frankenstein, a white whale, an extraterrestrial, or a man so vile we cannot see ourselves in him; he is as removed from us as a gorgon."

In other words, the images of religio-spiritual experience are seen to have roots in the world. And so, says Shinzen (2005): "Sometimes the content of this material may be pleasant and informative, but more often it is disconcerting, full of weirdness, destruction, sex and violence. (In other words, what the subconscious projects onto the internal screen of the mind is the same stuff the culture projects onto the external screen of TV and cinema.)"

Once in the world, the images become our responsibility. Frankfurter (2008) says of the periodic witch hunts throughout history, whether of accused witches in Belgium and Salem, Massachusetts or of accused child abusers in a North Carolina day care center—in none of which has any shred of reality ever been established—"That is, the real atrocities of history seem to take place *not* in the perverse ceremonies of some evil cult but rather in the course of *purging* such cults from the world. Real evil happens when people speak of evil."

Actual modern NDE images
What I have called the *theoretical* images would more properly have been called "imaginary," meaning that someone in waking consciousness creatively thought them up. In contrast, images that present themselves whole and spontaneously—in dreaming, say, or in an NDE or some other vision—are considered "imaginal," meaning that they occur without deliberate, conscious input from the person; they simply appear.

In looking at depictions of hell, the theoretical, imaginary images (the ones consciously thought up) seem often to be more interesting than the majority of those that actually appear in contemporary distressing NDE accounts. In these imaginal (spontaneous) images, landscapes typically describe something more like Sheol than the medieval Hell; almost always, the individual seems more like a tourist than a participant, seeing but not being part of the scene; the distress of others is often conjectural: "It *seemed* as if they were in torment."

In distressing NDEs, these are the characteristic imaginal images across cultures:

- Darkness, the infinite undifferentiated Void, outer space, emptiness
- Uncanny, bleak landscapes
- Fire, lakes of fire, cold, pits
- Murky swamps, mists, fogs, rivers, bridges and wells, a boat, a barrier
- Sometimes a guide, faceless presences, trapped or wandering people and/or spirits, unrecognized forms, wraiths, occasionally deceased family or friend

How these images might be understood will be discussed at the end of this chapter.

Similar or identical images elsewhere
A similar grouping appears in the work of medievalist Howard Rollin Patch (1970), in *The Other World, According to Descriptions in Medieval Literature.* Patch lists elements that appear in nearly all known accounts of Eastern and Western underworlds or the otherworld, including: a barrier, a river, a boat and boatman, a bridge, gates and guardians, an important tree. The images are instantly recognizable to anyone familiar with Native American, Egyptian and Mesopotamian mythology and the classical Greek and Roman literature. The only one of the images mentioned by Patch that has not appeared in any of the NDE accounts I have seen is the tree,

probably the World Tree of shamanic lore. In short, they are not unique to near-death experiences.

Emotions
The base emotions of a deeply harrowing NDE are those of cataclysm: shock, fear, horror, loss, abandonment, dread, terror, incredulity, sometimes despair, sometimes panic or guilt. Here is St. Teresa: "I felt a fire within my soul the nature of which I am utterly incapable of describing…The fact is that I cannot find words to describe that interior fire and that despair which is greater than the most grievous tortures and pains.…" (Teresa)

Here is psychotherapist Alex Lukeman (1998) again, describing such experiences as "the destruction of traditional and habitual patterns of perception and understanding, including religious belief structures and socially accepted concepts of the nature of human existence and behavior."

For Polish philosopher Mishka Jambor (1997, 163-176), it is a matter of asking the right questions—and her questions are breathtaking. "Let us explore then transcendent experiences," she says in "The Mystery of Frightening Transcendent Experience," explicitly considering both frightening and pleasant experiences "transcendent" because they move beyond ordinary waking consciousness toward something experientially more real.

Given their similarity, Jambor wonders, "Where do all of these experiences come from?" She calls the overwhelming emotional forces "deep-feeling," and asks, "What is its origin?" If the pleasant deep-feeling—that of a radiant NDE—originates in "ultimate reality," what of the frightening deep-feeling, which, she says, "deserves the name 'abyss': What is that force, an abyss, into which mundane and transcendent events plunge us?" And with that she arrives at her central question: "What kind of beings are we, that we can feel in such a profound way that the *feeling alone makes for heaven and hell* (for otherwise the experience would only be judged cognitively as unusual and interesting)?" It is a stunning question.

The emotions of fear in that "profound way" cover a range of intensities and types. Jason Bivins (2008, 240) mentions emotions listed by Robert C. Roberts, distinguishing "fear from anxiety (which is less tied to specific objects and possibilities), fright (which involves a more 'dramatic aversive possibility'), dread (which 'sees the aversive object not as present, but as inevitably approaching'), terror ('more or less paralyzing'), panic (specific spontaneous actions resulting from perceptions of aversion), horror (where aversion figures into one's perception in a way that is not tied into the situation's probability, e.g., one's horror at seeing corpses, and being spooked (reacting to 'the strange, the mysterious, the unknown') All of these have been specially mentioned or described in accounts of distressing near-death experiences. Panic also appears in nurses' accounts of the deathbed visions of some patients. (See Chapter 12.)

Whether or not the actual contents of an NDE are fearsome, Grof (1988, 72) notes that "The experience of extraordinary perception can be associated with deep metaphysical fear, since it challenges and undermines the world view that the Western culture typically subscribes to and associates with sanity."

For any experiencer, but especially for those with a troubling NDE, it may be years before Grof's statement can be read as comforting; yet I believe it to be true. As Lukeman says, it is all that collapse of perceptions.

Themes

The themes identified in these images are universal: these are experiences of important journeying, of directly confronting our mortality, of going into unfamiliar areas of discomfort and disruption, of entrances and discovery and profound change. They have great power as references to what is going on in our life, including our spiritual life. While it is true that they serve as reminders of physical death to come, they also carry messages about life in the here and now: about noticing the death of outgrown aspects of the self, about recognizing a time to move out of a previous stage of life, about enduring the dislocation of new ways of thinking and being.

The bottom line about distressing NDEs in general and the hellish ones in particular seems to be that hell, like heaven, is very real—as a product of the imaginal system that produces experience. It is not a place, not a destination, but a built-in range of ideas that are part of us, and that we must deal with. This concept is part of a much larger conversation involving the growing evidence that consciousness is not strictly located in the brain but has a much greater field, perhaps universe-wide. (See, for example, the splendid *Irreducible Mind* by Edward Kelly et al.) That being true, it seems likely that the better prepared we are for these kinds of experience, the happier will be the outcome. Whether approached religiously or from a secular point of view, awareness and preparation may well make all the difference.

13
Symbolic Language

Symbols

If the elements of near-death experiences were as easy to read as signs, it would be possible simply to hand out a list: Here are the pieces; here is their meaning. Inconveniently, that is not the case. Interiority works not through *signs* ("this points to that") but through *symbols* ("this points to a field of feelings and ideas").

John Sanford (1970, 22) says simply, "Conscious minds think conceptually; the unconscious expresses itself in symbol." Lionel Corbett (1996, 45) says, "The simplest way in which the Totality makes itself known to the ego is by means of an image." Edward Edinger (1972, 209) makes the important observation that a symbol is "an image or representation which points to something essentially unknown, a mystery." Discussing powers and principalities as personifications of such ideas as hell, greed, evil, theologian Walter Wink (1986, 172-173) gives this vivid portrait:

> "The new age dawning may not 'believe in' angels and demons the way an earlier period believed in them. But these Powers may be granted a happier fate: to be understood as symbolic of

the 'withinness' of institutions, structures, and systems. People may never again regard them as quasi-material beings flapping around in the sky, but perhaps they will come to see them as the actual spirituality of actual entities in the real world. They are not 'mere' symbols—that too is the language of the old worldview that is passing, for we now know that nothing is more powerful than a living symbol. As symbols they point to something real, something the worldview of materialism never learned to name and therefore never could confront."

Before an NDE or similar experience can be genuinely understood, some probably quite ordinary human individual must be able to translate it. But if the referents are not "quasi-material beings flapping around in the sky," what are they? The task is to look at the images of heaven and hell as carefully as scientists have looked at the atom, and ask, well, if it isn't what we thought, then what *is* it?

What has been largely missing from discussions about near-death experience is the explicit acknowledgment that *because* these experiences are ineffable, they have no precise denotation. Like the Sacred, they have many images but no physicality. It is exactly for this reason that the language of science cannot deal with them.

Listen to experiencers' accounts. The voice is not that of the research report or even journalism, with its characteristic objective voice; rather, these are personal narratives, stories, a universal form (characters, setting, plot) for the carrying of messages. Listen to experiencers analyze their accounts, and you hear the language of poetry: simile ("It was like, it was as if…") and metaphor ("It was…"). Their stories, as linguist Regina Hoffman has noted (1995a, 1995b), are told in layers, because no single descriptive element is big enough. The situation is analogous to that of conceptions of God, because no one denotation can encompass the entirety: Creator, Almighty, Most High, Shepherd, Rock, Father, Mother, Holy Spirit, Source, Ground of Being, King, Living Water, Other. (And for belligerent materialists, no, people do not believe that God is a rock.)

As a rule, we don't quite know what to do with symbol. ("Why can't they just come out and *say* it?") But just as a map cannot be the territory it represents, so NDEs cannot be the territory they represent: they are signposts, arrows; maps written in symbol. They point to a "territory" beyond the capability of language to describe, and beyond the ability of physical vision to image. They point in one great general direction but not down a single roadway. And so, the only route to them is through the same means as any ineffable experience: through suggestion and imaginal language and symbol and archetype.

Again, notice the difference between "imaginal" and "imaginary." What is imaginary does not really exist but is made up, pretend, fantasy. What is imaginal, on the other hand, as the earlier quote from Joseph Campbell (1986, 55) noted, "is *meta*physically grounded in a dreamlike mythological realm beyond space and time, which, since it is physically invisible, can be known only to the mind." Put more simply (Frenier), "There is…a place in our imaginations where things are 'real,' in the sense that they are not being 'imagined' by someone but are images that have some kind of integrity or existence on their own. Thus, the imagination appears to have two aspects: one is intentionally fabricated; the other presents itself to us intact." That latter one is the imaginal realm.

Admittedly, this is the stuff to drive mathematicians mad, for there is no observable single answer. In fact, the difficult truth is that some realities wiggle, as physicists discovered early in the last century. It is one reason 'spirituality' is so often perceived as totally ungrounded. The elements of spiritual experience, though, may be no more elusive than, say, quarks.

We begin by looking for patterns, for images and concepts that appear over and over in human experience. Symbols never have a single, denotative meaning; that is reserved for signs. Symbols work more like fields, so it is necessary to ask, what meanings do they have, where does the field go, what does it suggest? Consider the following examples:

Fire
Almost invariably, people who encounter fire in an NDE are panicked because they associate it only with punishment, with a wrathful God and eternal torment. They completely miss its older, richer associations. Fire signifies the all-enveloping presence of God, divine revelation—the burning bush, the ancient sacrifice, the burning lamp. It is a classic symbol of transformation. Fire both literally and figuratively cleanses, renews, and refines. It is the means by which earth is readied for new growth.

Darkness, weeping, gnashing of teeth
Theologian Hans Kung points out (1984, 140) that darkness and the sounds of weeping and the gnashing of teeth may be, not indications of a quasi-physical hell, but "harsh-sounding metaphors for the menacing possibility that a person may completely miss the meaning of his life."

Predictions of dying or geological cataclysm
As in dreams, a suggestion of death or end times may point powerfully to change—to the end of a life phase or a major change in one's awareness, the death of a particular time. When things in an imaginal state appear to be coming apart physically, that is a good signal that there is disruption in other areas of life.

Creatures
You are in a powerful dream, in which you have come out of deep woods and are crossing a great meadow. Suddenly you realize that you are being stalked by a lion. As you look for cover, the ground shakes and you see a great bull racing toward you. He is almost on top of you, running at your left, the lion on the other side. Now an enormous eagle swoops in. Up ahead stands an angel holding a sword.

Is this a dream about being killed by wild animals? A message about nature? Why would that angel have a sword? Surely this dream (which I have just invented) is about dying a horrible and violent death. And so it could be, unless you know that the lion, bull, and eagle are symbols for the evangelists Mark, Luke, and John, and the angel with a sword represents Matthew. Knowing that, you might, if you are a Christian, wonder if your dream is reminding you that you really want to become a theologian. If you are not a Christian, you may spend a good deal of time wondering how those symbols got into your dream, as I wondered how the Yin/Yang got into my NDE. The point is that the entire tenor and meaning of this dream changes from merely terrifying to personally significant when it moves from the literal interpretation to a metaphoric understanding. Now it makes sense—or can at least be worked with.

Many creatures have long-standing symbolic meaning. A bear has often represented wisdom and power; a horned goat, instantly terrifying as Satan, has an ancient history as a guide. The snake, which a narrow reading of Genesis associated with deception and the origin of sin, has an even older association with sacred mystery, completion, and new life. Any monstrous being may simply indicate that things are not what they seem.

This brief listing is the merest introductory suggestion of how a broader awareness of symbol can lead to reframing a distressing NDE so that it can become a source of growth and maturity rather than a paralyzing blockade.

Archetypes

Why are there such repetitive themes and images throughout human experience? Where do these recurring images, such as the elements of near-death experience, come from? Are they from external powers or are we making them up?

Some concepts seem built into human experience, patterns that are as natural as crystals are to salt. As Richard Tarnas (1991, 423) observed, although Kant saw that human experience "was permeated by a priori structures" it was Jung who "discovered the universal archetypes in all their power and rich complexity." Jung (1968, 57) called the recurring patterns *archetypes*, "mental forms whose presence cannot be explained by anything in the individual's own life and which seem to be aboriginal, innate, and inherited shapes of the human mind."

They are universal patterns in human consciousness that draw from, and in turn help shape The Way Things Are, like information fields within the larger field of the imaginal realm, the collective unconscious. The ancients called them *elemental spirits*. These were the patterns that became the gods and goddesses of ancient time (leading conservative Christians today to reject them as a concept, not recognizing that in the Bible they appear as powers and principalities).

Plato recognized the universals as Ideas that exist beyond the perceptible world. Stanislav Grof has observed (1980, 31), "These mythologies and concepts of…heaven and hell…are an intrinsic part of the human personality that cannot be repressed and denied without serious damage."

Where do they come from? From the deepest levels of the psyche, our mental operating system. Together, archetypes constitute what Jung called the "collective unconscious"; others call it the "imaginal realm." As the wisdom teacher quoted earlier (Frenier) says, alongside our daydreaming and conscious fantasizing, "There is also a place in our imaginations where things are 'real,' in the sense that they are not being 'imagined' by someone but are images that have some kind of integrity or existence on their own."

From the mid-20th century on, the work of psychiatrist and consciousness researcher Stanislav Grof has demonstrated both the reality of archetypes and ways in which they shape and reshape our functioning. With psychedelic therapy, Grof discovered that people in certain levels of altered states of consciousness have experiences that seem to replicate virtually every human archetype, from the tender and blissful to the murderous and grotesque. The *pattern* within those therapeutic experiences, observed over a period of time, can best be understood as replicating the birth-to-death cycle, a reenactment that themes of the birth process play out both individually and collectively on the universal world (Tarnas, 428). When, in a series of sessions, the birth-through-death pattern has been completely worked through, it results in a remarkable integration or wholeness of the individual.

Put this into the framework of a profoundly distressing near-death experience. Tarnas describes it (433):

> [A]n inexplicably incoherent situation of profound traumatic intensity… [becomes] a redemptive reunification of the individuated self with the universal matrix. Thus the child is born and embraced by the mother, the liberated hero ascends from the underworld to return home after his far-flung odyssey. The individual and the universal are reconciled. The suffering, alienation, and death are now comprehended as necessary for birth, for the creation of the self…A situation that was fundamentally unintelligible is now recognized as a necessary element in a larger context of profound intelligibility…The rupture from Being is healed. The world is rediscovered in its primordial enchantment. The autonomous individual self has been forged and is now reunited with the ground of its being.

In the best of worlds, that's how it happens. But what if only part of the pattern happens, one of the traumatic bits? And what if it happens only once, so there's no chance to reach integration? And what if it happens to someone who's never heard about such things and has no inkling how to handle the situation? In other words, what if the traumatic bit is a distressing NDE? As the vast majority of experiencers are unlikely to go through Grof's holotropic therapy, other ways need to be found for reaching resolution. (See chapter 16.)

Christopher Bache (2000, Chapter 4) has put forward the idea that a distressing NDE represents a painful fragment of a potentially transcendent experience that either has insufficient impetus to blast through to the transcendent level or that gets "stuck" in the tunnel so many near-death experiencers describe. (I believe this is what

Ken Ring was trying to suggest [Chapter 6] when he put forward his subway tunnel image, though he equated the situation to "the nature of the minds" of those having a distressing experience.) Actually, the majority of NDEs do not feature a tunnel, but the principle of Bache's idea seems helpful as a counter to the prevailing punitive theories, whether of theological hell or folkloric judgment.

The nature of the struggle was the subject of a conversation I had some years back with biblical and Jungian scholar Wayne Rollins, PhD, now Emeritus Professor of Theology at Assumption College in Massachusetts. He had just read one of my articles on frightening NDEs and said:

> Whether personified with gaping throat and jaws, devouring, or as emptiness—these experiences read like dream material. They are signposts of invitation to true maturity, the promise of integration precipitated by despair: Erikson's 'ego integrity.' Fear is psychological; anxiety is ontological: Kierkegaard's 'dread.' Ecclesiastes and 'all is vanity'—that's a canonical statement of ontological dread. The anxiety is objectless—ontological—from the threat of destruction, of non-being. It is indigenous to the human condition—Henley's 'Invictus'—the anxiety resolved by discovery of his unconquerable soul.

> The crisis [the horrifying or terrifying NDE] precipitates an answer to the problem of dread; it reflects one's unconscious state. For some individuals, this is the first time they have confronted the issue of their own mortality at a deep level. Irrespective of any objective referent, the experiences are intensely meaningful, the promise of integrity precipitated by despair, and the fatalistic despair after the experience crystallizes the recognition so it can be dealt with. The experiences are crying for integration.

> In the classical creeds, the descent to hell—that's not for nothing. It's recognition of the very real existence of evil, of emptiness, of Nothing as a real presence but not the end. It's very Joban, driven

to recognize apparent evil, destruction, chaos. The presence of apparent evil does not mean the absence of God; that will come as a more mature recognition. This is not simple resurrection theology but resurrection symbolized, not literal but real, a deep recognition of the power of Being that overrides Non-Being, with integration as representing true maturity.

As this powerful analysis indicates, it is not only by "letting go" *within* the experience that integration is achieved, that surrender so often mentioned by critics; but integration may come as a long process afterward. Awareness of developmental and cultural issues at this level is surely called for in understanding the impact of the frightening experiences and working through them, whether for ourselves or in the service of others.

These, then, are the raw materials—the elements, images, and emotions—from which we ascribe meaning to a near-death experience or similar awakening. As with any experience, we shuffle and sort these materials—our images and emotions—according to the particular cultural matrix in which we find ourselves, until our experience "makes sense." Doing this really well demands great honesty with ourselves. It is a lot of hard work. Back again to the image of the Olympic athlete—gold medals go only to those who make the effort. The more one knows about symbolic language, the wider the possible understanding of what an experience is about. We will also be learning how to meet the images that may come when we actually die.

My friend said, "An NDE isn't *about* the other side! It's about *here*! We have to go deep and mine ourselves until we understand." Poet and cancer survivor Mark Nepo (2007, unpaged) shows the struggle of doing that in his prose poem, "Upon Seeking Tu Fu as a Guide."

Upon Seeking Tu Fu as a Guide

And so I asked him, how is it God is everywhere and nowhere? He circled me like a self I couldn't reach, "Because humans refuse to live their lives." I was confused. He continued, "You hover rather than enter." I was still confused. He spoke in my ear, "God is only visible within your moment entered like a burning lake." I grew frightened. He laughed, "Even now, you peer at me as if what you see and hear are not a part of you." I grew angry. He ignored me, "You peer at the edge of your life, so frantic to know, so unwilling to believe." Indeed, I was frantic. He was in my face, "And now that you have cancer, you ask to be spared." I grew depressed. He took my shoulders, "For God's sake! Enter your own life! Enter!"

14
Coping

Anyone coming to terms with a strong NDE will resonate with the statement of William James (1958, 352), "Mystical states, when well developed, usually are, and have the right to be, absolutely authoritative over the individuals to whom they come." Authoritative, indeed. What that means is, they take over.

Relative to that "authoritative" effect, I repeat what psychotherapist and near-death experiencer Alex Lukeman (1998) has said of experiences like NDEs: that they are "the ego's encounter with the underlying unconscious and transcendent dynamics of the [Holy], and the accompanying destruction of traditional and habitual patterns of perception and understanding, including religious belief structures and socially accepted concepts of the nature of human existence and behavior."

No small challenge! In this chapter we will consider what that means, specifically to life after an NDE. Consider the impact of discovering that you have awakened to find all your "patterns of perception and understanding" destroyed, including your "religious belief structures." Go back into the world and discover that you have lost all "socially accepted concepts of the nature of human existence and behavior." Now what?

Six challenges

What are the problems after an NDE, whether blissful or horrifying? In the spring of 2006, a group of twenty-five NDErs gathered for a weekend retreat to discuss the challenges they were facing after their near-death experiences. The most recent of their NDEs was two years previously; the most distant, fifty-five years past; yet all remained a powerful force in the life of each experiencer. Over the course of three days, the participants identified an astonishing 115 challenges, later grouped into six major categories. Their experiences had been peaceful, some blissful; yet, they and people after a disturbing NDE share similar challenges. Here is their summary, as reported in the *Journal of Near-Death Studies* (Stout, 2006).

1. Processing a radical shift in reality

The group described this as "a permanent and complete paradigm shift in reality and view of themselves, a sudden correction in their accustomed path and perspective on life…a radically new concept of life, death, the afterlife, body, mind, and spirit." The average time required to adjust to life after the NDE was 12.7 years.

2. Accepting the return

One challenge not shared by people with a painful NDE is accepting the return. All of the retreat participants had pleasurable NDEs and felt intense longings to go back to the experience, which they consider "home." Several had considered suicide as a way to get there.

Following a disturbing NDE there is an inverse problem. The challenge for these people is to find a way to accept the experience without giving in to its destructive potential and to get past their fear of death.

3. Sharing the experience

Participants reported four types of difficulties in talking to others about the NDE: finding words in which to express the indescribable; choosing appropriate confidants; coping with negative reactions; and the tendency of confidants to be more interested in the details of the NDE than in the needs of the experiencer.

Ineffability is hard for anyone to live with—and can be exasperatingly hard on family, friends, and co-workers as the experiencer talks almost incessantly in the frustration of trying to describe the indescribable. Dorothee Soelle (1975, 57) has described the difficulty precisely: "Nothing incites speakers to talk as much as ineffability."

As for finding a confidant after a distressing NDE…to whom could you talk, if it were your own experience? Whose reactions would you trust?

4. Integrating new spiritual values with earthly expectations

The "values, message, and meaning of the experience were often completely inconsistent with the participant's life prior to the experience." New outlooks and changes "created friction in almost all aspects of participants' lives." There was a 74% divorce rate, 65% career change. A shift in religious views for many—usually to a less dogmatic position—"could evoke tension and even hostility among family members and religious followers," although some participants "found places of worship to be more comforting and affirming than ever before." With so many changes in such basic areas, the experiencers often felt isolated; depression was common. "Participants sometimes felt as if they no longer fit in [and felt] like strangers in an alien world where few people understood or believed them."

It is no wonder that theologian and mystic Dorothee Soelle (1975, 196) could say, "Mystical experience is bliss and simultaneously it makes one homeless."

5. Adjusting to heightened sensitivities and supernatural gifts

Seventy-eight percent of the group reported problems resulting from newly acquired awareness and/or psychic abilities. Every participant mentioned having to struggle with extreme empathy, sometimes to the point of feeling other people's unspoken anxiety or physical pain. Their physical senses had become acute, making the noise, lights, and busy-ness of a typical workplace almost intolerable. Some found themselves super-sensitive to electricity and other energetic fields.

New psychic abilities included intuitive, auditory, or visual knowledge of "what was to come"; the ability to heal; telepathy; seeing auras; and other "supernormal gifts." These were often frightening and difficult to explain or manage.

6. Finding and living one's purpose
Retreat participants all agreed, "We are here to serve and show unconditional love—a pretty tall order, but short on specifics and difficult to apply."

Few experiencers of a distressing NDE have reported that type of purpose; for most, their sensed purpose seems to be to explain their experience in a way that makes sense in the context of their lives.

In sum, the challenges described by these twenty-five experiencers—and the fact that they needed a retreat in order to speak about them freely—say a good deal about the pain inflicted by the "myth of the NDE," that a person returns from any near-death experience garlanded with saintliness and brimming with answers to life's questions.

It is reminiscent of an event years ago, at a meeting of a local IANDS support group. The non-NDE members had become frustrated because meeting after meeting, the experiencers sat, listening intently, but never describing their NDEs. Then an experiencer from out of state came as the guest speaker. She described her NDE and the excruciating depression she had suffered afterward, the difficulties in adjusting to life in the same old household. And suddenly, the group's NDErs began to talk. The stories of their depression, their challenges, their difficulties came pouring out...until one of the non-experiencers, a sweet, gentle person, cried out, "Oh, stop! You mustn't talk like this! You have been to the Light—tell us what we are to do!"

And the experiencers fell instantly into silence again.

Why me?: The dilemma of suffering
It is a commonplace within long-standing communities of faith that the divine sometimes manifests in ways that cause great suffering.

Saint Paul is said to have claimed (Hebrews 9:21) that "It is a fearful thing to fall into the hands of the living God," echoed two thousand years later by metaphysician William Carl Eichmann (1991, 134), "If you undertake spiritual practice you will be confronted by your dark side. This is an axiom. The spiritual quest is dangerous, just as the books say. Seeking truth means experiencing pain and darkness as well as the clear white light."

A good many of today's authors on spirituality, freed from what seem to be the strictures of organized religion, are consequently limited by their ignorance of spiritual suffering. Unfamiliar with spiritual anguish in the world of religious community and monasticism, the traditionless writers prefer to emphasize joyful motifs and repress the difficult side of existence, other than to dismiss it as an inability of the experiencer to achieve an adequately higher consciousness.

This book is being written in a culture of unparalleled privilege at a time of almost obsessive flight from even minor inconvenience and discomfort. Even in a decade of unaccustomed economic hardship, technology and material progress are shielding us from the magnitude of deprivation and sheer physical pain that the majority of others, including our ancestors, have taken for granted.

Ours is a seriously skewed perspective. As Greenspan maintains, for as long as dark emotions are believed to be negative, we will find sorrow unacceptable. Under these conditions, it is not surprising that the question "Why me?" flourishes. But of course, misfortune happens all around us, all the time. Why should it not happen here, to me? To you?

The interpretation of pain and misfortune as punishment or as self-inflicted, each with its attendant guilt, seems almost a human instinct, and there have been lengthy arguments about it throughout the history of philosophy, theology, and psychology. To avoid a lengthy discussion, I am taking the position expressed by Jung, that the meaningful outcome of suffering, whether physical or emotional, is transformation. Jung calls it *individuation*, which can also be thought of as the ultimate stage of psychological or moral development, or theologically as the sacrificial giving over of the self for the sake of others.

For example, the psychic dismemberment of a shamanic initiate, like the religious significance of the crucifixion of Jesus, is *not* a punishment but the indispensable means of leading him toward his destiny. For this reason, says Jung (1984, 167), "the moralistic view of suffering as punishment seems to me not only inadequate but misleading. It is obviously a primitive attempt to give an explanation" of an archetypal idea that has not been thought about previously. Yet, he continues, "This psychological process is admittedly painful… But, as always, every step forward along the path of individuation is achieved only at the cost of suffering."

The popular teacher of consciousness and healing, Caroline Myss (2010), states that a great deal of suffering in any life crisis comes from our insistence on finding logical reasons for why it has happened to us. We believe, logically, that once we find the reason for our misfortune, we can turn it around, and that will be the end of our suffering. She says, "Obviously, we just don't 'get it.' What we don't get is that life and all that is included in life is not a logical, reasonable, rational experience. Life does not operate according to a system of what is fair, who deserves what and only the bad get punished… The truth that we cannot reason with the unreasonable holds the potential of igniting an epiphany in you because such a truth does not just liberate you from suffering; it is the best preventive medicine you will ever take in terms of going forward in your life."

It seems a bit ironic that at a time when "No pain, no gain" is proudly accepted as evidence of progress in physical training, emotional pain is found so unacceptable. Yet just as great physical capabilities are brought about by sometimes excruciating struggle, so transformative changes are usually precipitated by stress and anguish, to which any spiritual director or therapist will say Amen.

Caroline Myss again (2010): "But what about the illness that comes as a necessity to the soul's awakening? What about the creative depression that must be experienced as an initiation into the unlived life inside of us? What about the financial straits that must be endured in order to squeeze choice out of our lives, not allowing us to choose out of the ego's pride—ensuring that the soul's journey is kept on course?"

Rabbi Harold Kushner (2004, 80) holds out similar advice about not trying to explain or justify the reasons for misfortune or tragedy, even events that leave our lives collapsed around us. He explains "Why me?" as a rhetorical question to which any answer we might give could compound the suffering. Rather, he suggests, a more useful focus looks forward, asking, "Now that this has happened to me, what am I going to do about it?"

These difficult questions may infuriate and frustrate us, but they need to be asked, and we must find ways of coming to terms with them.

Even the darkest of experiences can lead somehow to what I will call an "intuition of being." We are deeply called, not to mere cognition, not to a grasp of fact, although that may be a component, but to a recognition, at a profound depth, of emotion, of Being, and of rightness. I do not necessarily know how that happens, even in my own life. I do know that at some measureless point we are driven by (or in) our pain to recognize that the physical world is not all there is, that there is a great More that is heavy with nameless meaning; and that we touch all of human suffering with our own. It enlarges us, I think, so that we can move, ironically, into humility.

The hazard with blissful experiences is that people who believe themselves to have been sanctified or otherwise elevated may collapse when darkness comes; they are unprepared for pain and often disrespectful of it. With harrowing experiences, the danger is that the sheer weight of fear and despair will lead the person to give up prematurely and collapse inward into a kind of paralyzed oblivion.

Until the nature of the universe changes, pain will happen. Stars will explode. Tsunamis and earthquakes and volcanoes and tornados will do what it is their nature to do, tearing the earth apart, leaving human misery and renewal behind. Friends will hurt us, intentionally or not, and lovers leave us heartbroken; family will be impossible or sometimes downright cruel; our lives may be imperiled by distortions in other people's psyches—rape, brutality, meanness, betrayal, theft. Freak accidents will take the lives of adored children and loving adults. And horrifying NDEs will leave some people forever changed. All of these events will come to someone, and most of those someones will not deserve them. Yet the trouble will come. Why should it not come to me? Or you? This is where Rabbi Kushner's question becomes imperative: As this event has happened to me, how will I respond?

Some respond by rolling into a ball of misery and victimhood and deciding, as many do, to live there, wearing wounds as if they were trophies, pointing them out to ourselves and others—"and then he…and then they…and she…and see here, where…" We can feed our hurt and starve our healing, and keep doing that over and over for a lifetime. But our spirits will shrink and dry up like leaves past their season. When, then, will we live?

Here again, I have found one of the ancient stories helpful. You can find it in Genesis, chapters 19-33, one of the great stories.

Jacob had deceived his dying father, swindled his older brother, and fled to a neighboring country to avoid his brother's murderous rage. Now, some fourteen years later, he has two wives, eleven sons, servants, enormous flocks. He is a wealthy man who wants to take his family and his riches and go home to his parents. But Jacob is still a conniver. He does not tell his father-in-law they are leaving but sneaks his family and goods away under cover of night. He tries to bribe his brother with a gift of hundreds of sheep, goats, donkeys, and cattle; but his spies say that the brother is advancing with a force of four hundred men.

Here he is, alone by a river in the darkness, this smooth talking, manipulating, deceiving Jacob, at yet another turning point in his life. There is danger ahead, danger behind, and unknowns all around, and in the darkness a mysterious Presence confronts him. Sometime in the night, says Genesis 32:25, "some man wrestled with him until the break of dawn. When the man saw that he could not prevail over him, he struck Jacob's hip at its socket, so that the hip socket was wrenched as they wrestled.

> "The man then said, 'Let me go, for it is daybreak.' But Jacob said, 'I will not let you go until you bless me.'
>
> "What is your name?' the man asked. He answered, 'Jacob.'
>
> "Then the man said, 'You shall no longer be spoken of as Jacob, but as Israel [which means contended with God] because you have contended with divine and human beings and have prevailed.'"
>
> "And at sunrise, as he crossed the Jabbok, Jacob limped because of his hip."

For anyone who has been wounded by an experience such as an NDE that will not give its name, this story might be a talisman: The account is puzzling and mysterious and incomplete. Yet in it there is the presence of the More: "I will not let you go unless you bless me." We will wrestle indefinitely until that blessing comes to us. Our limp will be its reminder.

15
More Questions

1. Were these people in good mental health?
Fortunately, for three decades psychiatrist Bruce Greyson was the researcher who most consistently looked into this kind of question. He oversaw the IANDS Research Pool, a group of 300 individuals willing to take what seemed like never-ending batteries of standardized psychological tests. Of the group, 100 had experienced at least one NDE; 100 had been close to death without an NDE; and the remaining 100 had never been knowingly close to death. They took test after test designed or administered by Greyson; in addition, other researchers called on them for their own independent studies. The results indicate clearly that the psychological status of near-death experiencers is unremarkable (Holden, 126-128).

In other words, there is no reason to wonder about a person's psychological status simply because of an NDE. Among a large group of people who have had NDEs, there will be some in fragile mental health or with outright mental illness, just as there are among the population that has not had NDEs; but the majority will be in good mental health. It is, therefore, safe to conclude that the people in a general study of near-death events or in the population at large are simply ordinary people who have had an extraordinary experience.

As discussed in Chapter 1, it is not possible (at least, not at this time) to predict who is likely to have an NDE. There simply are no known indicators, leading to the conclusion that "it could be anyone." With no clues to indicate who might turn out later to be experiencers, getting "before" information would require testing the entire population. There are no reliable data on before and after status, whether of mental health, personality type, physiological traits, or any other measure. Frustrating but true.

2. *When the NDE happened, were they depressed?*
Were they very pessimistic people? Or did they have major problems going on in their lives?

Based on the limited information we have, there is no way to generalize about any possible connection between experiencers' temperaments or immediate life circumstances and the type of NDE they had. This would be valuable information, as the assumption is common that there must be some correlation. However, one of the principal difficulties with research into any near-death experiences is the just-mentioned absence of hard data about people's lives before the NDE. The difficulty is compounded when working with difficult NDEs and the reluctance of the experiencers to talk freely about them. Findings about temperament and life circumstances will have to wait for a later investigation.

3. *Couldn't these experiences be dreams?*
Without question, there are similarities between dreams and near-death experiences. They occur during times of an altered state of consciousness. They involve sometimes complex visual imagery and symbolic language and structure from the imaginal realm. They can be studied and interpreted using similar techniques of dreamwork and, to a lesser extent, literary analysis. A major difference is that dreams do not share a similar patterning in the way that NDEs do—they are typically idiosyncratic. Another difference is

that dreams do not routinely produce enduring memory, except in the case of the rare "great dream," and even then, they do not have the life-transforming qualities of an NDE. Most significantly, near-death experiences typically incorporate transcendent elements—a powerful sense of having gone beyond the material world—and of incontrovertible knowledge about that reality. Despite their differences, their similarity in tapping into symbolic imagery means that the techniques of dreamwork provide an exceptionally fine-tuned approach to exploring meaning within an NDE.

4. *In NDEs, do people see what they expect at death?*

It really is surprising that expectations seem to have so little to do with the contents of NDEs. Of all the thousands of radiant accounts we have heard and read over the years, no one has described pearly gates, Saint Peter, or angels with feathers and harps. I do not know of any Western person who expected (or had even heard of) the Void. Hellish imagery in an NDE is as likely to be of water and cold as of fires, and reports of anyone's seeing anything like Satan are so rare as to be almost invisible. (I recall hearing a single mention, many years back, about a person who reportedly saw an entity in a red patent leather suit, who he thought might be the Devil.)

In the experiences included in this book, the young Jewish mother certainly did not expect to encounter a presence like Jesus; on the other hand, she lives in a largely Christian nation, so the idea would have been part of her conscious awareness. The liberal Yankee Protestant did not expect or understand the Eastern Yin-Yang symbol. Homosexuals who have been taught by their religious tradition that they are damned for their sexual activity have reported radiant, accepting, life-affirming experiences; whereas self-satisfied church deacons who believed themselves beyond reproach have been horrified by frightening NDEs. Kenneth Ring has pointed out many times that atheists often have the hardest adjustment after an NDE, because, "They don't know what it was they encountered; they just know it wasn't supposed to be there."

5. Did these people feel sinful or expect to go to hell?

This is another case in which, because there is no objective data about the experiencers' beliefs before the NDE, we cannot say conclusively what they felt at that time. However, it is highly unlikely that such a varied group shares a common belief about their moral character or the afterlife, or that they all believed the same things about themselves. For adults in the United States generally, the Gallup Organization has repeatedly asked about American belief in "a Hell to which people who had led bad lives without being sorry are eternally damned." Over a 30-year time span, the percentage of people answering "yes," they believed that, held at roughly 55% (Gallup, 125). Interestingly enough, only 15%, on average, believed they might go there themselves.

Unlike people who had pleasurable NDEs, more people after a frightening NDE report being afraid of death and hell than they say they were before. Many cannot explain what it is about themselves or their lives that would justify the severity of their experience, so they feel powerless to correct it. They wonder, as one woman put it, if "something evil is hanging over my head that I don't know about, or if there's something almost congenitally bad about me." On the other hand, individuals who are highly self-critical may blame themselves for behaviors that others would consider trivial.

6. Does a person have to be near death to have an out-of-body experience?

In a word, no. Some people, especially children, seem to have out-of-body experiences fairly routinely (if being out of the body can be considered "routine"). Otherwise, the circumstances commonly associated with OBEs are physical abuse, criminal assault, severe pain. We have heard numerous reports of women as well as children going out-of-body while being beaten or sexually abused; of OBEs during criminal assault and political torture, and in conjunction with debridement, the excruciatingly painful cleaning of burns. Some people who find it easy to go out-of-body report using it as a recreational activity.

7. Do women who have had an abortion have hellish experiences?

Despite the powerful social prohibitions placed around abortion in the United States, I cannot recall any report of a distressing near-death experience in which abortion was a factor.

8. What are the statistical findings of the original study?

Because of the difficulties experienced in getting even those few volunteers to share information, the Greyson-Bush study was not one to produce much quantifiable data. Although it provides abundant food for thought and the beginnings of anecdotal data, the detailed demographic and statistical charts are missing which would ordinarily give the comfort of scientific credence to the report. Others have done that with pleasant NDEs (notably Ring, Sabom, and Gallup), and except where we note a difference of opinion, we are comfortable with the outlines they have drawn.

In this case, however, the absence of much hard data may actually prove helpful. It is not possible in this analysis to become entranced by percentages and probabilities, to seduce ourselves into thinking that by measuring we are discovering something about meanings. Meanings are not the subject of scientific method.

9. Are you anti-scientific? You're barely mentioning neuroscience.

Several scientifically trained and capable people have written entire books about neuroscientific and other clinical findings. Read Peter Fenwick, MD's *The Truth in the Light: An Investigation of over 300 Near-Death Experiences* (1997); Pim van Lommel, MD's *Consciousness Beyond Life: The Science of the Near-Death Experience* (2010); or Chris Carter's *Science and the Near-Death Experience: How Consciousness Survives Death* (2010). Or check out Bruce Greyson's impeccable summation in *The Handbook of Near-Death Experiences: Thirty Years of Research* (2009). You'll do far better with them on the science than you would with me.

10. Are you anti-Christian? You're not defending the beliefs.

The purpose of this book is to provide as even-handed a description as I can give of what is known about near-death experiences and how people of different backgrounds and faith standings make meaning of them, *depending on their own point of view.* My purpose is not to write a defense of any single perspective, even my own, although that view obviously leaks through. Maybe in another book…

16
Bringing the NDE Home: Integration

After the experience, the first day of the rest of life. Old reference points are gone, and it is new eyes that open. Here is what it comes down to, in the words of social worker, author, and near-death experiencer Sally M. Leighton (1991, 233):

> [W]ith work, the center will hold. The work is what the symbols of transformation are all about. A hope is given that integration is a possibility, if one contains the pain and does the work…All these [symbols] I consider signposts toward the transcendent, images pointing beyond themselves to an ordering process, an ultimate concern, streetlamps for dark stretches of road. …The images raised by the traumata caused me to detach from the concrete, putting me in touch with basic human elements behind them, universals in life stages… the protean forms [God] takes to entice and elude and drive us relentlessly on to grasp His reality in our own, to find Him in anguish as well as exultation.

What can help a person understand a terrifying near-death or similar experience? The suggestions offered here are based on fifty years of "been there, done that" and relentless exploration.

The model of the hero's journey

At its simplest, a personal connection with an archetype may be the "That's me!" identification with a fictional character, or a strong and unexplainable feeling of attraction to a theme or even a landscape. At Tillicum Village in Puget Sound, a Native American dance troupe dances the Sasquatch legend, the story of Bigfoot, the humanoid creature rumored to live in the Pacific Northwest region of North America. In the performance, an elusive dark beast, shadowed and not-quite-identifiable, appears and vanishes, glimpsed and then disappearing among the great trees. For some veterans of frightening NDEs, the performance has provided a powerful sharing of a nameless truth—the existence of a barely recognized "something" that is the archetypal ground of their experience.

The archetype of the hero's journey has enormous healing potential because it says there is something of great value in the tortuous challenge. It is an initiation into deep maturity: you are being challenged to the utmost, not damned. Keep on.

Throughout history, stories of descent into the Underworld share characteristics. Here is how author Richard Tarnas (2007, 43) describes it:

> In Joseph Campbell's classic description of the archetypal journey of the hero—the liberator, the shaman, the mystic, the creator, the discoverer of new worlds—a dramatic progression takes place that involves certain characteristic stages: a decisive separation from the community, detaching the self from the larger whole in which it has until then been embedded; an experience of the physical and spiritual life of the world as undergoing a great danger, an encroaching shadow, a fall into ruin; and a radical shift of emphasis from external

realities to the interior realm, moving from the world scene of secondary effects to the causal zones of the psyche where the difficulties really reside. There follows a dark night of the soul, an interior descent, bringing a crisis of meaning, a transformative encounter with human suffering and mortality, and a disorienting dissolution of the self's basic structures of identity and being. Only through such a descent does the hero penetrate to a source of greater knowledge and power opened by a direct experience of the archetypal dimension of life. Along the way of this perilous journey certain humble clues and anomalies unexpectedly appear that challenge and destabilize the confident knowledge of the old self, yet ultimately point the way to the threshold of another world.

The journey demands integrity and persistence from the one who is called; it is never easy but always worthwhile. This is worth remembering before making any rush to judgment about one's own character or psychology, or that of any other person reporting a dark NDE.

The trajectory is similar both to that of the biblical story of Eden and to the birth-death cycle in Grof's findings: the archetype of the coming into consciousness, moving from the perfection of Before (the womb, the mind of God, the garden where everything is provided) to the absolutely essential phase of pain and struggle to reach life in the world, to the journeying that is history and individual life, and eventually (so far incomplete, for humankind) a return to Home, to God, to true being. In a similar way, the constellation of elements in the hero's journey forms the template of the dark NDE.

Not surprisingly, all of these follow the universal general pattern of the great spiritual task, the movement through suffering to destruction and at last to restoration. Successful spiritual journeys always lead to restoration—which brings us to point two:

What has been lost over the centuries, at least in Christianity, is the sense of gift even within a difficult spiritual experience. Whereas the ancient wisdom held out a treasure at the depths of such journeys, over-intellectualization of doctrine has truncated the archetype by taking the journeyer only *into* torment and punishment, *not back out*. In Christian terms, this is like stopping the narrative at the crucifixion—a loss which has carried over into an entire culture's understanding of suffering.

When human intellect made hell eternal, we forgot about the treasure that is always in the deeps. As a consequence, we have learned suffering and judgment but ignore restoration. The experiences we are concerned with are incontrovertibly frightening; but it is our doing that they are labeled 'negative.' It is time, once again, to look for the richness that lies within these extraordinary encounters.

With this clearly in mind, it is possible to look at disturbing NDEs and from a fresh perspective, with a goal of healing our misunderstandings and growing into a fuller understanding.

Approaches

Trying to piece together the meaning of a near-death or similar experience, whether glorious or horrifying, is much like studying literature or scripture: There are always levels of meaning. A typical scenario involves a minimum of three levels:

The *literal* level treats the description of the experience as true, the elements as facts: I went to the place described, saw these things, and so on. This is almost always the level that has produced the emotional reaction to the experience. It is generally the least helpful level when probing deeply and integrating an experience into one's life.

The *metaphoric* level gives an opportunity to pull back a bit and make a comparison of an element image, or even the entire event, to something with similar characteristics. "It is as if…" or "What if…?" This level allows us to consider other perspectives, other possible meanings. It expands exploration from the literal level to the symbolic, opening to all the possible meanings of images and ideas—for instance, seeing that fire might be understood not only as punishment in hell but as the equally valid meaning of the presence of God. This is the most helpful and useful level for deepening one's understanding of an NDE, a nightmare, scripture, or any serious work of art and literature.

The *personal* level asks, "What does this understanding of the experience mean to me?" This question is worth asking at each level and of each of the possible interpretations.

At first

In the early days/months/possibly years following a deeply disturbing experience, it will be important to tread lightly. The only recourse may be to buy time until panic has subsided enough for cognitive process around the event even to be possible. Hope need not be reasoned to be sometimes most important. An exception may be made to taking time if you are in the care of a psychotherapist or counselor skilled at post-traumatic stress therapy.

Here are important reminders for the early stages:

There is absolutely no evidence that 'Good people have good experiences and bad people have bad ones.' Holy figures in all traditions have endured similar experiences—Krishna, perhaps Jesus, shamans, many saints including Teresa (see Chapter 6, The Unwelcome Dark). The experience certainly did not keep them from being holy. For those who are unimpressed by saints, there is still no evidence that bad experiences happen only to bad people.

There is some evidence that if a disturbing NDE resolves fully, it changes to a pleasant or better experience. This is the reasoning behind the assurance of physician Barbara Rommer (2000, 53), "I explained to [my patient] that I believe with all my heart that had she not been resuscitated so quickly, a wonderful experience would have unfolded." Christopher Bache (1994, 42), observing clients who have worked through the stages of Grof's therapy, has emphatically asserted that "a frightening near-death experience is an incomplete near-death experience." Reassurance sometimes has more value than data analysis.

It is helpful to defuse the emotional intensity by, literally, getting it out. Psychotherapist Alex Lukeman (below) suggests telling the story out loud three times; if there is no listener, saying it out loud anyway will help defuse the anxiety. From my own experience, this is highly effective. Some people may feel less threatened by writing the experience first, then reading the text out loud. See "Get out of your head," below.

The Void is traditionally considered the ultimate experience in spiritual practice. For a person who has not been engaged long-term in a spiritual discipline, an encounter with the Void is like tossing a non-swimmer off the high board. Back off, work slowly to build skills in meditative practice and prayer, watch Brian Greene's *Fabric of the Cosmos* program on space, and see how the perspective changes.

Later

Note: Everything that follows is based on the assumption that although a person may be troubled and fearful, there is no mental illness present. *In the case of severe emotional fragility, get psychotherapeutic help (or help the experiencer get help) before attempting any kind of mental or emotional techniques on your own.*

There is no timetable and no prescribed route for exploring ways of thinking about the experience or coming to terms with what it means for your life. Those suggested here are a few of many possible paths; they are here because they have been suggested by professionals and/or were helpful in resolving my own experience.

Dreamwork techniques

The techniques developed for dreamwork and imaging can be invaluable. As Wayne Rollins observed, NDEs read like dream material, and decoding symbols applies not only to dreams but to NDEs and similar experiences as well.

Psychotherapist Alex Lukeman (2000, 10), a near-death experiencer himself, has identified seven keys for finding relief from the fear of nightmares. They are equally applicable to NDEs and similar experiences. The keys are:

"Realize the [experience] didn't occur just to scare you, but has meaning and purpose. This is absolutely fundamental.

"You have an innate ability to understand and gain relief from the [experience].

"Don't be afraid to look at horrifying images, or think that bad images mean bad things about you.

Learn to step away and consider the image objectively, without emotion, if possible.

"If you get an idea of the meaning, you get two good results: You won't have to have the dream [experience] again and you have practical advice for your real, outer life.

"Remind yourself that [these experiences] can open the door to love and healing in both a psychological and a physical sense. They are a gift from your unconscious mind, even though they seem frightening when they occur.

"Let your mind relax; freely associate images, feelings, and memories."

A rich source of dreamwork techniques, especially for readers wanting a religious framework, is the work of respected psychologists Louis M. Savary and Patricia H. Berne (1984). Their *Dreams and Spiritual Growth: A Judeo-Christian Way of Dreamwork* remains in print and highly recommended. Among the recommendations they suggest is amplification.

Amplification. Give the experience a title; name the theme. What can you say about the theme?—free-associate a bit. Where else (in movies, literature, scripture) does that theme appear? What parallels are there between those stories and the NDE? Then sit with them for a while; how could you understand the theme and the parallels to apply to issues in your life?

Do the same thing with the elements (the places, the characters) of the experience.

Think of hero's journeys in legend and video games: The hero carries a talisman and goes with a companion. Approach your NDE mentally, carrying in your mind (or, for that matter, in your hand) a talisman to protect you; choose a companion—living or not, whom you actually know or not—to help you through the experience. Notice what and whom you chose and what significance they have for you; free-associate and amplify what you can say about them, as above. Then go back to your experience with them. See if events in your experience shift, and how.

What could you have done differently during the actual experience? Now that you can participate consciously in the events, you are able to change your responses, to observe relationships, to try "going with" the experience. What differences do new approaches make?

Another experienced therapist makes the same point about amplifying the content of an imaginal experience. Lois Sekarak Hogan says (Frenier) of a dream about a sea turtle laying her eggs,

> "To get the most out of the dream, the best starting point is always the dreamer's unique experience of the image. For example, in the turtle dream image: Is it day or night? How does the water feel? How is the turtle feeling (fearful, tired, impatient, in pain, joyful)? Where is that felt in the body? What comes up as you sit with that feeling? What does the turtle experience as it leaves the water, walks on the sand, digs the hole, lays the eggs? These nuances communicate enormously! And appreciating the nuances of the image is particularly important because many dream images are reflecting some kind of growth edge. When we're at the edge of something, we're at the boundary of the unknown and this is often experienced

as a somewhat chaotic experience. At the edge, images often come that we would say are 'not me.' However, while we may claim that the dream image may not be the 'me' that my ego consciously knows, it may be another part of me that is seeking to be experienced or to grow more in consciousness."

Working with archetypes or doing dreamwork does not mean simply pairing images from an experience with those listed in a booklet picked up at the supermarket. Lukeman's simple and excellent book *Nightmares* treats dreamwork with respect and groundedness. A grounded course or workshop may help (but beware of amateur facilitators!) or consider spending some time with a Jungian therapist, skilled at this kind of interpretation.

Use both sides of your brain

Get out of your head
Interpret the experience with your body. Paint your experience. Sculpt it. Weave it. Dance it. If you can't dance, walk it; if you are physically paralyzed, imagine how it would feel to dance it. If you do crafts, make something of it. Learn an instrument. We are most accessible to sudden insight from our weakest aspect: So, if you ordinarily function from strong verbal or analytical skills, try something kinesthetic. If you prefer physical activity, read poetry or keep a journal. If the results are awful, just don't show them to anyone.

Get into your head
This cannot be over-stressed: Find the best information you can from as many sources as you can. This is no time to go all right-hemisphere and say that intellectual learning is unhelpful. Find views you agree with and views you don't. Build an educated understanding of the subject, not simply the first you come upon.

Read, read, read, especially outside the near-death literature. If you're not a reader, get audio recordings. Vary your reading; do not read only near-death, only metaphysical, only evangelical, only scientific—only anything—material. You're looking for all the content you can find.

Read the history of science, the perennial philosophy, a modern translation of the Bible (not King James, for reasons there is not space to go into here), the Koran and Baghavad Gita; read the spiritual literature of your own tradition and general books about religions other than your own, and transpersonal psychology; the 'new physics,' consciousness studies, metaphysics, contemporary theology; read hymn lyrics and poetry; read the mystics and Joseph Campbell; read dreamwork and imaging techniques, and about energy work and healing. Look for common themes in all of them. If you are a spiritual person, read science; if you love science, read the mystics. (Sometimes the least comfortable ideas may trigger something and become the most useful in the long run.)

Especially when dealing with anger and resentment—the "Why me?" issues—there are approaches that can help. From a psychological perspective, there are these books from the bibliography: Pema Chödrön, *The Places That Scare You: A Guide to Fearlessness in Difficult Times*; Edward Edinger's *Encounter with the Self*, his commentary on Job, or virtually any of Stanislav and Christina Grof's many books. Rabbi Harold Kushner's *When Bad Things Happen to Good People* cannot be too highly recommended for all readers, or the beautiful introductions to Jewish mysticism in Rabbi Lawrence Kushner's *Honey from the Rock*, or his *God Was in This Place and I, I Did not Know*. For a Christian sense, Matthew Fox's *Original Blessing* has been an eye-opener for many people who have known nothing previously but the condemnation of the doctrine of original sin; or read any Alan Watts. For a fresh look at Christian thinking, follow some of the positive blogs: BioLogos, http://biologos.org Peter Enns, http://www.patheos.com/blogs/peterenns RichardBeck, http://experimentaltheology.blogspot.com, Andrew Perriman's http://www.postost.net, especially http://www.postost.net/node/571 for his ebook *Heaven and Hell in Narrative Perspective*.

There is no lack of recent titles with a metaphysical point of view, though the quality varies as much as in any religious category. These titles are merely a taste of what is available (and please do not limit yourself to only a single perspective).

Listen to tapes of conferences and lectures. Listen with a critical ear, not to find fault with the presenter but to hear patterns, themes, and inconsistencies. Beware of people who insist they have definitive answers, the only answer, special insight.

Go to conferences; take courses. If you cannot afford conferences, find inexpensive books and tapes at the public library; attend discussions at a compatible church or temple (if secular, try Unity, Bah'ai, or a Unitarian/Universalist church); find a pertinent short-term adult ed course at the nearest high school or community college. Always, always, be cautious of people who are absolutely certain their opinions are absolute Truth and that they have the only answer. Yes, I do realize that this flies in the face of a good many religious dogmas; it is entirely possible to be deeply religious while knowing more than a single point of view. If you cannot bring yourself to look outside your religious tradition, at least read widely within it. If there is no variety of opinion within the tradition, do the best you can to interpret the experience yourself.

To experiencers: Through it all, recognize that you are vulnerable to charlatans, bad information, and being ripped off. You will want a guru or teacher; be very careful in choosing your role models. The world is full of harm and bad advice from spiritual-sounding people whose primary interest is their own financial or ego-building interest rather than helping you.

Take your time. Do not commit to any person or group that will not easily let you go. Remember that spiritual growth cannot be bought; high price need not lead to higher consciousness. You are as likely to find genuine growth with a church or temple as by attending trendy but expensive workshops—and the support won't disappear at the end of a single weekend.

Find the story that speaks to you. Maybe Frodo, the peaceable hobbit, venturing into a realm of evil for the sake of his community.

Maybe Job; or Jacob wrestling all night by a river until he is wounded by an unidentified being; or the Aeneid. Maybe Harry Potter (look behind the scare-tactic criticisms) or the film *Avatar*. Read or see the film versions of Tolkein's *Lord of the Rings* and C.S. Lewis' *Chronicles of Narnia*. Explore reviews or other interpretations of these stories that can help deepen your understanding. Most of them are variations on the old, old story: challenge, sacrifice, restoration. Same as a distressing NDE.

Pay attention to interpretations of the experience that differ from yours. As Bruce Greyson noted years ago (personal communication, 1985), every interpretation represents a different model of the experience—and they are all models, not the real thing. Look at different versions—the concretist (literal) model, a variety of 'explain it away' reductionist models (that nevertheless contain useful information), the Jungian ego-Self model, a holographic universe model, an apocalyptic model, ecumenical religious, conservative religious, scientific, metaphysical…and on and on. Notice how they are alike, how different. Discover which ones feel most comfortable and uncomfortable, and then examine why: not, 'Why is my interpretation right and that one wrong,' but what do your choices say about what is important to you?

Identify the vocabulary that registers with you. Different models have different vocabularies. Find your vocabulary; for example, some people find that working with psychological terms opens doors, while others consider it psychobabble. Again, remember that the words build a *model*, not the real thing.

Ask, what is *the gift within the experience?* This is a question that may take years to answer. Insist on finding the gift, a blessing in your experience.

Use Other People's Thoughts

There is no "answer" to a near-death experience, any more than there is an "answer" to life itself. But there are a myriad of thoughts about related subjects. Use them; you are not expected to come up with an entire explanation by yourself. What there will be are approaches, ways of exploring and finding pathways to understanding, and the more you know of them…well, the more ways you will have to get you where you're going, which is to a sense of meaning that feels right to you. There are Western approaches, and Eastern; there are religious and secular, psychological and spiritual, intellectual and emotional, analytical and intuitive approaches. Using more than one or two will help integrate an experience into ongoing life.

Eastern thought: Equanimity, Chödrön, Shinzen

The conceptions of 'self' and 'reality' are very different in Western and Eastern faith traditions. The idea from Eastern thought that the physical world and ego are merely illusions may cause a struggling Western experiencer to become even more traumatized. Unless or until the person is already comfortable with those principles, it is wise to go very slowly with any arguments based on the idea of ego death.

A great many readers have found help in the writings of Pema Chödrön, the American Buddhist abbess. She is especially strong in her teachings about non-attachment, especially to destructive emotions. For instance, when identifying the chain reaction qualities of unhelpful emotions, can lead to stopping the pattern. Chödrön's books describe practices for such learning.

It is not unusual that students who are well along in the practice of a contemplative discipline may, in the depths of their prayer or meditation, encounter alarming images like those that appear in distressing NDEs. Mindfulness teacher Shinzen Young (2005) says of these, "Be happy that the deep mind is unburdening itself under these benign circumstances. Otherwise, there is every likelihood that it will come up under difficult ones such as illness or the dying process [when] it will cross-multiply with the other challenges present, vastly potentiating your sense of suffering. You are directly encountering the manifesting power of impermanence!" In other words, whatever the experience, it will pass; whatever it is, be still and know that it will change.

Western thought: Do the psychological work
If there is an eleventh Commandment, it must be, "Thou shalt do thy inner work." If that strikes too authoritative a note, consider that it is not possible to dance the spiritual dance while the floor is littered with psychodynamic rubble. To experiencers, my strongest recommendation is: Begin to clear the floor. Find a therapist to help you identify personal issues that may keep you from functioning at your best; if you can't afford long-term help, pick one issue and work with a counselor or psychotherapist short-term; if you can't afford that, apply to a clinic; and if you still can't afford that, get a library card and begin reading. This is not a short-term project and it is not the only task, but it is absolutely essential.

As soon as possible, it will be productive to name the issues that made the experience so frightening: Was it being out of control; or unfamiliarity, or oddness; the threats of perceived entities? What about that issue makes it feel like such a threat? Then work on that issue. And ask, what does that mean to you? If the threat was of ceasing to exist, what does *that* mean—physically dying? Spiritually disappearing? You are not the only one to feel this threat; what do other people say about it? This is when to become good friends with your local librarian, used-book dealer, and the power of Internet search engines. Some short-term therapy may be particularly useful here, especially with issues related to control and being.

Reframe Symbols : Other Meanings
As discussed in chapter 13, a first interpretation of images is likely to be far too shallow. In dealing with spiritual symbols, as with reading the Bible or other religious literature, a misplaced naïveté carries a high price. (For instance, God is not and was never literally a shepherd, nor a rock, nor a thunderbolt. Jesus was not an actual lamb. Interpreting symbolic language as if it were literally true leads to very bad comprehension.) Re-read Chapter 13 for reminders about all this.

Fire, for instance, which we generally interpret as the worst sort of punishment, has an honorable history as a symbol of God, of cleansing, purification, and rebirth (for example, the Phoenix rising). The Egyptian goddess Isis bathed the infant prince in fire, not as punishment but to grant him immortality.

Darkness, weeping, gnashing of teeth may take on new meaning when thought of, as theologian Hans Kung (1984, 140) points out, "harsh-sounding metaphors for the menacing possibility that a person may completely miss the meaning of his life."

As in dreams, a suggestion of death may point to much more than the end of physical existence—to the end of a project, relationship, or phase of life, or to a major shift in one's awareness and thinking.

The Void may feel like ultimate abandonment; but to someone who is ready to experience it that way it can also represent ultimate unity and potential.

A horned creature, terrifying when understood only as Satan, has an ancient history as a guide. The more one knows about symbolic language, the richer one's understanding becomes.

Recognize What a Resource Can Do

A clinical psychologist may be skilled at helping unravel life-history material but not dream symbols. A spiritual director works with a person's relationship to the sacred, not with deep-seated psychological problems. At any given point, one may be more helpful than another.

Identify a Community

The work is always done alone, but others will help. Caution and discernment are crucial; this is harder than finding a dentist.

Some IANDS support groups are able to be helpful; others are too fearful, or too enamored of the radiant experience to tolerate the depths.

For the person who has given up religion, it is worth the attempt to go back. Most experts recommend staying within your own faith, though perhaps not the same denomination, if your understandings have changed. If the tradition of your childhood was not harmful, it could be worth revisiting; or, if that is uncomfortable, look for one that better meets your understandings of today. ('Church shopping' is sensible, not a sin.)

In some geographic areas, it may be possible to find a spirituality group or book club. Be careful; these can be wonderful but are often the targets of especially needy and/or ungrounded folks who will drain emotional energy and talk nonsense rather than encourage genuine understanding and growth. This same caution applies to Bible study groups; if they demonstrate unbalanced interests in punishment and predictions of doom, or insist on a single interpretation (theirs), or are absorbed by warnings about satanic influence more than in living affirmatively with the Holy, find another group.

17
Conclusions

Just the Facts
What do we know about distressing NDEs? Basic facts about "less-than-positive" experiences, as author Barbara Rommer delicately termed them, can be summarized quickly.

Accounts of NDEs from around the world go back to antiquity. Some of them are challenging, including those described as frightening trips through an underworld.

1. All near-death experiences belong to a family of events of the deep psyche (some would say 'soul') that include profound experiences of prayer, meditation, shamanic initiation, near-death, and many other circumstances, known by a variety of names such as "mystical," "imaginal," and "spiritually transformative" experience. They occur in life-threatening and non-life-threatening situations.
2. From the neuroscientific perspective, of the many physiological explanations that have been put forward, some temporal lobe involvement seems central as a mediator of the affective

component of NDEs. Note that this is distinct from the content and meaning attributed to the event.
3. The primary effect of an NDE is usually a powerful and enduring awareness that there is more to reality than the physical world.
4. NDEs do not play favorites: they appear across demographic bases including age, race, ethnicity, nationality, gender, sexual preference, education, occupation, socioeconomic status, religious background and beliefs, level of religious activity, expectations of afterlife. Despite limited demographic data about distressing NDEs, they appear to show the same broad distribution.
5. Research indicates that the great majority of NDEs are pleasant or better, but that as many as one in five may produce intense terror, guilt, panic, loneliness, despair. As radiant NDEs represent the heights of spiritual/human experience, these represent the depths.
6. Because distressing NDEs appear across so many personal circumstances, there is no objective evidence that they are punishment for wrong beliefs or unaccepted behavior, or that they happen only to bad people. They are indiscriminate.
7. Both pleasant and distressing NDEs share some commonalities of pattern, which may include: an out-of-body experience; movement; special qualities of light or dark; a landscape; encountering presences; intense emotion; sometimes transcendent elements (symbols, archetypal images, etc.) a noetic quality. Some experiences include more of these elements than others. Distressing NDEs typically lack a life review, the positive emotional characteristics of pleasant NDEs, and loss of the fear of death.
8. There are at least three types of distressing NDE, four if we separate out an otherwise pleasant NDE with a guilt reaction to the life review: 1) Features common in pleasant NDEs, but experienced negatively; 2) the Void; 3) features interpreted as hell.

9. NDEs are not always static but may switch from unpleasant to pleasant or, less commonly, the other way around.
10. Distressing NDEs are underreported out of fear, shame, social stigma, the sense that the person cannot burden others with such horrific information, and other reasons.
11. A distressing NDE may produce long-lasting emotional and psychospiritual trauma.
12. The very fact of strong emotional response reported to have been present during NDE indicates that interpretation begins within the experience.
13. Any report identifying a presence as a particular individual, especially a spiritual figure, is a perception that may or may not be factual but cannot be confirmed either way. However, that identification is what the person was experiencing, so it contributes to meaning.
14. Encountered entities will be described according to the person's interpretation and available vocabulary: for instance, the unrecognized Yin/Yang images in my NDE, which for years I knew and described only as "circles." Further, an archetype may be given a name: a "Jesus look-alike" in the NDE of a non-Christian; "Oh, it was God," from a four-year-old. Again, there is no way to know whether the identification is factual or experiential; ultimately the only difference it makes is in the use to which the identification is put following the experience.
15. Pleasant NDEs tend to convey messages for living that are common across religious and philosophical systems: recognition of forces beyond observed physical reality, a mandate for love and compassion; the importance of learning; the centrality of service to others. Distressing NDEs have less focused messages but typically follow the ancient shamanic pattern of suffering/death/ resurrection, a universal pattern which in less metaphoric terms can be read as an invitation to self-examination, disarrangement of core beliefs, and rebuilding.
16. After a distressing NDE, a person may find meaning by

"reforming" his life, possibly with a convincing religious affiliation, or through reductionism; some struggle to find resolution. Beyond that, there is little information about how people cope.
17. NDEs do not conform to the exact teachings of any specific cultural, philosophical, or religious system. Because they appear unbidden and unscripted, their universality is understood by many people as revealing something vital about the nature of the universe, the human psyche, and core religious teachings. Their lack of particular doctrinal conformity leads some religious bodies to consider them false or satanic.

Beyond these observations lies little but conjecture—to which, let it be noted, this work is not immune.

Observations

Living things are designed to avoid death—bacteria, poison oak and rosebushes, clams, scorpions and butterflies, cocker spaniels and tree-climbing sloths—camouflaged, toothed, shelled, clawed, poisonous, quick, all to protect life. Move too close to an amoeba, and it will flee.

Designed to protect our life, nonetheless all of us will die. We humans live with the consciousness of that fact all the time, which flies in the face of our instinct for survival. A distressing near-death experience triggers that instinct. Threatened, we flee, big time. But we can never understand these experiences by running away. The way to understand anything requires that we get close, that we come to know it. Where do they come from, these life-burdening events? What do they mean?

My own experience was more than fifty years ago, and the better part of that time I have spent, first learning not to run away from it, and then trying to figure out what could be said about such intellectually, emotionally, and spiritually devastating experiences.

My answer: Look at the universe and understand that it is made up of both light and dark, swaths of tranquility and worlds of violence, powers and what we non-physicists persist in calling energies. None can be observed without the others. We, and our experiences, are part of that universe. The way the universe (Creation) works is reflected in how we and everything else on our planet are made up, how we are designed, how we function. It's an unsurprising maxim: As above, so below.

Why, then, should our inner experiences not mirror the characteristics spread throughout the universe—the light, the darkness, the silence, the violence?

What makes sense to me is the thought of those unseen, unknown forces that occupy all of space, which may be Brian Greene's cosmological constant or quintessence (an apt word), beyond and through which some of us believe there is the unseen force we call God.

What makes sense to me is the idea of the imaginal realm, what Jung called the collective unconscious, of symbols and images, the archetypes that pattern and populate our minds and understandings the way other invisible forces pattern space. They are the raw materials of our philosophical and religious constructions, the carriers of messages and meanings about the universe. Whether the imaginal realm, the collective unconscious, is actual or metaphoric makes no difference to me, because, like gravity, the concept works too well and explains too much to be ignored. It is the source, I believe, of our transformative experiences, as it has been the source of every creative act.

It is such a mystery! Out of it humankind has forged explanations, some of which have grouped into cultures and belief systems, not all of them religious, with doctrines and dogmas and ritual practices; they operate as closed systems and can be lived in. All of them, whether religious, philosophical, scientific, economic, are attempts to understand and explain the universe. Some, like this, become books.

What makes sense to me is to take those products which constitute the mental materials of the world—the findings of science, the sacred writings, the cultural teachings and art, the scholarship and creativity of good minds—and put my own near-death experience and those of others up against them to see where they touch, how they reflect similar or different ideas, how they picture reality, the body of Creation.

Resolution

We have been talking about the work of a lifetime.

The twin temptations of light and dark near-death experiences are paralysis and flight. After a glorious experience, the temptation is, oddly enough, to a paralysis of spiritual self-satisfaction, even of grandiosity, and flight away from the bodied world in an insatiable hunt for more light, more bliss, more "home." It is too often a denial of life. By contrast, with a horrifying experience, the temptation is to the paralysis of despair, a desperate fear of both living and dying, a flight from engagement.

Neither approach is complete. As William James (319) observed, a characteristic of all mystical events is that they are the experience of an instant in a life, not the entirety of that life. The event will shape but must not consume everything that comes after.

No one would wish for the task of clearing the ghastly wreckage of the Twin Towers, or for the work of those volunteers in the Middle East, or anywhere, who take upon themselves the collecting of body parts of people blown apart by bombs. Yet it is those labors, and the persistence and integrity of those who do them, that make heroes in the modern archetypal descent to an underworld beyond imagining.

No one would wish for such experience; yet, once it arrives, one wishes to meet it with courage and compassion, recognizing that eventually the world will be remade, the dead given the respect they deserve. Some workers will be crushed by the burden; for most, the gift may be to recognize themselves as part of such an archetypal restoration, marked to perpetuity by a depth and knowledge of suffering. These are not the gifts one asks for, but in the incomprehensible fullness of human experience, they are sometimes those we are required to find.

One can draw similar conclusions about dark near-death experiences. They are neither trivial nor meaningless. As radiant experiences represent the heights of numinous encounter, those that are distressing represent the depths. Neither is conclusive about the perfection or brokenness of the experiencer nor the reach of the heavens.

If a single conclusion is to be drawn here, it may be that we are called to a higher level of understanding: to recast the ubiquitous assumption that pain is equivalent to punishment, that suffering is *per se* malevolent (although some surely is). Certainly it is possible to discount or deny an unwelcome distressing event, to disavow its significance. But those are avoidance techniques, as they are in any effort to escape an unwanted reality. Significance need not mean grandiosity but simply growing into a more nuanced sense of being. It can be possible, then, given time and care, to face the experience and find that worthwhile meaning can come from it. This is not a naïve romanticism, though it is a flag in the face of nihilism.

At the simplest possible level, I am convinced that the most helpful approach to these experiences is to think about them not in the language of daily news, as being factually true, but in the language of spirit, as figures of meaning sent out in disguise. Read them as symbols and metaphors, as pointers beyond themselves. If your religious training is such that a metaphoric response feels blasphemous to you, try approaching it with "What if…?" Or if skepticism immobilizes your imagination, do the same. What if there were another explanation beyond the literal? What might it be?

Approached that way, the experiences reveal themselves to be not threats or harsh sentences but solemn invitations. They are variations on ancient messages, largely a beckoning to love and to suffering as a way to crack through to understanding: There is a great More (I call it that so as to include those who reject whatever distortion they perceive as "God"; call it whatever you want) in which we are called to participate. At its heart is compassion. Come and be an intentional part of it.

You are not who you think you are; none of us is. It is time to change, to open to a wider understanding. Because this feels so threatening to our felt sense of being and identity, it is terrifying. Yet as Rilke said, "Every angel is terrifying." The answer is to change perspective.

I say this to experiencers:

Distressing NDE, afraid of the light: It's true. You are not in control. Work on understanding that. Then loosen the way your ego is held. There's a More in the universe—called Universe, Force, Spirit, God, *something*—that permeates the world, your life; there's more than your own control. It's ok. You can learn to trust it.

The Void: It's true. Objects are not reality in the way you think they are. Not even your self. You are being asked to let go of the transitoriness of objects, including yourself, and understand that ultimately there is only Being. It's ok. There's More.

Hellish: It's true. Your very self knows it is threatened, even attacked. You are being required to let go of yourself, to die to self so you can be renewed, yes, even "born again," though not in a narrow, doctrinal sense. From your present position, it feels like hell; but it is really an invitation to open your mind. Learn to live bigger, wider, more inclusively.

All of us: It takes an open heart, an open way, to learn to live wider. It is the way of compassion, of faithfulness, of trust that darkness will not have the final word. I call it sacred.

One might say: Amen. Or, from Steve Jobs: "Oh wow. Oh wow. Oh wow."

APPENDIX 1

Interventions for Caregivers

Experiences that suggest a near-death experience or deathbed vision are not news to caregivers in hospice, hospital, or emergency services who work with seriously ill and dying patients. Fortunately, the great majority of such visions are affirming and reassuring. However, some are deeply distressing, and caregivers need to be prepared to deal with them. As examples, here are quotes from a nursing blog (allnurses.com) about seriously distressing deathbed visions.

"I also have seen many of the beautiful peaceful scenes just described. But, (y'all knew it was coming, didn'y ya?) I saw one young man, early 20's, losing to cancer, who woke up in the middle of the night SCREAMING at the top of his lungs "HE is coming to get me HE is coming to get me!!!!" We all rushed into the room and it was horrible. The pt was backed up into the corner (he was too weak earlier to make the bathroom, used a [bedside commode]), IVs out, blood everywhere and pointing to the crucifix on the wall and SCREAMING. As we tried to get him back in bed he grabbed a nurse by the throat and then…simply fell over with the most horrified look on his face and died. When the mortuary came and picked him up he still had that expression on his face. I believe in a peaceful afterlife…BUT…There is also a not peaceful one also…I think."

"Another lady patient…Was a very prominent member of the community and church member all her life. The night before she died we had her in a recliner at the nurse's desk because she didn't want to be alone. She would scream out, "OH MY GOD!! THE DEVIL'S COMING FOR ME! HE'S GOING TO TAKE ME!" and did not stop all night. She was doing it when I left that morning, and she died that afternoon. The other nurses said she was screaming it up until the instant she passed."

"I too, have seen these type deaths. what's interesting, is these [patients] i'm thinking of, didn't have any beliefs about afterlife. they believed in nothingness, total nothingness. Kaput. it's over. it's obvious to me they did see something…whether it was a religious figure, an angel or something totally unfamiliar to them…and it scared the begeezuz out of them, thinking all this time that nothing was going to happen. it's a horrifying event to witness and more, to experience. whenever i have a pt who believes in 'nothingness', i have to tell them 'don't be frightened if you see _____.' they snort. i wait."

General suggestions

Those experiences are not at all typical of deathbed visions, but they do occur. They were perhaps as horrifying to the nursing staff as to the patients themselves, as they triggered universal anxieties about dying, and feelings of helplessness and fear violated the caregiving desire to *do something* to help. Nurses and aides, like the rest of the population, almost certainly have too little information to understand what is happening. Second, they are likely to have no idea how to respond, which is not surprising, considering that most clergy feel the same way. Third, depending on their own religiously inspired fears, they may be traumatized themselves. The suggestions in this chapter may be helpful in establishing a protocol and offering at

least some basic scripting of response. The four essential steps are:
1) preparation; 2) assessment; 3) acting; 4) responding.

Be prepared

Information

Ignorance is never useful at the bedside. As counseling psychologist Marilyn Mendoza observes (2008), it is not helpful when a caregiver with insufficient information encounters this kind of situation and runs from the room screaming. Information can be provided through classwork, reading, or audiovisual materials.

All critical care, hospice, and end-of-life hospital staff, including chaplains and volunteers, need at least an introductory class on death-related experiences, both pleasant and distressing—nearing death awareness, near-death experiences, and deathbed visions. The class should include at least a brief mention of common interpretations of what is happening with deathbed events. Are they evidence of:

- A psychotic break
- Simply a neurological disturbance
- An hallucination
- Something really weird and scary from another world
- The Devil at work
- An eruption from the subconscious
- A common end-of-life event of unknown origin
- Literal evidence of an afterlife

These are *not* evidence that the patient is going crazy or has become psychotic; the visions are probably more than the typical hallucination. They are neurological in the sense that every human physical or mental experience is transmitted by neurological means. They are weird to the extent that they are unusual in the day-to-day run of ordinary consciousness; however, they are not unusual in these circumstances, as being close to death is not an ordinary event. The existence of the devil is not something that can be proven, though a good many people believe there is such an entity; if that is what the person believes, then that is the way the situation should be approached. Also, many people believe these kinds of event point to the reality of life after death, which also cannot be proven in any scientific sense but to which the same response is applicable.

The most useful answer to the question of "What is happening?" is that these are expectable end-of-life events of unknown origin. They happen. They can be interpreted from religious or secular perspectives. They are intensely meaningful to the person having the experience and to the family.

Whether or not a class can be offered, make reliable reading material available. If a small actual library is not possible, at least provide a list of books and articles.

For an easy-to-read introductory look at death-related events, Mendoza's (2008) easy-to-read book *We Do Not Die Alone* gives an anecdote-filled overview of a broad variety of situations and types of experience, including distressing ones. The book *Final Gifts* by hospice nurses Maggie Callanan (1997) and Patricia Kelley introduced the term "nearing death awareness" to describe the way persons close to death often express their needs in metaphoric terms. The book has become a staple for hospice personnel and the family members and friends of people who are close to death.

The most reliable source of information about these types of event is IANDS, the International Association for Near-Death Studies. They can provide reading and audiovisual materials, a comprehensive bibliography, suggested speakers, a list of local support groups, and more. Contact information is on their very interesting website, http://iands.org

Action resources

Protocol
Because a deathbed panic or severe agitation is so upsetting for staff

and family members as well as for the patient, it is helpful to develop a protocol for how to deal with such a situation.

Patient spiritual history
More and more research demonstrates the value of knowing something about a patient's background and interests, at least to the extent of knowing the person's attitude toward religious practice, religious beliefs or lack thereof, childhood religious training, favorite music, anxieties or fears about dying, interest in talking with a chaplain.

Staff
Be sure there is at least one staff member who has had training, experience, or at least a reading background on distressing NDEs and deathbed visions and is prepared to handle a difficult situation. Put that person's contact information on the posted protocol. In a facility with a chaplaincy service, list the chaplain; in fact, make friends with the chaplain. Although it may sound odd in a clinical setting, know who on staff is a good pray-er. As with any other activity, some people have more skill at prayer than others; include cleaning staff and aides as appropriate. (It is not necessary for all praying to be done aloud, and it can be done from a distance, but the warmth of hands-on prayer by a person of faith is legendary.)

Materials
Build a small library of patient aids: music CDs to play for the dying (quiet hymns, harp music, instrumental music); a loose-leaf notebook or small book of prayers, scripture, and the words to well-known hymns that can be read aloud. In my view, every caregiver at every level should have a stash of brief memorized prayers, affirmations, and poems or song lyrics to call on when needed.

What to do
Having theoretical information is important, but even more essential is knowing what to do should a crisis arise. Instances of a patient's

severe distress or outright panic are fortunately not common, but no hospital or hospice should be unaware of the possibility. Some hints:

Accept that the person is actually experiencing whatever is going on, so it matters that you respond accordingly. Shouting, "There's nothing there!" will not help.

Having essential background information on patients will suggest what an individual may respond to.

Assessment

As with any clinical emergency, when a distressing deathbed event occurs, check what is going on in the room. Hearing is the last of the senses to remain clear, but a disoriented person may not be able to translate sound accurately.

What is the patient seeing or hearing? Difficult experiences for patients have been precipitated by family members arguing over the bed of a semi-comatose parent; by hellfire preaching or warnings of doom coming from a radio or television; by noisy equipment or harsh noises from radio or TV; by loud staff joking and talking nearby; by a busy setting, as when a confused patient is left unattended by the nursing station or in a heavily trafficked hallway. Restoring a peaceful environment may make all the difference.

In case of a patient's deathbed panic

Some situations break too fast for intervention, like that of the young man cowering in the corner. In that case, the caregivers' own prayers and visualizations have to suffice. They can be very powerful. Even in the midst of such a rush and confusion, it is possible to quickly visualize the person in a circle of light, and to pray whatever is quick and meaningful—"Lord, have mercy"; the Shema—"Hear, O Israel, the Lord our God, the Lord is one", "Guides, come to him!"; a heartfelt "*God, help!*"; or simply "Peace!" Supplications like this can run in the mental background while physical attention goes to the tasks at hand.

When there's no time for conversation, offer something sustaining in place of the terror. Having essential background information on patients will suggest what an individual may respond to—a psalm, a prayer, a popular song.—say it out loud; sing it. If you don't know, try "Amazing Grace," try the 23rd Psalm.

In case of drawn out fear (the woman at the nursing desk)
Any person going through prolonged, obvious distress needs assistance. Reassurance is key. Assure the person that she is not alone, and that help is available.

At eye level with the person, offer assurance. Say, "It will be all right. *You* will be all right." Mean it. The reassurance can be as simple as, "I'm here with you to help." "You are safe now."

Consider small amounts of relaxing medication as a first recourse (I am told by an experienced hospice nurse this should not include Ativan).

Help them put something in place of the terror. Often this is singing—back to "Amazing Grace," or it could be a simple children's song like Mr. Rogers' "It's a beautiful day in the neighborhood." "Jesus Loves Me," or "Sesame Street." Even a sweetly sung "Itsy bitsy spider" will do. If you don't know any hymns, sing whatever you do know; and it doesn't matter if you can't carry a tune. Sing part of a line and see if the person can fill in the last word. Make your own list of things you can memorize. Tuck a list somewhere in the nursing unit.

Call on the chaplain. The authority of clergy is a great gift at such a time, and in some instances a ritual may be helpful. If the person is afraid, as this woman was, of the prospect of hell, a reminder is appropriate of Bible teachings about God's love and forgiveness; the chaplain can make a brief ceremony of forgiveness to help.

There are, of course, patients who have said they do not want to see a chaplain or any member of clergy. The approaches mentioned here are suggested because they can be done by clergy or any lay person.

Sometimes a more visual suggestion of protection can get through to a frightened person. Here, keep in mind that *what the patient can use is more important than your own beliefs* (or lack thereof). This is not the time to discuss or even consider your own theological or philosophical views. It may be helpful to keep repeating out loud a phrase appropriate to the person's beliefs, if you know them: "You are safe in a bubble of light." "You are in a circle of the white light of Christ," "Jesus, come to this child," or simply, "I have put up a shield to protect you." Use your own words; the point is to get across that protection is standing between the person and the danger. In the case of the specific woman mentioned earlier, it would have been appropriate to say firmly, "The devil can't reach you. You are safe in a circle/a fence of light. You are protected. Christ/God/Elijah is with you." A down-to-earth prayer might say, "Oh, honey, I'm praying that devil away. You're safe now."

Enlist the person's participation. "Who is there to help you? Look for your guide/ /your angel/your friend." If she says no one is there, suggest she invite someone. Who would they like to have with them? Living, dead, known personally or not—the point is that the patient is not going alone.

Depending on what is known about the patient's personal background, one can say, "Call God (or Jesus/Mary/Elijah/Allah to be with you." "Surround yourself with the white light of Christ." "Ask your guardian angel to help." "Go toward the light."

If it is not upsetting to the patient, hold the person's hand or lay a hand on the shoulder while talking. Be aware that a person in an alarmed state of consciousness may experience touch as an attack; it may help to say you are going to touch them before actually doing so.

Out loud, say the Lord's Prayer or a psalm. It should be easy enough to locate a Christian Bible; for Jewish patients, here is the 23rd psalm in a translation from the Jewish Study Bible:

Psalm 23

> The Lord is my Shepherd, I need nothing more.
> He makes me lie down in green pastures;
>   He leads me to water in places of repose;
>   He renews my life;
> He guides me in right paths as befits His name.

> Though I walk in the valley of the shadow of death,
> I fear no harm, for You are with me;
> Your rod and Your staff, they comfort me.
> You spread a table before me in full view of my enemies.
> You soothe my head with oil; my drink is abundant.
> Only goodness and steadfast love shall pursue me all the days of my life, and I shall dwell in the house of the Lord for many long years.

In case of processing after a difficult experience
Give reassurance: Yes, a distressing near-death or similar experience is difficult to go through, but this is a puzzle, not a punishment. It does not mean the patient is a bad person, or doomed. Saints have had experiences like these. There is no evidence supporting the common assumption that a good person will have a good NDE, and a bad person will have a frightening one. Some people who have had more than one NDE have had both pleasant and difficult kinds.

Saints and holy people throughout time have reported having terrifying spiritual experiences (see St. Teresa's description in Chapter 6). Like them, try to look for the message behind the fear. Keep praying. If the person does not pray, try affirmations.

There is some evidence (Bache, 2000) that a frightening NDE or similar event is simply incomplete. Based on many years of therapeutic experience, there is reason to believe that when a difficult NDE has discharged fully or goes on long enough (whatever "long enough" may mean), it becomes blissful.

As a basic exercise, do deep breathing with imaging: breathe in light, breathe out all darkness and fear; breathe in peace, breathe out fear; modify for the individual

As an ongoing technique, suggest the visualization of being protected within a circle: "Think of yourself surrounded by a bubble of light/by the white light of Christ/by an invisible shield."

As I hope this book has indicated, for the universe (and for us, living in it), reality includes both darkness and light. The darkness is never solely conclusive. For easily available books with accounts of pleasant and radiant NDEs, read the original book, Raymond Moody's *Life After Life*; or, for a sound research perspective, especially for Christian readers, Michael Sabom's *Light and Death*; or, for a comprehensive view with a more New Age approach, P.M.H. Atwater's *The Big Book of Near-Death Experiences*. See the website of www.iands.org for experience accounts, most of which are positive. Their stories of light-filled accounts balance the negativity of distressing NDEs and need to be heard or read again and again.

Suggest that the person choose a friendly guide as a companion (who may be living or dead, someone known or perhaps a religious or heroic figure).

See the suggestions in the previous chapter about reframing: what other meaning might there be for the images from the frightening experience; what other interpretations could be given?

Tell the wonderful stories, the radiant NDEs. Play the audio of any IANDS conference panel of experiencers describing their NDEs.

See nurse comment #3 above: "If you see _____, you can do this _____."

See all the techniques suggested in Chapter 10.

Look for the Light and go for it.

If the person has time enough, it is helpful to do some of the end-of-life things that hospice helps with and that may enable the person to feel proactively engaged. Even a very frail person can do some things to prepare for the journey—what people have done for centuries when going on a pilgrimage. Some version of the following advice from a sermon delivered in the year 1125 (Zaleski, 40) is found in almost any hospice today:

- Think of the people who have injured you, and forgive them.
- Think of any person you have injured, and apologize (the person need not be there physically) and ask forgiveness. Give back anything that is not rightfully yours.
- Find a peaceful solution for conflicts that are within your

control; visualize a peaceful solution for conflicts that are not in your control.
- Put your house in good order; or ask someone to write down some things that need to be done.
- Tell God (or the Universe) you are sorry and are doing what you can to make things right; let God (or the Universe) forgive you

Responding to family and friends
When a patient has had a difficult NDE, family and friends are almost certain to be distraught. Helping them involves most of the same approaches that are suggested with patients. They need the same assurances, the same techniques for getting past their anxiety.

Whether or not the person dies, staff and family will need support afterward. Many people have been comforted to know that a good deal of research has shown that a terrifying spiritual experience that runs its course will transform into an experience of bliss and acceptance. Howard Storm's story may be helpful. Saints have reported terrifying spiritual encounters; the experience does not automatically mean that the patient is in hell. Recognize that this information may not be welcomed by people who are tightly bound by religious views of literal hell fire and damnation, who may believe that talk outside their vocabulary is a satanic delusion; their pastor will be the necessary resource.

APPENDIX 2

Experiencer Accounts

These additional accounts offer a fuller picture of the range and variety of distressing near-death experiences than the few examples provided earlier.

Afraid of the light

Donald
A 64-year-old man developed a postoperative infection following surgery for an aneurysm. At first he felt motion and seemed to be traveling, on a train, he thought, nearly filled with passengers. They were wearing black hats with black veils which covered their faces and were tied under the chin. The train made several stops, and at each one some passengers got off. After a while he realized that he was the only passenger remaining. Then:

"I was now in the last row of the train, alone. The train started with an awful jerk and stopped short, and I was jerked from my seat and tossed in the air away from the train. As I looked under me, the train was melting. [A] strong wind was pulling me into what seemed to be a funnel shaped like a cornucopia, only opened at both ends.

I was flying and drawn directly into the vortex or funnel. At the end the lights were blinding and crystal flashing was unbearable. As I neared the very end I was reaching for the sides, trying to stop myself from falling off the end into the flashing crystal. I felt that I did not want to go on. If there were some way I could explain to you what happened! I vividly remember screaming, "God, I'm not ready. Please help me." As I write this letter I am reliving it. I remember [that] when I screamed an arm shot out of the sky and grabbed my hand, and at the last second I was kept from falling off the end of the funnel, the lights flashing, and the heat was really something."

The Void

Iris

Not uncommonly, a person who has had a near-death experience will recall it in fragments over a period of time, not all at once. That may be what happened with this young woman four months after her NDE in 1986.

"It was close to Christmas, and my cat had died three days before. I was getting dressed this particular morning, brushing my teeth, and as I looked into the mirror I started to grieve over the cat, realizing that I would never see her again... It was four months after my NDE, and I was so completely open with the absolute knowledge that Everything Is Love that I knew there was nothing that could hurt me... As I looked into the mirror I realized I was, at that very moment, floating in space. "Almost simultaneously the deep Realization or Total Knowledge hit me that I had died and I was completely alone, never to be with any loved ones, or for that matter, no living thing again in any form... Even though this experience only lasted about ten seconds, I was in a place or state of consciousness that I didn't know [the time]. To me it was for all eternity.

"There is really no way to describe or explain what this experience felt like, except to say that if a person was to allow himself or herself to mentally conjure up a scenario that represented the greatest amount of fear and terror that individual could imagine and then multiply it by five billion, it still wouldn't equal what I felt.

"As this horrible feeling overtook me I started screaming "No! No!" I could see my body on the other side of the mirror, and hard as I tried to pull myself back into it, it was as if some huge force was pulling me back out into space. I finally, with the hardest struggle, made it back into my body, which was just standing there at the sink. . . and I wanted to call my husband to confirm that I was in fact here. I actually wondered if my body had enough gravity to hold me on the earth since I had just been in a weightless situation."

In comments she sent later, the same experiencer says,

"The emotional pain of complete separation and isolation was terrifying and horrible! [I tried to escape] by screaming "No! No!' and clawing my way back into my body. As I struggled to get back in my body I suddenly found myself back. I don't know how it happened. I felt this place in space holding the pure energy of Aloneness ('hell') was an accumulation of all the fears ever felt in the world. (Even a lobster, with its nervous system, can perceive pain in its last few seconds boiling alive. That pain, fear, etc. goes into the 'hell Energy' we must ultimately resolve)."

Jeannie
"Eleven years ago I had a near death experience. I found myself floating in a void and nobody was there, not even God. I was overwhelmed with loneliness and despair because I knew this was eternity. I don't know how long this lasted or if I stopped breathing. I was being strangled at the time. If you need to know these things the man who attacked me might remember. . . Just don't tell him where I am. I hope this will help your research."

Kyle
This is from the recollection of an accident when the writer was eleven:
"I lost consciousness again and all that I remember was being very alone. I could hear a high piercing sound, and all that existed was

a white light. I was afraid that this was eternity and I would be lost here forever with nothing but my consciousness."

Louis
Finally, this was the experience of a 50-year-old man, suffering an episode of angina pain at home, for whom the Void suggested an impending hell:

"The thought occurred to me that I might be passing into another life or something. But—there was no color, no sound, no heat, no cold. Nothing! I asked myself if this was what I had been working toward?—is this all there is? Is this what I would get for faith and abstinence?...Lutherans are taught that one is justified by faith alone...and I was doubting! I was really frightened! Terrified! I was weak in faith! I was going to go to hell! I started praying, real sincere prayer...prayer for faith. 'Don't let me go to hell! Strengthen my faith! Give me another chance. Send me back! Give me faith! More faith! "I was back and up by the ceiling and then back in my body. My doctor says it was a dream. No way! My eyes were open and I was in pain. . . My pastor, who is completely lacking in emotion and extremely anti-spiritual, says it was hallucinations."

Hell

1. "When I convulsed and lost consciousness I will never forget the terrible horror it was as though screaming demons were pulling at me. I can't think of anything more terrifying. I came to for a couple of minutes, then began to go under again, and I screamed to the doctors not to let me go back to that terrible place. Of course they didn't know what I was talking about. However, this time when I lost consciousness I knew nothing. It has left a horror in my mind. I have never spoken about it until now [29 years later]."

2. "I underwent the operation. I was supposedly dead for fifteen minutes. [The doctor] thought he lost me, but I fought back

for I was fighting the Master of Death. Master of Death was in an alcove all covered. Couldn't see face only form. I won the battle for I told him that I wanted to see my son get married. When I won the battle from him, I saw the most beautiful picture. Which is very hard to describe."

Elise

A licensed practical nurse, Elise had a hysterectomy at age 36, followed by a pelvic abscess with a fever documented at 105.6 degrees Fahrenheit. She describes shaking uncontrollably, being unable to hold a thermometer and accidentally breaking it with her teeth, and then…

"I don't know what happened next or how, but I was no longer in my hospital bed, but I—not as we know me, a solid human form, but myself, my energy, or my mind—was in a place surrounded by a misty gray cloudlike substance. I then began to see lights flashing in a circular shape, advancing towards me at a rapid speed, then retreating after coming inches from my face. This continued for a period of time, and I was terribly frightened. I felt as if I were transfixed.

"Then I began to talk to myself nonverbally. I said to myself, 'You can handle this; you're strong; you'll be okay,' and continued to repeat this and pray to God. I felt near death.

Then suddenly I was overcome by a feeling of *complete peace*. [Her italics.] My feelings were that I was safe, and it was beautiful, weightless. I loved it. I felt at one with all, a great joy and ultimate peace of mind and body. I knew no harm in any way would come to me. All was peaceful, and profound love surrounded me. There is no description on earth that can compare with this place and feeling. I felt something was saying, 'You're safe now; don't be afraid; this peace will help you.'

After this happened, I just came back. I refer to this as leaving and coming back, as that's how I feel. My body was there, but where was I?…Anyone who has felt this peace would never want to leave or have it leave them."

Fleur

Another young woman tells of resisting an out-of-body experience in the initial stages of a vivid NDE. She was 27 and immediately postpartum, in surgery for repair of extensive uterine lacerations.

"Suddenly I became aware that something really strange was happening. It was as if I had pulled up and away from my body, and from a corner of the room near the ceiling I found myself watching my doctor and his nurse working on my body. I felt so startled at being able to hover above like that. And I wanted to feel in control of my situation, but I was unable to do anything except watch helplessly. I made some attempts to get the attention of the other two [people] in the room, but they were totally oblivious to anything I was saying to them.

"Then I found myself no longer in the room but traveling through a tunnel, slowly at first, then picking up speed as I went. As I entered the tunnel I began hearing the sound of an engine, the kind that operates heavy machinery. Then, as I was moving slowly I could hear voices on each side of my head, the voices of people whom I've known before, because they were vaguely familiar. About this time I became frightened, so I didn't concentrate on trying to recognize any of the voices.

"I found myself growing more and more afraid as the speed picked up, and I realized that I was headed toward a pinpoint of light at the end of the tunnel. The thought came that this was probably what it was like to die. I decided then and there that I wanted to go no further, and I tried to backpedal, stop, turn around—but to no avail. I could control nothing, and the pinpoint of light grew larger and larger. Before I knew it, that light exploded around me. I should also report that my attitude at this time was quite terrified I did not want to be there, and I was determined that I was not, by God, going to stay.

"There were beings all around me and they acknowledged my presence. The beings were quite amused at me. They totally accepted me into their midst and didn't seem to mind one bit that I was cranky and demanding to know where I was, and who did they think they were anyhow, snatching me away like that! 'Put me back, damn it, put me back!'

"Slowly my ruffled feathers became smoothed, and I felt peaceful and calm. So I began going along with this weird experience and became accepting of them, too. We began to have a question and answer time. I would ask the questions and instead of receiving a wordy reply, they would show me the answer. We moved from place to place with no effort at all, and I learned a great deal.

"Finally the beings made it clear to me that I could return to the delivery room, and I found myself traveling back through either a tunnel or a hallway of some sort. This went very quickly, and I became aware of my doctor and his nurse again. Within a brief instant, I was inside my head…Then I felt the sensation, throughout the rest of my body, that we would have if we slipped on a glove over our hand."

Curt

The last experience in this section, another "transformed" account, is also not from the Greyson/Bush study, but is included here because it contains elements familiar in world mythologies of hell but which did not appear in our study sample. Stories of the harrowing of hell appears throughout history, stories in which an individual voluntarily undertakes the perilous journey into the otherworld on a quest, sometimes to rescue someone who has died. Not only is this account startling in its echoing the Greek myth of Orpheus and Eurydice, but the theme is apparently universal. Eliade mentions such stories from China; Wikipedia refers to the same in Japan, Akkadia/Sumer, and the Mayans; and Barry Lopez (1977, 131-134) has recounted a similar tradition involving Coyote from the Nez Perce. Here is a modern version (Fiore and Landburg) that occurred when the German actor Curt Jurgens had an episode of clinical death during heart surgery with the famed Dr. Michael DeBakey.

"I had been looking up into the big glass cupola over the operating room. This cupola now began to change. Suddenly it turned a glowing red. I saw twisted faces grinning as they stared down at me. . . . I tried to struggle upright and defend myself. . . Then it seemed as if the glass cupola had turned into a transparent dome that was slowly sinking down over me. A fiery rain was now falling, but though the drops were enormous, none of them touched me. They splattered down around me, and out of them grew menacing tongues of flames. . . . I could no longer shut out the frightful truth: beyond doubt, the faces dominating this fiery world were the faces of the damned. I had a feeling of despair, of being unspeakably alone and abandoned. The sense of horror was so great that it choked me, and I had the impression that I was about to suffocate. Obviously, I was in hell itself.

"In this situation, the black silhouette of a human figure suddenly materialized and began to draw near. At first I saw it only indistinctly amid the flames and clouds of reddish smoke, but quickly it became clearer; It was a woman in a black veil, a slender woman with a lipless mouth, and in her eyes an expression that sent icy shudders down my back. When she was standing right face to face with me, all I could see were two black, empty holes. But out of these holes the creature was nonetheless staring at me. The figure stretched out her arms toward me, and, pulled by an irresistible force, I followed her. An icy breath touched me, and I came into a world filled with faint sounds of lamentation, although there was not a person in sight.

"Then and there I asked the figure to tell me who she was. A voice answered: 'I am death.' I summoned all my strength and thought: 'I'll not follow her anymore, for I want to live.' Had I betrayed this thought?

"In any event, she moved closer to me and put her hands on my bare breast so that I would again be under the spell of her magnetic force. I could feel her ice-cold hands on my skin, and the empty eye sockets were fixed immovably on me. I concentrated all my thoughts on living, so as to escape death in this womanly guise.

"Before entering the operating room, I had embraced my wife Simone. Now the phantom of my wife came to rescue me from hell and lead me back to earthly existence. When Simone appeared on the scene, the woman with the black veil departed soundlessly, on her lipless face a dreadful smile. Death could avail nothing against Simone, all radiant with youth and life.

"I felt only freshness and tenderness as she led me back by the hand along the same way that just before had been under the dark figure's spell.

"Gradually we left the fearful realm of shadows behind us and approached the great light. This luminousness guided us on, and finally became so bright that it began to blind me, and I had to close my eyes.

"Then suddenly a severe, dull pain set in, threatening to tear apart my chest cavity. I clutched Simone's hand harder and harder after my sudden return to consciousness. I found Simone sitting on my bed wearing a white nurse's uniform. I just had the strength to muster a weak smile. It was all I could do to utter one word: 'Thanks.'

"With this word I concluded a fearful but still fascinating journey into the afterworld, one I shall never forget as long as I live."

APPENDIX 3
IANDS
The International Association for Near-Death Studies

As an educational nonprofit 501(c)(3) organization, the International Association for Near-Death Studies (IANDS) focuses most of its resources on providing the highest quality information available about NDE-related subjects. Now in its fourth decade of service, it remains the only such membership group in the world.

The Association's purpose is to promote responsible, multi-disciplinary exploration of near-death and similar experiences, their effects on people's lives, and their implications for beliefs about life, death, and human purpose. Where scholarship does not indicate a reasonably clear position on the origin or interpretation of these experiences, the Association's position is to remain impartial and open to the presentation of varying points of view. IANDS never supports proselytizing.

IANDS maintains an information-rich website and an online archive of experience accounts, publishes a peer-reviewed scholarly journal and a member newsletter, sponsors conferences and other programs, works with the media, and encourages the formation of regional discussion and support groups.

Contact information is at the website: www.iands.org

Acknowledgments

Over the years, so many people have contributed to the making of this book, I have in all likelihood omitted some of their names, and for that I ask forgiveness. My conscious and heartfelt thanks—make that unconditional love—go to them and all the following:

IANDS, the International Association for Near-Death Studies, the home ground for thirty years of incomparable transformation; and Ken Ring, who invited me in. Diane Corcoran, who got me to stay longer than either of us dreamed. Bruce Greyson, whose collaboration on the first study opened the door; who has always, sometimes hilariously, answered emails; who said I must write this book, and who has given more than he knows.

To the fifty who first shared and to all those since, for whom speaking has taken sometimes great courage; you have enabled all the rest.

To every author named in the References; for at the beginning, there was nothing.

Wayne Rollins, scholar, light in a darkness, friend—and what an editor! Peter Grandy, pastor and friend, for insights that cut through the…well, that cut through. J. Harold Ellens, respected for his scholarship, blessed for his support, now adored for his outlook. The late Richard Underwood, who was planting seeds. Lou Savary and Pat Berne, exemplars.

"The Revs," ordained and not: Marilyn Mendoza, Carolyn Fleming-Sawyerr, Fran Sansone-Pelletier, Mickie Norman, Gerald Blackburn, David Suggs. Thanks always and blessings, from me and the caregivers.

Margot Gray, and Kimberly Clark Sharp and P.M.H Atwater for all the years, and for knowing what was out there. Allen Kellehear, Michael Grosso, and Carol Zaleski for support you didn't know you were providing.

To manuscript readers who talked back: Madelaine Lawrence, Maggie Callanan, Mary Fond Daughtridge, the Rev. Barry Kubler, and my daughter Leigh Gray Kenyon. My daughter Katy Evans-Bush for knowing about everything I didn't. Nancy K. Humphreys, Susan Pomeroy, and Natasha Fondren for going so far beyond the expected and making things happen. Henry Brand for unfailing support, matchless enthusiasm, and filling in the blanks.

For being in my life and sustaining sanity: Anneliese Fox, Jayne Smith, Ed Bosk, Allen Katzoff, the late and much-grieved Leslee Morabito and Bonnie Johnson Shurman.

My family: my sisters: Barbara Keating, Mary Evans Vink'Lainas, Rhondda Hardy; my children: Katy Evans-Bush, Leigh Gray Kenyon, Adam Bush; yes, the grandkids: Daniel, Emil, Nat, Daisy, Maggie Pearl, and Katya Rose, and Peter and Xander; and beyond expressing, Nancy Poe Fleming, who for three decades and counting has made everything possible.

References

Allnurses.com (2008). Death bed visions. Created May 8, 2008 Retrieved from http://allnurses.com/general-nursing-discussion/death-bed-visions-301825.html October 18, 2010.

Almond, G., Appleby, R. & Sivan, E. (2003). *Strong religion: The rise of fundamentalisms around the world.* Chicago: University of Chicago Press.

Armstrong, K. (2007) *The great transformation: The beginning of our religious traditions.* New York: Anchor.

Atwater, P.M.H. (1992). Is there a hell? Surprising observations about the near-death experience. *Journal of Near-Death Studies* 10:149-60.

Atwater, P.M.H. (1994) *Beyond the light: What isn't being said about near-death experience.* New York: Birch Lane.

Atwater, P.M.H. (1988). *Coming back to life.* New York: Dodd-Mead.

Aztec mythology and their underworld, Mictlan. Retrieved from http://www.river-styx.net/aztec-myth-mictlan.htm July 16, 2010.

Bache, C. (1994). A perinatal interpretation of frightening near-death experiences: A dialogue with Kenneth Ring. *Journal of Near-Death Studies* 13:25-45.

Bache, C. (2000). *Dark night, early dawn: Steps to a deep ecology of mind* (SUNY Series in Transpersonal and Humanistic Psychology) Albany, NY: State University of New York Press.

Bailey, L & Wade, J. eds. (1996). *The near-death experience: A reader.* New York: Routledge.

Beck, R. (2006). Retrieved from http://experimentaltheology.blogspot.com/2006/06/game-theory-and-kingdom-of-god-quirky_07.html April 21, 2011

Beck, R. (2006b). Retrieved from. http://experimentaltheology.blogspot.com/2006/10/why-i-am-universalist-part-3-gift-of.html April 18, 2011

Beck, R. (2007). Retrieved from http://experimentaltheology.blogspot.com/2007/11/death-and-doctrine-part-1-need-for-ante.html April 18, 2011.

Beck, R. (2007b). Retrieved from http://experimentaltheology.blogspot.com/2007/11/death-and-doctrine-part-2-on-why-hell.html April 20, 2011.

Becker, Ernest. (1974, 1991). *The Denial of Death.* New York: Free Press.

Bernard. (2010). Cantica Canticorum, Sermon LXXIV, in Underhill, E. (2010). *Mysticism.* Charleston, SC: Nabu Press.

Bivins, J. (2007). The religion of fear: Conservative evangelicals, identity, and anti-liberal pop. *Journal for Cultural and Religious Theory*, 8.2, 2007. p 82. Retrieved from http://www.jcrt.org/archives/08.2/bivins.pdf July 8, 2009.

Bivins, J. (2008). *Religion of fear: The politics of horror in conservative evangelicalism.* New York: Oxford University Press.

Borg, M. (2002). *Reading the Bible again for the first time.* New York: HarperCollins.

Borysenko, J. (1993). *Fire in the soul: A new psychology of spiritual optimism.* New York: Warner Books.

Brashler, J. and Bullard, R., translators. *The Apocalypse of Peter.* The Nag Hammadi Library / The Gnostic Society Library Retrieved from http://www.gnosis.org/naghamm/apopet.html November 7, 2009

Bratcher, D. (2011). Interpreting the book of Revelation. Retrieved from http://www.crivoice.org/therevelation.html November 20, 2011

Brinkley, D. (1994). *Saved by the light.* New York: Villard.

Bro, H.H. (1993). New Age spirituality: A critical appraisal. In Ferguson, D. *New Age spirituality: An assessment.* Louisville, KY: Westminster/John Knox.

Buber, M. (1947). *Tales of the Hasidim: Early masters.* New York: Shocken Books.

Bush, N.E. (1994). The paradox of Jonah: Response to "Solving the riddle of frightening near-death experiences." *Journal of Near-Death Studies* 13(1), 47-54.

Bush, N.E. (2002). Afterward: Making meaning after a frightening near-death experience. *Journal of Near-Death Studies* 21(2), 99-133.

Bush, N.E. (2009). Distressing Western near-death experiences: Finding a way through the abyss. *Handbook of Near-Death Experiences: Thirty Years of Scholarly Inquiry.* Praeger.

Byrne, R. (2006). *The secret.* New York: Atria/Beyond Words.

Callanan, M. and Kelley, P. (1997). *Final gifts: Understanding the special awareness, needs, and communications of the dying.* New York: Bantam.

Campbell, J. (1986). *The inner reaches of outer space: Metaphor as myth and as religion.* New York: Harper & Row, 1986.

Carlson, R. Demon. Retrieved from http://theophiliacs.com/2008/09/14/demons/ (2008, November 3)

Carter, C. (2010). *Science and the near-death experience: How consciousness survives death.* Rochester, VT: Inner Traditions.

Chödrön, P. (1997). *When things fall apart: Heart advice for difficult times.* Boston and London: Shambhala.

Chödrön, P. (2001). *The places that scare you: A guide to fearlessness in difficult times.* Boston and London: Shambhala.

Chödrön, P. (2010 reprint). *Taking the leap: Freeing ourselves from old habits and fears.* Boston and London: Shambhala.

Chopelas, P. (Undated). Heaven and hell in the afterlife, according to the Bible. Retrieved from http://aggreen.net/beliefs/heaven_hell.html. September 12, 2001.

Conze, E. (1981). *Buddhism: Its essence and development.* New York: Harper & Row. In Smith, H., (1991, 115). *The world's religions.* San Francisco: Harper.

Corbett, L. (1996). *The religious function of the psyche.* London: Routledge.

Corneille, A. (1989). Death: A beginning?, *Everybody's News,* October 27-November 9, 1989, 4.

Courant. (2010). Retrieved from http://articles.courant.com/2010-0112/news/10011212532342_1_ home-language-non-english-west-hartford January 12, 2010.

Cousins, E. (1994). *Christ of the 21st century.* New York: Continuum.

Cuneo, M. (2001). *American exorcism: Expelling demons in the land of plenty.* New York: Doubleday.

Dawson, S. (2004). Jesus' teachings on hell. Retrieved from http://www.tentmaker.org/articles/jesusteachingonhell.html January 14, 2011.

Dorsey, G. (1995). *Congregation: The journey back to church.* New York: Viking. 1995.

Eadie, B. (1992). *Embraced by the light.* Placerville, CA: Gold Leaf Press.

Edinger, E. (1986). *Encounter with the self: A Jungian commentary on William Blake's Illustrations of the book of Job.* Toronto: Inner City Books.

Edinger, E. (1972). *Ego and archetype.* New York: G.P.Putnam's Sons.

Eichmann, W. (1991). In Zweig, C. and Abrams, J. *Meeting the shadow: The hidden power of the dark side of human nature.* Los Angeles: Jeremy P. Tarcher/Perigee.

Eiseley, L. (1959). The snout. *The immense journey.* New York: Vintage.

Eliade, M. (1964). *Shamanism: Archaic techniques of ecstasy.* Princeton, NJ: Princeton University Press (Bollingen).

Eliade, M. (1954). *The myth of the eternal return: cosmos and history.*

Princeton, NJ: Princeton University Press (Bollingen).

Ellens, J. H. (1981). Biblical authority and Christian psychology: II. *Psychology and Theology, 9*, 318-325.

Elliott, A. (2011, March 20). A marked man in America. *The New York Times Magazine.* http://query.nytimes.com/gst/fullpage.html?res=9B03E4D81F3EF933A15750C0A9679D8B63&pagewanted=1

Ellwood, G. F. (2001). *The uttermost deep: The challenge of near-death experiences.* Brooklyn, NY: Lantern.

Enns, P. (2011). (Shut up, already) and listen to the desert. Retrieved from http://www.patheos.com/blogs/peterenns/ 2011/12/shut-up-already-and-listen-to-the-desert/ December 10, 2011.

Farnáz M. (2002). *Life after death: A study of the afterlife in world religions.* Los Angeles: Kalimat Press.

Fenwick, P. and Fenwick, E. (1997). *The truth in the light: An investigation of over 300 near-death experiences.* New York: Berkly Trade.

Ferguson, D. (1993). *New Age spirituality: An assessment.* Louisville, KY: John Knox.

Fiore, C. & Landsburg, A. (1979). *Death encounters.* New York: Bantam.

Flynn, C. (1986). *After the beyond.* Englewood Cliffs, NJ: Prentice Hall.

Foster, R. (1978). *Celebration of discipline: The path to spiritual growth.* San Francisco: Harper & Row.

Fowler, J. (1981). *Stages of faith: The psychology of human development and the quest for meaning.* San Francisco: Harper & Row.

Fox, M. (1983). *Original blessing: A primer on creation spirituality.* Los Angeles: Jeremy P. Tarcher/Putnam.

Fox, M. (1988). *The coming of the cosmic Christ.* San Francisco: HarperOne.

Fox, M. (2002). *Religion, spirituality and the near-death experience.* London: Routledge.

Franklin Institute (2004). Stress and noise. Retrieved from http://www.fi.edu/learn/brain/stress.html#stressnoise June 6, 2009

Frankfurter, D. (2008). *Evil incarnate: Rumors of demonic conspiracy and satanic abuse in history.* Princeton, NJ: Princeton University Press. Retrieved from http://press.princeton.edu/chapters/s8135.html May 7, 2009

Frenier, C. and Hogan, L. ( ) Engaging the imaginal realm: Doorway to collective wisdom. Retrieved from http://www.collectivewisdominitiative.org/papers/frenierimaginal.htm November 26, 2011.

Gallup, Jr., G. & Proctor, W. (1982). *Adventures in immortality.* New York: McGraw-Hill.

Givens, D. (1998-2010). Retrieved from Center for Nonverbal Studies. http://center-for-nonverbal-studies.org/aromacue.htm June 5, 2007

Goodrick-Clark, N. (1985) *The Occult Roots of Naziism.* Retrieved from https://secure.wikimedia.org/wikipedia/en/wiki/Occult#cite_note-8 June 8, 2010.

Gray, M. (1985). *Return from death: An exploration of the near-death experience.* London: Arkana.

Green, A. (2004). *A guide to the Zohar.* Stanford, CA: Stanford University Press.

Greenspan, M. (2004). *Healing through the dark emotions: The wisdom of grief, fear, and despair.* Boston: Shambhala.

Greer, J. (2001). *Monsters: An investigator's guide to magical beings.* Woodbury, MN: Llewellyn.

Greyson, B. (1983). The Near-Death Experience Scale: Construction, reliability, and validity. *Journal of Nervous and Mental Disease 171*:369-75.

Greyson, Bruce. The psychodynamics of near-death experiences, *Journal of Nervous and Mental Disease,* 1983, 171, 376.

Greyson, B. (2000). Near-death experiences. In E. Cardeña, S.J. Lynn, and S. Krippner (Eds), *Varieties of anomalous experience: Examining the scientific evidence,* 315-53. Washington, DC: American Psychological Association.

Greyson, B. and Bush, N.E. (1992). Distressing near-death

experiences. *Psychiatry*, Vol 55, February.

Greyson. B. and Flynn, C.P., eds. (1984). *The near-death experience: Problems, prospects, perspectives.* Springfield, IL: Charles C. Thomas.

Grof, S. (1975). *Realms of the human unconscious.* New York: Dutton.

Grof, S. (1985). *Beyond the brain: Birth, death, and transcendence in psychotherapy.* Albany, NY: State University of New York Press.

Grof, S. (1988). *The adventure of self-discovery.* Albany, NY: State University of New York Press.

Grof, S. (1994) Alternative cosmologies and altered states. *Noetic Sciences Review,* Winter 1994, 21-29.

Grof, S. (2006). *The ultimate journey: Consciousness and the mystery of death.* Ben Lomond, CA: Multidisciplinary Association for Psychedelic Studies.

Grof, S. & Grof, C. (1979) *Spiritual Emergency: When personal transformation becomes a crisis.* Los Angeles: Jeremy P. Tarcher.

Grof, S. & Grof, C. (1980) *Beyond death: The gates of consciousness.* NY: Thames and Hudson.

Grosso, M. (1983). Jung, parapsychology, and the near-death experience: Toward a transpersonal paradigm. *Anabiosis: The Journal for Near-Death Studies* 3:3-38.

Grosso, M. (1986). *The final choice: Playing the survival game.* Walpole, NH: Stillpoint.

Hanson, J.W., DD. (1888). *The Bible Hell.* Boston: Universalist Publishing House. Retrieved from http://www.tentmaker.org/books/TheBibleHell.html#Gehenna May 2, 2011.

Haule, J. (1999). *Perils of the soul: Ancient wisdom and the new age.* York Beach, Maine: Weiser.

Heelas, P.(1996). *The New Age movement: Religion, culture and society in the age of postmodernity.* Oxford, UK: Wiley-Blackwell.

Hoffman, R. (1995a) Disclosure needs and motives after a near-death experience. *Journal of Near-Death Studies* 13, 237-266.

Hoffman, R. (1995b) Disclosure habits after near-death experiences:

Influences, obstacles, and listener selection. *Journal of Near-Death Studies* 13:29-48.

Holden, J. Long, J., & McClurg, B.J. (2009). Characteristics of Western near-death experiencers. In Holden, J., Greyson, B., & James, D. (Eds). *The handbook of near-death experiences: Thirty years of investigation.* Santa Barbara, CA: ABC-CLIO/Praeger.

Holy Bible: New International Version. (1993). Grand Rapids, MI: Zondervan.

Horgan, J. (2006). The God experiments: Five researchers take science where it's never gone before. *Discover.* From the December 2006 issue; published online November 20, 2006. Retrieved from http://discovermagazine.com/2006/dec/god-experiments January 7, 2008.

Houlihan, J. (2005) I=N=C=O=H=E=R=E=N=T: How contemporary American poets are denaturing the poem, *Web del Sol.* Retrieved June 7, 2005 from: http://www.webdelsol.com/LITARTSBoston_Comment/

Hurd, R. http://dreamstudies.org/2008/10/13/lucid-nightmares-fear-initiation-and-beyond/

Ingall, M. (2000). Stairway to Heaven? *Mademoiselle,* July, 94-96.

Jambor, M. (1997). The mystery of frightening transcendent experiences: A rejoinder to Nancy Evans Bush and Christopher Bache. *Journal of Near-Death Studies* 16(2), 163-176.

James, W (1988). *William James: Writings 1902-1910 : The varieties of religious experience / Pragmatism / A pluralistic universe / The meaning of truth / Some problems of philosophy / Essays.* New York: Library of America.

Jaspers, K. Retrieved from http://www.newworldencyclopedia.org/entry/Axial_Age September 5, 2009

Jung, C. (1933). The spiritual problem of modern man, *Modern Man in Search of a Soul.* London: Routledge & Kegan Paul,

Jung, C. (1945). The Philosophical Tree. In *Collected Works 13: Alchemical Studies.* 335

Jung, C. (1968). *Man and his symbols.* New York: Dell.

Jung, C. (1979). *Answer to Job: Researches into the relation between psychology and religion.* London: Routledge & Kegan Paul.

Jung, C. (1968). *Psychology and western religion,* Princeton, NJ: Princeton University Press.

Kastenbaum, R. (1996). Near-death reports: Evidence for survival of death? In Bailey, L. and Wade, J. *The near-death experience: A reader.* New York, Routledge.

Keats, J. (2005). Letter to his brother, in Douglas Wu, Ed. *Romanticism: an anthology,* 3rd ed. New York: Wiley-Blackwell.

Kellehear, A. (1996). *Experiences near death: Beyond medicine and religion.* New York: Oxford University Press.

Kelly, E. & Kelly, E. (2009). *Irreducible mind.* New York: Rowman and Littlefield.

Kelsey, M.(1972). *Encounter with God.* Minneapolis, MN: Bethany.

Kelsey, M. (1976). *The other side of silence.* New York: Paulist Press.

Kruglanski, A. (2004). *The psychology of closed mindedness.* East Sussex, UK: Psychology Press, 2004.

Kubler-Ross, E. (1969). *On death and dying.* New York: MacMillan.

Kung, H. (1984). *Eternal life? Life after death as a medical, philosophical, and theological problem.* Garden City, NY: Doubleday.

Kushner, H. (2004). *When bad things happen to good people.* New York: Anchor.

Kushner, L. (1977). *Honey from the rock: Visions of Jewish mystical renewal.* New York: Harper & Row.

LaBerge, S. & DeGracia, D.J. (2000). Varieties of lucid dreaming experience. In R.G. Kunzendorf & B. Wallace (Eds.), Individual Differences in Conscious Experience (pp. 269-307). Amsterdam: John Benjamins. Retrieved from http://www.lucidity.com/VOLDE.html August 5, 2009

Laing, R.D. (1979). "Transcendental Experience in Relation to Religion and Psychosis," in Grof, *Spiritual Emergency.*

Lambert, Y. (1999). Religion in modernity as a new axial age: Secularization or new religious forms? *Sociology of Religion.* Volume: 60. Issue: 3, 303. Publication Year: 1999. *Groupe de Sociologie des*

Religions et de La Laïcité Retrieved from http://www.questia.com/PM.qst?a=o&d=98493653

Leighton, S. (1991). God and the God image. *Journal of Near-Death Studies* Summer 9(4), 233-246

Lewis, C.S. (1956). *The Last Battle*, Book 7 of *The Chronicles of Narnia.* New York: MacMillan.

Lindlay, J., Bryan, S. and Conley, B. Near-death experiences in a Pacific Northwest American population: The Evergreen study, *Anabiosis*, (1)2, December, 1981, p. 113.

Lopez, B.(1977). Giving *birth to thunder, sleeping with his daughter: Coyote builds North America.* New York: Avon.

Lukeman, A.(1998). Book review of Edward F. Edinger, *Encounter with the self.* Retrieved from. *Tiger's Nest Review.* Created 3/25/98; accessed 9/4/01. http://www.frii.com/~tigrnest/encount.htm.

Lukeman, A. (2000). *Nightmares.* New York: M. Evans.

Machida, S. (1997). The soteriology of the Noh theater. Session 177: Japan. The world of demons and hells: The premodern and modern images. Association for Asian Studies conference 1997, Retrieved from http://www.aasianst.org/absts/1997abst/japan/j177.html June 18, 2009

Mack, C.K. & Mack, D. (1999). A field guide to demons, fairies, fallen angels and other subversive spirits. New York: Holt Paperbacks.

Marty, M. & Appleby, R.S. (1992). *Fundamentalisms observed (The fundamentalism project.)* Chicago: University of Chicago Press.

May, G. (1982). *Will and spirit: A contemplative psychology.* New York: Harper & Row.

May, R. (1969). *Love and will.* New York: Dell.

Meador, B. (2000). *Inanna Lady of Largest Heart: Poems of the Sumerian High Priestess Enheduanna.* Austin, TX: University of Texas Press.

Mendoza, M. (2008). *We do not die alone: "Jesus is coming to get me in a white pickup truck."* Dahlonga, GA: ICAN Publishing.

Montreal Zen Center. Retrieved from http://www.zenmontreal.ca/en/center/index.htm October 15, 2011.

Moody, R., Jr. (1975). *Life after life.* St. Simons Island, GA: Mockingbird Books.

Moody, R. Jr. (1977). *Reflections on life after life.* Covington, GA: Mockingbird Books.

Morse, M. (1990). *Closer to the light.* New York: Villard.

Morse, M. (1992). *Transformed by the light: The powerful effect of near-death experiences on people's lives.* New York: Villard, 1992.

Myss, C. (2010). You can't reason with illness, catastrophe, or God. Retrieved from http://www.oprah.com/spirit/You-Cant-Reason-with-Illness-Catastrophe-or-God-Caroline-Myss Retrieved January 30, 2010.

Naisbitt, J. and Auberdene, P. (1990). *Megatrends 2000.* New York: William Morrow.

Needham, R. (1978). *Primordial characters.* Charlottesville, VA: University Press of Virginia. Retrieved from : http://www.jstor.org/pss/2066002 May 14, 2009

Okeowo, A. (2008). Portal to Maya 'Hell' found in Mexico? November 10, 2008. Retrieved from http://news.nationalgeographic.com/news/2008/11/081110-maya-road-to-hell.html June 6, 2009.

Orne, R. M. (1995). The meaning of survival: The early aftermath of a near-death experience: *Research in Nursing & Health,* 18, 239-247.

Orr, J. (1915). Hell. *The International Standard Bible Encyclopedia.* Chicago: Howard-Severance.

Otto, R. (1958). *The idea of the holy.* Oxford: Oxford University Press.

Owens, J. (1992). In Klinkenborg, V. At the edge of eternity. *Life,* March 1992 (Vol. 15, No. 3), 64-73.

Pasarow, R. (1981). A personal account of an NDE: Reinee Pasarow. *Vital Signs,* December, 1981, 11.

Patch, H. (1970). *The otherworld, according to descriptions in medieval literature.* London: Octagon. In Turner, A. (1993) *The history of hell.* New York: Harcourt Brace.

Plott, J. (1977). *Global history of philosophy (Vol. 1) The Axial Age (250 B.C.)* Delhi: Motilal Banarsidass.

Ram Dass. (1989). Promises and pitfalls of the spiritual path. In Grof, S. and Grof, C. *Spiritual Emergency*. Los Angeles: Tarcher.

Rawlings, M. (1978). *Beyond death's door*. Nashville, TN: Thomas Nelson.

Rawlings, M. (1993). *To hell and back*. Nashville, TN: Thomas Nelson.

Rilke, R.M., transl. S. Mitchell. (1989). The Duino Elegies. *The selected poetry of Rainier Marie Rilke*. New York: Vintage.

Ring, K. (1980). *Life at death: A scientific investigation of the near-death experience*. New York: Coward, McCann and Geoghagen.

Ring, K. 1984. *Heading toward omega: In search of the meaning of the near-death experience*. New York: William Morrow.

Ring, K. (1994). Solving the riddle of frightening near-death experiences: Some testable hypotheses and a perspective based on A Course in Miracles. *Journal of Near-Death Studies*, 13:5-24.

Ritchie, G. (1978). *Return from tomorrow*. Carmel, NY: Guideposts.

Robbins, B.D. (1999). Emotion, movement, and psychological space: A sketching out of the emotions in terms of temporality, spatiality, embodiment, being-with, and language. Retrieved from http://mythosandlogos.com/emotion.html June 6, 2009

Roberts, R. (2003). Emotions: An essay in aid of moral psychology. Cambridge: Cambridge University Press. In Bivins, J. (2008), *Religion of fear: The politics of horror in conservative evangelicalism*. New York: Oxford University Press.

Roemischer, J. (2005). A new Axial Age. Interview with Karen Armstrong. Retrieved from http://www.enlightennext.org/magazine/j31/armstrong.asp?page=1 September 8, 2009.

Rogo, S. (1990). *The return from silence: A study of near-death experiences*. New York: Harper & Row.

Rommer, B. (2000) *Blessings in disguise. Another side of the near-death experience*. St. Paul: Llewellyn.

Ruysbroeck, Blessed John. The book of supreme truth. Retrieved from http://saints.sqpn.com/the-book-of-supreme-truth-by-blessed-john-ruysbroeck/ May 4, 2011

Sabom, M. & Kreutziger, S. (1982). *Recollections of death*. New York:

Harper & Row.
Sanford, J. (1989). *Dreams, God's forgotten language*. New York: HarperOne.
Sanford, J. (1970). *The kingdom within*. New York: Paulist Press.
Savary, L.M. and Berne, P.H. (1984) *Dreams and spiritual growth: A Judeo-Christian way of dreamwork*. New York: Paulist Press.
Sharp, K. C. (1986). In. Flynn, C. *After the beyond*. Englewood Cliffs, NJ: Prentice-Hall.
Sharp, K. (1995). After the light: What I discovered on the other side of life that can change your world. New York: William Morrow.
Shunyamurti (2011). Beyond the singularity: This is the end of what world? Retrieved from http://www.realitysandwich.com/beyond_singularity_end_what_world August 29, 2011.
Smith, H. (1977). *Forgotten truth: The primordial tradition*. New York: Harper & Row.
Smith, H. (1958, rev. 1991). *The world's religions*. San Francisco: Harper.
Sobol, E. (2009). Do we really create our own reality? Retrieved from http://www.realitysandwich.com/node/12915 August 25, 2011.
Soelle, D. (1975). *Suffering*. Philadelphia: Fortress.
Spangler, D. (1993). New Age Spirituality: The movement toward the divine. In Ferguson, D. *New Age spirituality: An assessment*. Louisville, KY: Westminster/John Knox.
Spong, J. (1992), *Rescuing the Bible from fundamentalism: A bishop rethinks the meaning of scripture*. New York: HarperOne.
Stace, W. (1960). *The teachings of the mystics*. New York, Mentor.
Storm, H. (2001). *My descent into death: A second chance at life*. East Sussex, UK: Clairview.
Stout, Y., Jaquin, L., Atwater, P.M.H. (2006). Six major challenges faced by near-death experiencers,. *Journal of Near-Death Studies* 25:1, Fall 2006, 49-62.
Strassman, R. (2001). *DMT: The spirit molecule. A doctor's revolutionary research into the biology of near-death and mystical experiences*. South Paris, ME: Park Street Press.

Sutherland, Cherie. (1992). *Transformed by the light.* New York: Bantam.

Swidler, L. (2000). *The study of religion in an age of global dialogue.* Philadelphia: Temple University Press.

Swidler, L. (2008). Retrieved from http://www.astro.temple.edu/~dialogue/Swidler/ September 7, 2009.

Synod of Constantinople. (2011). In Encyclopædia Britannica. Retrieved from http://www.britannica.com/EBchecked/topic/134061/Synod-of-Constantinople , May 1, 2011.

Tarnas , R. (2007). *Cosmos and Psyche: Intimations of a New World View.* New York: Plume.

Tart, C. (1979). *Altered states of consciousness.* New York: Wiley.

Tart, C. (1996). Who might survive the death of the body? In Bailey, L. and Wade, J. *The near-death experience: A reader.* New York, Routledge.

Taves, Ann. (2009). *Religious experience reconsidered: A building-block approach to the study of religion and other special things.* Princeton, NJ: Princeton University Press.

Taylor, E. (2000). *Shadow culture: Psychology and spirituality in America.* Berkeley, CA: Counterpoint.

Teresa of Avila. *The collected works of St. Teresa of Avila, Volume 1.* Washington, DC: Institute of Carmelite Studies Publications

Thayer, T. (1855). The biblical doctrine of hell: The word "Sheol" or the biblical doctrine of hell. *The Origin and History of the Doctrine of Endless Punishment.* Retrieved from http://www.auburn.edu/~allenkc/tbhell.html June 6, 2010.

Titus Flavius Domitianius. Retrieved from http://www.roman-empire.net/emperors/domitian.html June 9, 2009

Turner, A. (1993). *The history of hell.* New York: Harcourt Brace.

Underhill, E. (Reprint, 2010). *Mysticism, a study in the nature and development of man's spiritual consciousness.* Charleston, SC: Nabu Press.

van Lommel, P. (2010). *Consciousness beyond life: The science of the near-death experience.* New York: HarperOne.

Watchman Fellowship. (2001). Watchman Fellowship's 2001 index of cults and religions. Retrieved from: http://www.watchman.org/cat95.htm November 1, 2009.

Wakabayashi, H. (1997). The demonization of "Other" in medieval and modern Japan. Session 177: Japan. The world of demons and hells: The premodern and modern images. Association for Asian Studies conference 1997, Retrieved from **http://www.aasianst.org/absts/1997abst/japan/j177.htm** June 18, 2009

Weiss, Rabbi A. (5767 [2006]) Shabbat forshpeis. *Toras Aish* XIV:4, 1. Retrieved from http://www.aishdas.org/ta/5767/simchasTorah.pdf May 11, 2011

Wiese, B. (2006). *23 minutes in hell.* Lake Mary, FL: Charisma House.

Wiesel, E. (1972). *Souls on fire: Portraits and legends of Hasidic masters.* New York: Random House.

Wink, Walter. (1986). *Unmasking the powers: The invisible forces that determine human existence.* Philadelphia: Fortress Press.

Wu, Douglas. (2005). *Romanticism: an anthology*, 3rd ed. New York: Wiley-Blackwell.

Yoffe, Emily. (2010). Negativity. Dear Prudence. *Slate*, Monday, March 22, 2010.

Young, Shinzen. (2005). *The Science of Enlightenment* (Audiobook), disc 6. Sounds True.

Zaleski, C. (1987). *Otherworld journeys: Accounts of near-death experience in medieval and modern times.* New York: Oxford University Press.

Zaleski, C. (1996). *The life of the world to come: Near-death experience and Christian hope.* New York: Oxford University Press.

Zevit, Ziony, *The Religions of Ancient Israel: A Synthesis of Parallactic Approaches.* London: Continuum, 2001.

Zingrone, N. & Alvarado, C. (2009) Pleasurable adult near-death experiences: Features, circumstances, incidence. *The Handbook of Near-Death Experiences.* Santa Barbara, CA: ABC-CLIO/Praeger.

Zweig, C. & Abrams, J. (1991). *Meeting the shadow. (A consciousness reader).* Los Angeles, CA: Tarcher.

Index

Abandonment. *See also* Depression; Doubt
  by God 34, 167
  of others, by experiencer 34
  the Void as the ultimate 239
Absence. *See* Void (Abyss)
Adventures in Immortality 11–12, 20–21
Afterlife. *See* Life after death
Aloneness in a NDE 4, 21, 34. *See also* Abandonment; Darkness
Amplification of inexplicable experience 231–233
Angels 143. *See also* Guides; Messengers
Anger, Madness, and the Daimonic 191
Anger (Why me?) 234
Anxiety 197, 206. *See also* Death anxiety; Fear
Apocalypse. *See also* Cataclysmic events; Hell
  "Apocalypse of Peter" 90
  Book of Revelation 86, 89–91
  in Zoroastrian and Israelite religions 85
Archetypes. *See also* Images; Symbolic language
  demons as 193–194
  of suffering 212–216
  significance 203–207
  the hero's journey 226–227
  working with 230–232
  Yin/Yang symbol (taijitu) 6
Armstrong, Karen 163
Asian religions. *See* Eastern religions
Attacks in NDEs 41–42. *See also* Violence in NDEs

Atwater, P.M.H.
  books on NDEs by 12
  claims about experiencers of distressing NDEs 66
  comparison of blissful and distressing NDEs 61
  "myth of the near-death experience" 15
Axial Age 161–165
Aztec concept of hell 83

Bache, Christopher
  theory about incomplete NDEs 43–44, 205
  views on experiencer responses 45, 205
Bardo Thodol (Book of the Dead) 154
Beasts. *See* Creatures (beasts, monsters)
Becker, Ernest 69, 110
Beck, Richard 108–113
  Experimental Theology (blog) 109
Berne, Patricia, H., *Dreams and Spiritual Growth* 231
Beyond Death's Door (Rawlings) 18–19
Bible, misinterpretations of "hell" in 94–95. *See also* Gospels, references to heaven or hell in; Revelation, Book of
Birth-to-death cycles in archetypal journeys 204. *See also* Death, resurrection, and rebirth cycle
Bivins, Jason C.
  Religion of Fear 99–100, 197
Blissful NDEs. *See also* Distressing NDEs; Hybrid NDEs

accepting return from 210
appeal of 74–75
as impediment to exploration of distressing NDEs 181–183
as Satanic delusions 119
as sign it is safe to die 7–8
compared with distressing NDEs 26–29, 61
early books and TV programs about 9–14
findings about 223
hazard to experiencers 215–216
Books of the Dead 154–155
Borg, Marcus 66
Borysenko, Joan 72
Brain hemispheres 156–157. *See also* "Dying brain" theory of NDEs
Bratcher, Dennis 90
Brinkley, Dannion, *Saved by the Light* 12
Bro, Harmon 121–122
Buber, Martin 134
Buddha (quoted) 136
Buddhism. *See also* Nirvana; Tibetan Buddhism
  concept of detachment 135–136
  concept of hell 98
  concept of self 137
  origins 147
  roots in mysticism 157
Bush, Nancy Evans (Nan)
  about her own NDE 3–7, 117
  beliefs about science and religion 224
  work, at International Association of Near-Death Studies (IANDS) 7

Campbell, Joseph 186, 201
Caregivers (Appendix 1) 249–260
Carlson, Reed Anthony 45, 56
Cataclysmic events 202. *See also* Apocalypse

Causes of NDEs. *See* Explanations of NDEs
Changing one's life. *See* Conversion, as response to NDE
Chaos 29
Chinese dragons 192
Chödrön, Pema 237
  The Places That Scare You 234–235
Christian fundamentalism. *See also* Evangelicals; Rawlings, Maurice, *Beyond Death's Door*
  about 96–100
  reaction to New Age movement 177–178
Christianity. *See also* Judeo-Christian tradition
Christians. *See also* Evangelicals
  ex- 123–125
  helpful books and blogs for 234
  interpretations of NDEs by 116–118
  origins 147
  reaction to distressing NDEs 18
Clergy. *See also* Caregivers; Experts
  lack of public commentary on NDEs by 13
  reactions to reports of NDEs 169–171
Cognitive closure 119
Collective unconscious (Jung) 245
Communities for healing 239–240
Congregational Church parish (United Church of Christ)
  response to members' mystical experiences 170–171
Consciousness
  role of otherwordly creatures in 191–192
Consciousness (human)
  difficulties in finding meanings of symbols 199–203
  location of 198
  role of emotions in 184

Control 28
  living with the lack of 248
Conversion, as response to NDE 47–49. *See also* Warning, NDE as
Copernicus 127
Corbett, Lionel
  on conflicting religious beliefs 137
  on "meaning" as "dispositional power of event" 46
  on reductionism 49, 51
Cosmology. *See* Universe, the
Cousins, Ewert 163
Creatures (beasts, monsters). *See also* Demons; Satan; UFO abductions
  as archetypes 225–226
  in Book of Revelation 90
  multiple meanings attached to 239
  prevalence, in conservative Christian accounts 101–102
  roles assigned to 191–192
  symbolism of 202–203
Cultural milieu. *See* Axial Age; *See* Eastern culture; *See* Western culture

Daimon(es) 148, 191–192. *See also* Demons
Damnation. *See also* Eternity; Hell Houses
  as condemnation of political liberalism 100
  as human need for reassurance about death 110–111
  as only a part of a restorative process 226–228
  of souls for eternity 92, 108–109, 222
Dante's conception of hell 93
Dark NDEs. *See* Distressing NDEs
Darkness. *See also* Aloneness in a NDE

  as companion of light 212–213
  ignoring of, by contemporary metaphysics 122–124
  in NDEs 202
  making it conscious 69–74
  sense of, in distressing NDEs 20
Dass, Ram 29
Death. *See also* Life after death
  as cause of NDEs 77–80
  as cause of out-of-body experiences 222
  ego, resistance to dying 154–155
  equating NDEs with 183–184
  of the ego 155
  symbolism of, in NDEs 201–202, 238–239
Death anxiety 69–70, 109–112
Deathbed visions 103, 249–260
Death, resurrection, and rebirth cycle 41–44. *See also* Birth-to-death cycles in archetypal journeys; Salvation
Demographics. *See also* Experiencers
  of experiencers 11
  of experiencers of distressing NDEs 22
Demons. *See also* Creatures (beasts, monsters); Daimon(es); Satan; UFO abductions
  as elements of the human mind 192–193
  in distressing NDEs about Hell 37
  in hybrid NDEs 41–42
  in medieval images of hell 93
  in medieval Japanese images of hell 190
Denial of Death (Becker) 110
Depression. *See also* Therapy
  after a NDE 212
  as reason for distressing NDEs 220
Deservingness. *See* Goodness
Despair, after distressing NDE 5–6, 34, 51–54. *See also* Abandonment; Depression

Detachment. *See also* Non-attachment (Buddhist concept); Otherness (ontological)
   as a cornerstone of Eastern religions 135–137
   felt by experiencer of hybrid NDE 31
   felt by experiencers of hellish NDEs 44, 138
Devil or devils. *See* Daimon(es); *See* Demons; *See* Satan
Diamond, Stephen A.
   Anger, Madness, and the Daimonic 191
Dionysius the Areopagite 159
Dismemberment 105, 106, 214
Dissociation and distancing. *See* Detachment
Distressing NDEs. *See also* Blissful NDEs; Hellish NDEs; Hybrid NDEs; Void (Abyss)
   accepting the experience and getting past it 210
   achieving resolution about 246–248
   as a gateway into the spiritual world 141–145
   as incomplete NDEs 205–208, 229
   as sign person "not right with God" 119
   as sign person not "right" with God 47
   compared with blissful NDEs 26–29, 59–60
   defined 30, 141
   experiences similar to 79, 103–107
   Greyson/Bush study 21–24
   impediments to examining 181–182
   initial reports about 17–21
   rates of occurrence 20, 58
   rituals that prepare people for 154–155
   summary of facts known about 241–243
   three basic patterns 24
   three types of responses to 46–54
Divine, the, describing 157–160
Dorsey, Gary 171–170
Doubt. *See also* Abandonment; Religious beliefs
   about meaning of distressing NDEs 51–54
   complete loss of faith in one's religion 20
   loss of belief in God 32–34, 53–54
Dragons 192
Dread 197, 206. *See also* Fear
Dreams. *See also* Nightmares
   amplifying their content afterwards 232
   differences from NDEs 220
   during hypnogogic state of consciousness 104–105
   similarities with NDEs 78
Dreams and Spiritual Growth (Savary and Berne) 231
Dreamstudies.org 107
Dreamwork techniques 230–232
Drug reaction, NDE as 51
"Dying brain" theory of NDEs 59, 79

Eadie, Betty, *Embraced by the Light* 14
Eastern culture 135–137. *See also* Western culture
Eastern Orthodox Christians 96, 157
Eastern religions. *See also* Buddhism; Hinduism
   conceptions of 'self' and 'reality' 237
   demons and monsters in 190–192
   embracing of detachment 135–136
   familiarity with the Void 138–140
   roots in mysticism 157
Eckhart, Meister 158

Edinger, Edward 199
   Encounter with the Self 234
Ego, the. *See also* Individuation (Jung)
   about 131–132
   challenge of the Void to 138
   maturity and maturation 141, 155, 206–208
   resistance to dying 154–155
Eichmann, William Carl 213
Einstein, Albert (quoted) 7–9
Elemental spirits 204
Eliade, Mircea 106
Ellens, J. Harold 154
Ellwood, Gracia Fay, *Uttermost Deep, The* 79
Embraced by the Light (Eadie) 12
Emotions. *See also* Movement in distressing NDEs; Stress; Suffering; specific emotions, e.g., aloneness, despair, fear, etc.
   alleged to cause distressing NDEs 67
   avoidance of uncomfortable 73
   connection with human consciousness 184
   expressed by demons 191
   felt after NDE 211
   felt while in distressing NDEs 196–197
   felt while in hellish NDEs 44
   felt while in the Void 30–32
   human brain hemispheres 156
   of different individuals with same experience 25–27
   reactions to distressing 72–74, 210
   Seen in first accounts of NDEs 9
   understanding, after inexplicable experience 231–232
   unresolved, after a distressing NDE 51–54, 69–70
Empathy 211
Emptiness. *See* Aloneness; *See* Space, the nature of

Encounter with the Self (Edinger) 234
End of the world. *See* Apocalypse
Enoch, Book of 86
Episcopalian view of hell 96
Eternity. *See also* Damnation
   as part of Hell 37
   as part of the Void 32
   early Judeo-Christian concept of 89
Evangelicals. *See also* Fundamentalism
   modern conceptions of hell 96–97
   reactions to distressing NDEs 18–19
   relationship with American popular culture 98–100
   symbolism used by 203
Evil, done by human beings 194
Evil Incarnate (Frankfurter) 193
Exorcisms 102
Expectations and content of NDEs 221
Experiencers. *See also* Emotions; Integration; Near-death experiences (NDEs); Out-of-body experiences (OBEs)
   accounts by, in Appendix 2 261–270
   as observers of other's pain in NDEs 44
   assisting the family of 259
   books and blogs helpful for 233–234
   brain scans of 55
   characteristics and lifestyles 57, 219–224
   Greyson/Bush study 21–24
   Kenneth Ring's survey 9
   mental health of 219
   moral judgments about 65–68, 222, 229
   Nan Bush's advice for 248

narrative "voice" used in accounts of NDEs 200
need for protection, after NDEs 235
personal filters used by, to understand NDEs 113–124
religious backgrounds of 57
reluctance to discuss distressing NDEs 22–23, 69–70
responses to NDEs 10, 45–54, 215–218
six challenges faced by 209–212
whether they were really dead 77–80
who have multiple NDEs 50–51
who is likely to be one 11, 22
Experimental Theology (blog) 109
Experts. *See also* Clergy; Therapy
　inability to help experiencers of distressing NDEs 53, 169
　lack of acknowledgment of distressing NDEs 70
　NDE researchers 8–16
Explanation of NDEs
　medical 59
Explanations of NDEs 57–58. *See also* Experiencers; Greyson, Bruce; Interpretations of NDEs
　abortion as reason for hellish NDEs 223
　death 77–80
　emotions alleged to cause distressing NDEs 67
　medical 57
　psychological problems 66–67, 115, 219
　reductionistic 49–51
　religious beliefs 67–68

Fabric of the Cosmos (Greene) 139–140, 230
Fairness. *See* Justice
Faith. *See* Doubt; *See* Religious beliefs
Faith model 129
Family of experiencers, assisting 259
Fantasy and science fiction stories 235. *See also* Hero's journey (archetype)
Fear. *See also* Death anxiety
　an instrument for ensuring salvation 93
　dealing with 72–74
　during a distressing NDE 25–26, 43–44
　of death after blissful NDE 10
　of death after distressing NDE 53–54, 222
　of nightmares 230–231
　ontological fear of the Dark 69–74
　role, in conservative religious groups 49
　synonyms for 197, 206
　that hell exists 81, 222
Feelings. *See* Emotions
Finding one's purpose. *See* Purpose in life
Fire 202
　multiple meanings of 238
Flynn, Charles P. 21
Foster, Richard J. 133, 157
Fox, Mark, *Religion, Spirituality, and the Near-Death Experience* 170
Fox, Matthew 122–124
　Original Blessing 234
Frankfurter, David, *Evil Incarnate* 193
Fright 197. *See also* Fear
Frightening NDEs. *See* Distressing NDEs
Fundamentalism. *See also* Christian fundamentalism; Islamic fundamentalism; Orthodox Judaism
　as filter for interpretations of NDEs 118–119
　fear and repentance within 47–48
　secular 118

Gallup, George Jr. 20
  Adventures in Immortality 11
Gallup polls on belief in hell 222
Garfield, Charles A. 19
Gehenna (biblical image) 88, 89, 95
Ghosts. *See* Spirits
Givens, David B. 188
Gnosis 137
God. *See also* Religious beliefs
  Abraham's covenant with 133
  as an explanation for all events 168
  loss of belief in 32–34, 53–54
  Seeing in a NDE 39–40
  unknowability of 157–160
Goodness. *See also* Morality; Punishment
  idea it will be rewarded 58, 65–68
Gospels, references to heaven or hell in 87–89
Greek concept of life after death 94–95
Greene, Brian, *Fabric of the Cosmos* 139, 230
Greenspan, Miriam 46, 73–74
  Healing Through the Dark Emotions 46
Greer, James 192
Grey, Margot 61, 187–188
Greyson, Bruce *See also* Foreword to this book
  early interest in distressing NDEs 22
  on interpretation of experiences 236
  on the causes of NDEs 59, 144–145, 156
  on the ego 132
  research on experiencers of NDEs 219
  The Handbook of Near-Death Experiences 59, 223
Greyson/Bush study 21–24
  findings 223
  volunteers 57

Grief, in reaction to a NDE 3–6
Grof, Christina 234
Grof, Stanislav
  on archetypes as psychologically healing 204–205
  on concept of heaven and hell 154, 204
  on effect of an extraordinary perception 197
  on the Void 33
Grof, Stanislav and Christina
  on medical perspective of distressing NDEs 144, 172
  on spiritual/mystical perspective of distressing NDEs 172
Grosso, Michael 184
Guides. *See also* Angels; Messengers
  demons in Hell Houses as 99
  for dreamwork 232
  horned creatures as 239
  religious figures within NDEs 39–40, 116–118
  Satan as 203
  "Upon Seeking Tu Fu as a Guide" 207

Hades 86, 94
  mistranslation as "hell" 95
Hallucination 104–105
Handbook of Near-Death Experiences, The (IANDS) 59, 223
Haule, John Ryan 185–187
Haykel, Bernard 118
Healing Through the Dark Emotions (Greenspan) 46
Heaven. *See also* Nirvana; Void (Abyss)
  as a real, human construct 198
  concept of, in the Gospels 87–89
Heaven and Hell in Narrative Perspective (ebook) 234
Heelas, Paul 153
Hell. *See also* Apocalypse; Damnation; Hellish NDEs; Life after death

xxvii

as a creation of biblical misinterpretation 94–95
as a place in a NDE 67–68
as a place separate from God 83–84
as a real, human construct 198
as a situational hallucination 104–105
Buddhist conceptions 98
distressing NDEs as warning against going to 47
early Christian conceptions 87–91
experiencer's accounts of 264
fear of its existence 81
Gallup polls about Americans' belief in 222
Hindu conceptions 82
Hindu concepts 83, 98
how the idea has shaped human thinking 79
hybrid NDE experiences of 37–44
images of 188–198
in modern NDEs 20, 100–102, 195–196
medieval conceptions 44, 102, 191
Medieval conceptions 93–94
modern conceptions 96–100, 195
pre-Christian conceptions 82–86
pre-Columbian conceptions 83
reasons for its existence 107–111
sense of, in distressing NDEs 20
St. Augustine's conception 92
theoretical images of 189–193
variety of descriptions about 103
Hell Houses 99–100, 102
Hellish NDEs. *See also* specific images, e.g., Darkness; Demons; Fire, etc.
abortion as reason for 223
accounts of experiencers 43–44
coming to terms with having 248
images 100–102
Hero's journey. *See also* Fantasy and science fiction stories; Jacob (Biblical character)

Hero's journey (archetype) 226–228
Hinduism
concept of detachment 135
concepts of hell 82, 83, 98
iconography 190
roots in mysticism 157
History of Hell, The (Turner) 44
Hogan, Lois Sekarak 232
Holy Spirit (Christian concept) 149
compared with Psyche (psychological concept) 150–151
impact on the experiencer 209
problems in describing 159
Honey from the Rock (Kushner) 234
Horror 197, 206. *See also* Fear
Houle, John Ryan, *Perils of the Soul* 104–103
Human Potential movement 177
Hurd, Ryan 107
Hybrid HDEs 37–44
Hybrid NDEs. *See also* Blissful NDEs; Distressing NDEs; Inverted near-death experiences

IANDS. *See* International Association for Near Death Studies (IANDS)
Iconography. *See* Images
Ideas (Plato) 204. *See also* Archetypes
Identity. *See* Ego, the; *See* Self, the
Ideology, relationship with religion 165–167
Images
from medieval literature 195
in Book of Revelation 90
psychological/spiritual significance 141–145
Images in distressing NDEs 189–193. *See also* Archetypes; Odors in distressing NDEs; Sounds heard in distressing NDEs; Symbolic language; specific images, e.g. Creatures, Light, Tunnels

actual (non-theoretical) 195
Imaginary (theoretical) images 190–194
in hellish NDEs 100–102
in the first accounts 20–21
metaphysical themes identified with 197–198
Nan Bush's "circles" 4–5, 6
"Imaginal" 201
Imaginal realm 204
versus "imaginary" realm 201
Imaginary (theoretical) images 189–193
Immortality 75
Impermanence (Buddhist concept) 237
Inanna (goddess) 82
Individualism. *See also* Self, the
a self-divination 151–153
as lens to view meanings of words 165–167
societies without the notion of 135
Individuation (Jung) 213–214
Integration. *See also* Interpretations of NDEs; Self-help techniques after a NDE; Therapy
achieving, by using a literal filter for NDE 123
achieving, by working birth-through-death pattern 205
after a frightening NDE 206–208
cultural barriers to achieving 141–145
of a NDE into rest of one's life 197, 226–240
of new spiritual values 211
the need to make sense of mystical experience 45
Integrity. *See* Self, the
International Association for Near Death Studies (IANDS)
about 271
definition of NDE 59

Handbook of Near-Death Experiences 59
Journal of Near-Death Studies 22
media requests for information 13–14
Nan Bush's work for 7
purpose 9
Interpretations of NDEs. *See also* Dreamwork techniques; Explanations of NDEs; Meaning-making
as sign of personal worth 122
by psychologists 154–156
effect of word choice on 24
fundamentalist filter 118–119
making use of many different 236–240
metaphysical filter 120–124, 201
Nan Bush's observations about 244–246
non-fundamentalist religious filter 116–118
using other people's thoughts about 236–240
Interventions, used for ill and dying patients with distressing NDEs 249–260
"Intuition of being" 215
Inuit concept of hell 83
Inverted near-death experiences 28–30. *See also* Hybrid NDEs
Irreducible Mind (Kelly) 198
Islam
about 131
origins 147
role of mysticism in 157
Islamic fundamentalism 28. *See also* Fundamentalism
about 98
as filter for interpretation of NDEs 118
Israelites' concept of life after death 84

Jacob (Biblical character) 216–217. *See also* Lazarus and the rich man in heaven
Jambor, Mishka 183, 196
James, William
  on mystical experiences 60, 209, 246
  on validating the truth by "roots" rather than "fruits" 122
Japanese iconography of hell 190
Jobs, Steve, last words 74, 248
Journeys, as part of NDEs 189, 204–208. *See also* Hero's journey (archetype)
Judaism. *See also* Orthodox Judaism
  Israelites' concept of divine punishment 84
  origins 147
  views about afterlife 96
Judeo-Christian tradition. *See also* Christians; Fundamentalism
  concepts of hell 83–99
  emphasis on relationship with God 133–140
  esoteric tradition 175
  role of mysticism in 157
  view of the universe 8
Jung, Carl. *See also* Archetypes; Synchronicity
  "collective unconscious" 204
  discovery of archetypes 203
  "individuation" 213
  Man and His Symbols 6
  on enlightenment 69
  on the need for new shared myth 165
  "The Spiritual Problem of Modern Man" (lecture) 173
  view of the "Self" 148
Justice 108. *See also* Punishment; Suffering

Keats, John, on respect for "negative capability" 79
Kelly, Edward, et al., *Irreducible Mind* 198
Kelsey, Morton 158
Kruglanski, Arie 119
Kushner, Harold 215
  When Bad Things Happen to Good People 234
Kushner, Lawrence, *Honey from the Rock* 234

Laing, R.D. 169
Lambert, Yves 167
Landscapes, in distressing NDEs 100
Language. *See* Words
Lazarus and the rich man in heaven 88. *See also* Jacob (Biblical character)
Leighton, Sally M. 225
Lewis, C.S., *Narnia* series 236
Life after death. *See also* Apocalypse; Heaven; Hell; Spirits
  effect of NDEs on belief in 10
  Judeo-Christian beliefs 96
  NDE experiencer's expectations of 221
  NDEs as proof of 74–76
Life After Life (Moody) xvii, 258
Life at Death (Ring) 9–10
Light
  fear of 261–262
  in distressing NDEs 20, 26
  in hybrid NDE experience 38–40
  significance of, in contemporary metaphysics 122–124
Literal level of meaning. *See also* Warning, NDE as a
  about 228
  alternative way of interpreting spiritual events 247
  ambiguousness of 238–239
  as cause of confusion 53–54, 115
  as distraction when interpreting NDEs 118, 168, 183

as only level that will be attained 113
Loneliness. See Aloneness
Loss of belief in God 33–35, 53–54. See also Abandonment
Loss of faith. See Doubt
Lucid nightmares 107
Lukeman, Alex
  Nightmares 233
  on events like NDEs 184, 196
  on relief from fear of nightmares 229, 230–231

Machida, Soho K. 191
Materialist worldview. See also Reductionist response to NDEs; Science (scientific study)
  impact on our ability to acknowledge NDEs 143–145
  in the face of a NDE 15, 28, 115
  of the universe 8
Mayan concept of hell 83
May, Gerald 132, 138, 172
May, Rollo 191
Meaning-making. See also Conversion, as response to NDE; Integration; Purpose in life; Self-help techniques after a NDE
  about 46
  after a distressing NDE 46–54, 229–232
  by experiencers of NDEs 113–124
  obstacles to 141–145
  three levels involved in 228–229
  through learning what others think 236–238
  through learning what others think of NDEs 239–240
  through reframing symbols 238–239
Media, early reporting about NDEs 13–14

Medical evidence for NDEs 57, 58–59, 79
Medical evidence of NDEs. See also Brain hemispheres; Reductionist response to NDEs
Medieval conceptions of hell 93
Meditation
  alarming images during 237–238
  in Eastern versus Western religions 157
  similarities with NDEs 55, 192
Memory, human 184
Menahem-Mendl, Reb 159
Mental health
  of experiencers after NDE 230
Mental health of experiencers 219–220. See also Therapy
Messengers 4–5. See also Angels; Guides
Metaphoric level of meaning 228–229, 238–239. See also Symbolic language
Metaphysics. See also Archetypes; Mysticism; Spirituality
  as filter for interpreting NDEs 120–122, 186
  as part of human culture 56
  books on 235
  difference from materialism 167–168
  of fear 197
Minimizing NDEs. See Reductionist response to NDEs
Ministers. See Clergy
Miriam Greenspan 72
Modernity
  adaptation and reinterpretation 172–178
  religious effects 167
  secularization 168–172
Monsters. See Creatures (beasts, monsters)
Moody, Raymond 17, 182

Life After Life xvii, 258
Reflections on Life After Life 9–10
Morality. *See also* Conversion, a response to NDE; Goodness; Justice
  development of, in human history 162
  moral judgments about experiencers 65–68
  of experiencers before a NDE 222
  of experiencers of distressing NDEs 229
Movement in distressing NDEs 3–4, 28, 30–32, 36. *See also* Out-of-body experiences (OBEs)
  connection with emotions 189
Myss, Caroline 214
Mystical experiences. *See also* Metaphysics; Reality; Spiritual experiences
  as part of human culture 56
  compared with NDEs 60
  impact on the experiencer 60
  responses of clergy to parishioner accounts 171
  the need to make sense of 45
Mysticism. *See also* Psychology
  intersection with the Void 157–160
  labeling of, as pathology 143–144
  of Eastern and Western religions 157
  relationship with religion 165–167
Myth of the NDE 15, 182

Naisbitt, John 120
Nakedness in a NDE 32
Narnia book series (C.S. Lewis) 236
Native North Americans' concepts of hell 142
Near-death experiences (NDEs). *See also* Blissful NDEs; Distressing NDEs; Hybrid NDEs; Experiencers; International Association for Near Death Studies (IANDS)
  as a matter of life, not death 183–184
  as a religious experience 165–167
  common characteristics of 60, 187
  conventional wisdom about 57–58, 65–68
  coping with 209
  definitions of 60
  discomfort with talking about 143–144
  experiences similar to 78
  first known account of 81
  interpreting as sign of personal worth 122
  myth of 15, 182
  phenomena commonly found in accounts of 22
  reported rates of 11
  the shocking nature of 184–187
Needham, Rodney 193
Negative NDEs. *See* Distressing NDEs
Nepo, Mark, "Upon Seeking Tu Fu as a Guide" 207
Neurophysiological explanations of NDEs 59. *See also* Medical evidence for NDEs
Neuroscience studies of NDEs 223
New Age movement 120–121, 172–178
Nightmares
  lucid 107
  relief from fear of 230–231
  working with 231–232
Nightmares (Lukeman) 233
Nirvana 136, 139–140. *See also* Void (Abyss)
Noh plays 190–191
Non-attachment (Buddhist concept) 237. *See also* Relationship
Non-physical presences. *See* Spirits
Nothingness (feeling). *See* Void (Abyss)

Obedience 137
OBEs. *See* Out-of-body experiences (OBEs)
Odors in distressing NDEs 188. *See also* Sounds heard in distressing NDEs
Organized religion, defined 146
Original Blessing (Fox) 234
Orthodox Judaism 48
Otherness (ontological)
 as the human shadow self 194
 relationship with the Void 138–140. *See also* Detachment
 emotional impact of falling into 29
 use, in dreamwork 232
Otherwordly Beings. *See* Angels; *See* Creatures (beasts, monsters)
Other World, According to Descriptions in Medieval Literature, The (Patch) 195
Otto, Rudolf 149–150
Out-of-body experiences (OBEs) 36, 184–185
 as part of a NDE 3–4, 36
 as part of blissful NDE 26–27
 as part of distressing NDEs 27, 30–32
 causes associated with 222
Owens, Justine 49

Pain. *See* Suffering
Panic 197. *See also* Fear, dealing with, after distressing NDE 229–230
Pastors. *See* Clergy
Patch, Howard Rollin, *The Other World, According to Descriptions in Medieval Literature* 195
Pathology
 consequences of labeling suffering as 73–74
 labeling mysticism as 143–145
 labeling NDEs as 91–93, 169
 of medieval images of hell 93

Perils of the Soul (Houle) 104–103
Persian concept of hell 85
Personal filters 113–124
Personal level of meaning 229
Physical reality. *See* Materialist worldview
Physical sensitivity after NDEs 211
Physical sensitivity in NDEs 28. *See also* Movement; Out-of-body experiences (OBEs)
Physiological explanations. *See* Medical evidence for NDEs
Places That Scare You, The (Pema Chödrön) 234
Plato, account of NDE 81
Plott, John C. 162
Post-traumatic stress therapy 229–230. *See also* Suffering
Powers and principalities. *See* Elemental spirits
Prayer, similarities with NDE 78
Predestination (Calvinism) 5, 117
Protective rituals 154–155
Psychedelic experiences 193
Psyche (psychological concept) 150–151. *See also* Soul(s)
 defined 146
Psychic abilities after a NDE 211
Psychological problems. *See also* Emotions; Stress; Therapy
 after a distressing NDE 51–54
 as a catalyst for a NDE 59
 as reason for NDEs 66–67, 115, 219
Psychology. *See also* Mysticism
 books helpful for experiencers 233–234
 defined 146
 interpretations of distressing NDEs 154–156
 relation to spirituality and religion 146–154
Punishment. *See also* Goodness
 expectation that wicked people will receive 57, 65–68

Israelites' concept of divine 84
notion it should fit the crime 108
notion that suffering is 214
Purpose in life. *See also* Meaning-making; Warning, NDE as a
finding and living, after a NDE 212
finding, in an NDE 39–40, 39–44
the hero's journey (archetype) 226–228

Ram Dass story and quotation 29
Rawlings, Maurice, *Beyond Death's Door* 18–19
Reading as therapy 234–235
Reality. *See also* Eastern religions; Materialist worldview; Mystical experiences
Buddhist view 136
"creating one's own" 122
exploring transcendent 142–145
of NDEs 55–56
of symbolic images 201–202
point of intuiting there's more than 215
processing a radical shift in 210
rupture between physical and psychic/spiritual 42, 184–186
shattering of, by NDE 3–6, 138–140
what to do with an imageless 157–160
Recollections of Death (Sabom and Kreutziger) 11
Redemption. *See* Salvation
Reductionist response to NDEs 49–51, 144–145. *See also* Materialist worldview; Medical evidence for NDEs
psychological and spiritual components 146–148
Reflections on Life After Life (Moody) 9–10

Relationship. *See also* Aloneness; Non-attachment (Buddhist concept)
as cornerstone of Western religions 131–134
obliteration of, by the Void 138–140
to the sacred 239–240
with one's own self 137
Relationships
after a NDE 211. *See also* Detachment
communities of healing 239–240
Religion
defined 146, 166–167
distinguished from secular ideology 146–147
impact of modernity on 167–172. *See also* Theology
NDE as a religious experience 166–167
relationship with politics 167
Religion of Fear (Bivins) 99, 99–100, 197
Religions. *See* Eastern religions; *See* Western religions
Religion, Spirituality, and the Near-Death Experience (Fox) 170
Religious beliefs. *See also* Doubt; God; Mystical experiences
as reason for content of NDEs 67–68
influence on NDEs 103
questioning of one's own 3–6, 67
variety of, in United States 172–178
Religious conservatives. *See* Fundamentalism
Repression
as a reaction to a NDE 46–47
as fear of death 110
as reaction to a NDE 115

Responses to NDEs. *See* Experiencers
Resurrection. *See* Death, resurrection, and rebirth
Return from Tomorrow (Ritchie) 9
Revelation, Book of 87, 90. *See also* Angels; Creatures (beasts, monsters)
Reward, expectation good people will receive 58
Righteousness. *See* Goodness; *See* Morality
Ring, Kenneth
  Life at Death 9–10
  notion of "inverted" experiences 28–29
  on distressing NDEs 17, 18, 44, 51
  subway tunnel image 71, 206
  "Weighted Core Experience Index" 9, 24, 71
Risk 29
Ritchie, George, *Return from Tomorrow* 9
Rituals, that prepare one for death 154–155
Robbins, Brent Dean 189
Roberts, Keenan 99
Rollins, Wayne 141, 206, 230
Roman Catholic Church, view of hell 96
Rommer, Barbara 67, 229
Ruysbroeck, Blessed John 159

Sabom, Michael
  on distressing NDEs 17
  on hybrid NDEs 43
  Recollections of Death 11
  report about distressing NDE 20
Saint Augustine 92
Saint Paul 213
Saint Teresa
  circles of Avila 68, 196
Salvation. *See also* Death, resurrection, and rebirth cycle
  and death anxiety 110–111
  effect on intrepretation of NDE 119
  in Eastern religions 135, 191
  through a distressing NDE 47
  through Hell Houses 98–100
Sanford, John 199
Satan. *See also* Creatures (beasts, monsters); Daimon(es); Demons
  NDEs as Satanic delusions 119, 170
  rarity of sightings of, in NDEs 221
  symbolic significance 203
Savary, Louis M., *Dreams and Spiritual Growth* 231
Saved by the Light (Brinkley) 12
Science (scientific study). *See also* Materialist worldview; Medical evidence for NDEs
  impact on modern consciousness 163–165
  research studies about NDEs 223
  view of reality 55–56, 144
  view of the universe 8, 127–128
Secular ideology
  difference from religious beliefs 146–147
  impact of secularization on religion 168–172
  of self-interest 151–153
  relationship with theology 165–167
  responses to NDEs 115
Self-help techniques after a NDE 233–236. *See also* Meaning-making; Therapy
Self, the. *See also* Eastern religions; Ego, the; Individualism; Otherness (ontological)
  about 131–132
  death of 138–140
  integration, after dreadful experience 197, 226–240
  the Janus self 141–160

Sensitivity, changes in, after a NDE 211
Shadow self. *See* Otherness (ontological)
Shamanic initiation experiences 41–42, 105–106
Sharp, Kimberly Clark 22, 70
Sheol (region of the dead) 84
  translation of, as "hell" 85–86
Shock. *See* Fear
Shunyamurti (quoted) 128
Silence. *See* Void (Abyss)
Sin. *See* Morality
Smells in NDEs 188. *See also* Sounds heard in distressing NDEs
Smith, Huston 8
Soelle, Dorothee 34, 211
Soul(s). *See also* Psyche (psychological concept)
  as immortal 75, 77
  awakening of 3–6, 214
  eternal damnation of 92, 108, 222
Sounds heard in distressing NDEs. *See also* Odors in distressing NDEs; Voices heard in distressing NDEs
  multiple meanings of 238–239
  unseen sources of 101, 188
  weeping and gnashing of teeth 202
Space, the nature of 139–140
Spangler, David 151–153
Spirit. *See* Holy Spirit (Christian concept); *See* Psyche (psychological concept)
Spirits. *See also* Life after death
  communicating with, during a NDE 30
  elemental 204
  seeing, within a NDE 20
Spiritual directors 171, 239
Spiritual experiences. *See also* Mystical experiences
  interpretation of 247–248
  suffering from 214
Spirituality. *See also* Metaphysics
  defined 146–147
  integrating new values after a NDE 211
  relationship with religion 165–167
  relation to religion and psychology 146–148
  the Void as part of 33
"Spiritual Problem of Modern Man, The" (lecture by Jung) 173
Stace, Walter 157
Stories. *See also* Hero's journey (archetype)
  earliest intact 82
  Jacob's battle 216–217
  Lazarus and the rich man 88
  narrative 'voice' used by NDE experiencers 200–201
  Ram Dass' pig and chicken story 29
  Sasquatch legend of Bigfoot 226
  told by children 72
Storm, Howard (NDE experiencer) 41–42, 189
Storytelling. *See also* Amplification of inexplicable experience; Meaning-making
  as first response to dreams and NDEs 113–114
  healing through doing 229
  healing through hearing 235
Strassman, Rick 193
Stress
  association with distressing NDEs 188
  correlation with, in NDEs 11
  post-traumatic-stress therapy 229–230
  transformative changes precipitated by 214–218
Strong Religion (Almond) 98

Suffering. *See also* Justice; Therapy
  as initiation into deeper maturity 226–240
  consequences of labeling it as pathological 73–74
  coping with 212–218, 246–248
  followed by death and dismemberment 42, 205
Suicide
  as reason for distressing NDEs 11, 17
  consideration of, after a blissful NDE 210
  NDEs of those attempting 36–37
Sumerian concept of hell 82
Supernatural. *See* Mystical experiences; *See* Sensitivity; *See* changes in, after a NDE
Surrender
  to death of self or ego 138–140, 154–155, 207–208
  within a distressing NDE 29, 44
Swidler, Leonard 146, 163, 167
Symbolic language. *See also* Archetypes; Images; Words
  metaphoric level of meaning 228
  reframing symbols 238–239
Symbolic Language
  about 199–208
Synchronicity 7. *See also* Jung, Carl

Taoism. *See* Yin/Yang symbol (taijitu)
Tarnas 205
Tarnas, Richard 203
Tartarus 86
Tart, Charles 76, 129–130, 143
Taves, Ann 166
Television shows that popularized NDEs 13–14
Terminology. *See* Words
Terror 197, 206. *See also* Fear
The Life of the World to Come (Zaleski) 75
Themes identified in NDE images 197–198

Theology 165–167, 171–172. *See also* Religion
Theoretical (imaginary) images 190–194
Therapy. *See also* Amplification of inexplicable experience; Dreamwork techniques; Interventions; Self-help techniques after a NDE
  finding good confidants 210–211
  for experiencers 229–230, 238
  kinds of therapists and group therapy 239–240
Tibetan Buddhism 154
Transbodily experience 37
Transcendent, the
  defined 146
  experiences of 196, 205–206
Trivializing NDEs. *See* Reductionist response to NDEs
Tunnels in NDEs 71, 205, 266–267
Turner, Alice D., *The History of Hell* 44
Turning one's life around. *See* Conversion, as response to NDE; *See* Purpose in life

UFO abductions 103
Underhill, Evelyn 159
Understanding NDEs. *See* Interpretations of NDEs
United Church of Christ parish response to parishioners' mystical experiences 170–172
Universe, the
  as a lens for interpretation of NDE experience 245
  as empty space (the Void) 138
  Eastern view 135–137
  existence of suffering in 215–218
  is friendly? 7–8
  Judeo-Christian view 8, 125–126, 129–134
  scientific view 127–128
  the ancients' view of hell 82–83

"Upon *Seeking* Tu Fu as a Guide" (Nepo) 207
Uttermost Deep, The (Ellwood) 79

Values, integrating new 211
Violence in NDEs 102. *See also* Attacks in NDEs
   as part of Eastern religions and culture 138–140
Vocabulary. *See* Words
Voices heard in distressing NDEs 3–5, 32, 41–42. *See also* Odors in distressing NDEs
Void (Abys)
   in Book of Enoch 86
Void (Abyss). *See also* Space, the nature of; Aloneness; Heaven
   about 33–35
   accepting the reality of 248
   as only an emotional construct 196
   as part of Eastern religions and culture 157, 237
   as part of mystical experience 157–160
   as path to the Divine 159
   as ultimate experience in spiritual practice 33–34, 230
   experiencer's accounts of 262–264
   in Christian religious traditions 157–160
   interpretation of, as hell or torment 20
   multiple meanings of 238–239
   Nan Bush's experience 3–6
Vulnerability. *See also* Surrender
   after a NDE 122, 235
   during a NDE 29

Wakabayashi, Haruko 190
Warning, NDE as a 47, 119. *See also* Conversion, as response to NDE; Literal level of meaning; Purpose in life

Watts, Alan 234
Western culture. *See also* Individualism; Science (scientific study)
   about 129–135, 143, 161–164
   impact of secularization 168–172
   two views of the Universe 8, 56, 127
Western religions. *See also* Islam; Judeo-Christian tradition
   compared with Eastern religions 237–238
   emphasis on control 42
   minorities' spiritual traditions within 178
   role of mysticism in 157
When Bad Things Happen to Good People (Kushner) 234
Why me? question 212–215, 234
Wiesel, Elie 133, 159
Wink, Walter 199
Words. *See also* Bible, misinterpretations of "hell" in; Symbolic language
   complete lack of, to describe a NDE 116, 231–232
   describing a mystical experience with 157–160
   effect of wording on interpretations of NDEs 24
   inadequacy of, for describing NDEs 114, 210–211
   literal and metaphorical meanings 228
   used to describe hellish NDEs 43–44
   used to describe human experience 165–167
   using, to understand NDEs 236
   vs. emotions, their impact on memory 184
Worldview. *See* Axial Age; *See* Materialist worldview

Yin/Yang symbol (taijitu) 6
Young, Shinzen 192–193, 194, 237–238

Zaleski, Carol
   on desire for immortality of the soul 76, 77
   on distressing NDEs 21
   on Eastern societies 135
   on imagining death 78
   The Life of the World to Come (Zaleski) 75
Zevit, Ziony 83–84
Zoroastrianism 85
Zweig, Connie 151

CPSIA information can be obtained at www.ICGtesting.com
Printed in the USA
BVOW03s0448290813

329772BV00006B/131/P

9 781936 912537